SENNA VERSUS PROST

Also by Malcolm Folley

Borg Versus McEnroe
A Time to Jump: The Authorised Biography
of Jonathan Edwards
Finding My Feet (with Jason Robinson)
From Red To Amber (with Ginger McCain)
Hana (with Hana Mandlikova)

SENNA
VERSUS
PROST

MALCOLM
FOLLEY

C

CENTURY · LONDON

Published by Century 2009

6 8 10 9 7 5

First published in Great Britain in 2009 by
Century
Random House, 20 Vauxhall Bridge Road,
London SW1V 2SA

www.randomhouse.co.uk

Addresses for companies within The Random House Group Limited can be found at:
www.randomhouse.co.uk

The Random House Group Limited Reg. No. 954009

A CIP catalogue record for this book is available from the British Library

ISBN 9781846055409

The Random House Group Limited supports The Forest Stewardship
Council (FSC), the leading international forest certification organisation. All our
titles that are printed on Greenpeace approved FSC certified paper carry the FSC
logo. Our paper procurement policy can be found at
www.rbooks.co.uk/environment

Mixed Sources
Product group from well-managed
forests and other controlled sources
www.fsc.org Cert no. TT-COC-2139
© 1996 Forest Stewardship Council
FSC

Typeset in Bembo by Palimpsest Book Production Limited
Grangemouth, Stirlingshire

Printed and bound in Great Britain by
Clays Ltd, St Ives plc

To Rachel, Sian and Megan for brightening each day more than they will ever know

PROLOGUE

JE NE REGRETTE RIEN

Paris, summer 2008

Almost noon and the streets in the prosperous 16th *arrondisse-ment* will soon be bustling with people seeking out a restaurant for lunch. But for now there is hardly a person in sight and no one within fifty yards of the address I have been given in a quiet road not far from the Place des Etats-Unis. The gigantic thick wooden double doors, guarding the building, look capable of delaying the progress of an invading army, but, fortunately, on closer inspection one is slightly ajar.

Once inside, there is a cobbled courtyard leading to a set of garages in the distance. On the left is an apartment belonging to the concierge of the building and beyond this there are double doors opened by an intercom situated on the facing wall. There is no obvious indication which apartment I am looking for – and so the wife of the concierge, deaf to my knocking, is startled to find a stranger in her home as she prepares lunch. I explain in halting French that I am expected. Brusquely, she accepts my apology and walks to the intercom and pushes the button for the top floor apartment.

Silence.

An unwanted thought occurs: is this the right address . . . Or, worse, have I come a day after our scheduled appointment? Reluctantly, the woman tries the buzzer again. And this time a voice answers: another woman. Gratefully, I hear a click as the main doors open to grant access to the lift. On the fourth floor, a housekeeper waves me into the only apartment. In the high-ceilinged entrance hall there is a table displaying a golden miniature racing car with an inscription. It turns out to be the only piece of motor racing memorabilia on display in the home of Alain Prost, four times world champion.

'I was never close to the trophies anyway,' says Prost, after showing me into his drawing room. 'I have my four cups I received from the FIA for winning the world championship. I have four helmets I wore in those championship years – and that's it. The rest I gave away.'

Prost looks to have stepped from a time machine. Older looking, yes; but his dominant features from photographs of twenty or more years ago remain the same. His hair is still a shock of curls, if cut shorter and greying at the temples. His crooked nose still creates a prominent and easily caricatured profile, while his smile is warm and accommodating. His finger-nails are bitten to the quick, just as they were when he was driving, and he is small enough not to look out of place in the weighing room at Longchamps, the Parisian racetrack to which thousands of English flock each year for the running of the Pny de l'Arc de Triomphe. 'It is true, I have not put on any weight,' he says, laughing. 'I am fifty-seven and a half kilos, and if anything

I might be a little lighter than when I was in Formula One.' At fifty-three, it is an enviable trick.

Tony Jardine, who was team manager at McLaren when Prost first drove for the team in 1980, the year before Ron Dennis and John Barnard arrived to reshape the team's history, had called him 'Little Napper'. Teams were small and intimate then, and Prost was bright eyed and new to the game and watched in bemusement as Jardine, an art school graduate, caricatured him as Emperor Napoleon Bonaparte perched on a front wheel of his McLaren. Perhaps no one ever really improved on the imagery of that epithet, for Prost possessed an imperious superiority in a racing car that enabled him to conquer the world unchecked; at least until Ayrton Senna materialised. But it was not as 'Little Napper' that Prost was to be known, but rather by another nick-name given to him by Pierre Dupasquier, from Michelin, which struck a universal chord and accurately described the elan and intelligence of his undramatic driving style. Prost became simply: *Le Professeur*.

As one of a small number of sportswriters who travelled the world with the Formula One circus writing for English news-papers, I had been acquainted with him throughout most of his career as a grand prix driver. He was media-savvy from the beginning, but he will tell you that he was an innocent abroad in comparison to Senna. Indeed, it was Senna who had a full-time travelling press officer, Betise Assumpcao, a multi-lingual, effervescent Brazilian with a swift mind and a faster tongue, who later married Williams director Patrick Head, with whom she has two children. From 1990 Betise ensured that all of Brazil's media, print and broadcast had a daily bulletin on Senna's activities because he was coherent with the law of economics that prevented all but a handful of journalists from his South America

3

heartland from following him in person. She was an invaluable ally to Senna, who also kept a large office and a substantial staff in São Paulo.

Prost was for the most part a lone agent, dependent on his team's publicity machine and a coterie of trusted journalists from France to spread his message. He had a pleasant and open relationship with those of us from the British media. He has always felt undervalued in France, and winning his four titles in British teams, three for McLaren and his last for Williams, did not elevate his status. 'Because the relations between the French and the English people are always a little tricky, it is perhaps difficult to be a French driver in an English team,' he suggests, drawing on centuries of turbulent Anglo-French history. 'But because I never had the French mentality, I always had a good relationship with the English people and English teams I drove for. I always said I don't like some French attitudes. Sometimes, to be honest, I never felt one hundred per cent French!' Prost was the first Frenchman to be Formula One world champion – and still the only one – but there is no residual sense of patriotism in his achievement. 'Being world champion for France was never my target,' he says.

His willingness to invite me to his home in Paris to discuss and answer questions on his relationship with Ayrton Senna for this book is an example of the man's generosity of spirit. But his collaboration is possibly motivated by another unspoken force. His invitation for me to be here with him is a reflection, perhaps, of his desire to ensure his voice is heard amid the clamour of testimony that he suspects, rightly, will be heard through these pages as a ringing endorsement of Senna's passion for driving on the limit; and sometimes beyond. No matter.

Prost's recollections and opinions convey in this modest

attempt to recreate a stormy, vibrant and wholly unpredictable chapter of Formula One an authenticity that cannot be denied. He never asked for a transcript of our interview, nor demanded any access to the words being ascribed to him. It is to be hoped that his trust is rewarded through the honesty and balance of this account of two compelling champions colliding with the inevitable, ugly consequences of two juggernauts coming together on an autobahn.

'Ayrton was different, nobody really understands this,' says Prost, who is dressed in jeans and a brown, long-sleeved Lacoste sweater. 'You can say all good things about him, and he had lots of qualities, but you cannot compare him to a normal racing driver. Never. Ayrton was completely apart. You do not realise that immediately. It takes time. I don't know if I can remember one precise day, but, slowly, I realised that his motivation was not just to beat me, but it was to destroy me. I was not prepared to die in a racing car. Honestly, I never felt that another racing driver had any value to hurt me at all.'

Ironically, Prost had pressed for Senna to be appointed as his new team-mate ahead of another Brazilian, the vastly experienced and politically adroit Nelson Piquet, a three-times world champion and a couple of years older than the Frenchman. 'I had nothing against Nelson, nothing at all, but I thought it better for the team to have the younger driver,' says Prost. As a competitor, Senna had already assumed the way to the summit of Formula One was to target the man with his flag planted on the highest peak. With two world titles, as well as two near misses to his credit, Prost was the acknowledged master of all he surveyed when the Brazilian joined him at McLaren for the 1988 season.

The first season they were together, they were virtually invincible. McLaren won fifteen of the sixteen rounds of the world championship, with Senna claiming eight victories to seven from Prost without a team order to be heard. There had been a moment or two of friction, notably in Portugal where Senna drove Prost to within inches of the pit wall at screaming full power, but peace was maintained. Just. Yet the writing, if not Prost's car, was on the wall. Senna's political acumen, on top of all his driving attributes, made him the most formidable F1 driver the world had encountered. The second year, uncivil war broke out between the two men. '1989 was really a nightmare,' admits Prost. By early summer, he felt obliged to tell McLaren team principal Ron Dennis that he was leaving the team. 'In effect, I was driven out by Senna . . . by Honda a little bit . . . and by Ron,' he claims.

'I realised in 1989, and even later on when I was driving for Ferrari, and then later still Williams, that Ayrton's motivation was much more than I thought. It was something you could not understand, you could not expect. When you want to be good in life, you need to be challenged. That is a good experience. But if I have learned anything it is this: it is forbidden to have enemies. Life is short and you must be very careful with the relations you have with people.'

His lessons had been absorbed in a hard manner. Prost's older brother, Daniel, died of cancer in 1986; and he came from a time when men, tragically, still lost their lives in racing cars with an unhealthy frequency. 'You can have people challenging you, you can have rivals, but you can't have enemies,' says Prost. 'I felt from 1989 Ayrton made me an enemy. It was not correct. As I said, I was not prepared to lose my life against another driver.'

As he pours sparkling mineral water into two glasses, he concedes that his career, and his life, were informed by the calamitous events of Formula One's desperate summer of 1982.

He was stripped of his innocence – and cavalier attitude – in a matter of months during which Gilles Villeneuve and Riccardo Paletti were killed and Didier Pironi so badly crippled that he never drove a Formula One car again. Villeneuve and Pironi, both close friends of Prost, both Ferrari drivers, and once thick as thieves, were not speaking at the time of Gilles' death. Villeneuve justly accused Pironi of betraying a pact at the San Marino Grand Prix at Imola – an accusation Prost would level with similar justification at Senna at the same racetrack seven years later. 'After Imola, Gilles was calling me every day,' says Prost. 'He was angry with Pironi and Ferrari, absolutely furious. Later on I would fully understand his feelings because I had this with Ayrton. At the next race in Belgium, Gilles went too far in the car in practice. He killed himself because of that dispute with Didier.'

Pironi's career in Formula One lasted just three months longer. During practice for the German Grand Prix at Hockenheim, Pironi drove his Ferrari into the rear of Prost's Renault that was invisible to him because of blinding spray being flushed in his face. Pironi had been out in the heavy rain earlier than most other drivers. He was pushing his Ferrari near the limit for lap after lap. 'Didier was hot, the car was good,' recalls Prost. 'He had strong possibilities to be world champion and he had a new girlfriend. He was strong – at the top.' And then – disaster. Pironi became airborne after he hit the back of Prost's car. When his Ferrari thundered back to earth it broke around him like a balsawood model. Prost, rushing back to the wrecked Ferrari, heard the medics discussing the need to amputate one, or both, of Pironi's legs that had been mangled in the footwell of his car. Prost says he pleaded loudly with the doctors: 'NO . . . NO . . . NO.' Pironi was in agony, but, with or without Prost's protestations, his legs were spared.

7

As he came to terms with the latest catastrophe, Prost, a saddened and disillusioned man, took refuge in the tranquillity of Renault's motorhome. He had seen two men's lives stolen by accidents and now a third was being cared for by medics in terrible pain and facing an uncertain future. He wondered to himself if the risks were worth taking any more, no matter that driving a racing car was the most natural instinct in the world to him. He shared his anxieties with key figures in the Renault team and they granted him the space to come to his own decision. 'I really thought about not going back in the car,' he admits.

An hour passed, maybe less, but Prost's mind had crystallised. He announced he would continue to drive, but with a rider. 'I told them that from now on I would do things my way,' he remembers. 'From this point, I changed the way I drove. I realised this day that from now I had to be more careful.' He would later call his autobiography, written just three years afterwards with his friend Jean-Louis Moncet, *Maître de Mon Destin*: master of my own destiny. 'I remember 1982 as a defining moment. When Didier was in the hospital in Paris I went to see him many times. Every time, he liked to show me his leg. I felt sick.'

In later years, Prost chose to face ridicule by refusing to race in heavy rain, at Silverstone, then at Adelaide, rather than risk being party to another horrendous accident like the one which destroyed Pironi's career and reshaped his life. 'Everyone thinks I don't like driving in the wet, but it was almost my preference before this accident with Didier,' explains Prost. Four years after crashing at Hockenheim, Pironi died in a powerboat accident. 'He was still living the same way, you know, going over the top.'

Prost was now being prudent, or as prudent as you can expect from a man piloting a racing car at speeds approaching 200mph. He explains his changed mentality like this: 'When you have a child, and I already had a son before this terrible summer, okay motor racing is your passion, it's your job, but you want to come home at the end of the day.' He would retain this philosophy through his career, and you will hear through these pages from many drivers, and team personnel, how Prost won races as slowly as possible. 'I spoke to Frank Williams once and I said to him: "I want to drive all the time if I can at ninety-five per cent. Maybe for one lap I will use ninety-nine per cent, but that you must accept."' Prost releases a slow chuckle: 'Frank did not like this, perhaps.' But here is the strength of Prost's deception at the wheel: how *slow* is a man who wins fifty-one grands prix?

Senna, however, fooled no one. His style was to drive every lap as hard and uncompromisingly as the last one. Prost says now, just as he did all those times when he was feeling the heat from the Brazilian, 'Ayrton went maybe too far in the way he was thinking and driving and competing,' he sighs, and his voice carries a sombre note.

I had offered to take Prost to lunch, but generously he arranged for his housekeeper to prepare a meal in order that we should not be disturbed. The dining room, along the entrance hall in the opposite direction from the drawing room, was sprinkled with original pieces of art, subtle and tasteful, as you would expect. Nothing about Prost, then or now, has ever been ostentatious. We talked as we worked our way through mozzarella and tomatoes, followed by haricot beans, thinly sliced pork, with a dessert of strawberries before finishing with coffee, all brought to the table by his housekeeper silently at work in the adjacent kitchen. An impeccably mannered man, Prost is the perfect host.

After all these years, he remains puzzled by the memory of Senna's lack of respect for his own safety; or that of others. 'You know, Ayrton was prepared to be in a crash and maybe kill himself, or hurt himself,' he suggests. 'It was always his rules. If they are your rules, it follows you believe they are right.'

By dying young, Senna lacquered his life with a romantic veneer that has protected him from ageing or from being accountable for his past, or his future. Others have manifested this subterfuge: did James Dean ever make a bad movie? Is Princess Diana ever going to be seen grey or wrinkled?

Prost knows he cannot compete with the ghost of Senna. He accepts and understands this as the inevitable consequence of being the survivor of the deadly duel they once waged. In most eyes, Senna's daring, commitment and mystique will leave him always revered ahead of Prost. One powerful example: Lewis Hamilton, now the chosen one at McLaren-Mercedes, and the youngest world champion in Formula One history with endless possibilities stretching before him, grew up in Hertfordshire idolising Senna, not Prost. 'I recognise that and I find that normal,' says Prost. 'I don't want to challenge it. What I didn't find normal was that at one stage people around us were not very objective. I was hurt quite a lot. Ayrton has never been hurt in his career, never. I mean, psychologically. He has been hurt only once – and that is terrible, of course. But I had many, many tough moments. That is what I learned in this part of life, the part that is over.'

Yet after his retirement at the end of 1993, Prost started to receive innumerable telephone calls from Senna. 'Clearly Ayrton asked someone who knew me for my number, because he never had it before!' laughs Prost. 'He told me he was not motivated against the other drivers and pleaded with me to come out of retirement. I told him that he was unbelievable.'

But there were more meaningful strands to the conversation, offering an insight into his mood and mind in those final weeks of his life. Senna told Prost he was intensely worried about safety issues because of the new regulations, and he was bothered by his switch to an unfamiliar Williams team, and an uncomfortable car that only the previous season had been driven to the world title by the Frenchman before Senna staked a claim to it. 'Okay, we had one page of a book, Ayrton and me,' says Prost, sombrely. 'Obviously, I had some tough moments, but it was part of our history. If he wanted a new page, this was something that I could understand. After all, I was retired. And I would no longer be a threat on the racetrack. I really had some sympathy because Ayrton was feeling so bad. He seemed to be troubled by many things, professionally and personally. It's important to know he was a completely different man – and a completely different driver.'

Neither Prost – nor the world – would ever discover to what extent Senna had changed or the truth behind his downbeat mood. On 1 May 1994, Senna was killed when he was leading the San Marino Grand Prix, with Prost describing the scene for French television station TF1 from a trackside commentary booth. 'You have no judgement any more, you are not in a rational state,' he recalls. 'It's an unbelievable destiny.'

Three years later, Prost came back to Formula One, only this time there was to be failure and perhaps a degree of humiliation. His ill-fated attempt at running his own Formula One team was, by his account, little more than a French farce. 'It was not a good idea,' he admits. 'The day before I signed an engine deal with Peugeot I didn't want to do it any more. We were having a strategy for five years, but every day they were changing the deal.' Only a call from Jacques Chirac, the President of the Republic, persuaded Prost to go ahead with the announcement. 'The President said, "Please, Alain, do it for France. Be sure, that we will be behind, we will do our best." This was not the case.

The president of Peugeot changed – and the company decided to go rallying. Then the National Assembly changed to the other side.' At the end of the Peugeot deal, he admits to having to pay Ferrari $30 million dollars a season for engines. 'We had no more help,' he says. 'I had a big experience of how France works.' How much did Prost lose? 'A little, for sure; but I don't care or think about the money.' It is the boldest of statements, as sources in France suggest that Prost's losses ran into millions of dollars. Instead of dwelling on the financial hit he took, Prost is embittered by the politics that conspired to hasten the downfall of his team. The return to Formula One by Renault in 2001 signalled the end for him as a team proprietor; their clout within the French Establishment meant his vision could no longer be sustained.

These days he is an avid cyclist and he races cars on ice ovals during the winter, and he has looked into proposals that one day could bring the French Grand Prix, ousted from the 2009 world championship calendar, to the streets of Paris. He is available to his three children, Nicolas, twenty-six, Sacha, eighteen, and twelve-year-old Victoria. 'Being in Formula One, you are a mono-maniac,' he says, and there is a real validity to his argument. 'When you are involved, there is a lot of money and there is feeling from inside the paddock that this is the centre of the world. I would advise those in F1 to take a step back, look outside.

'I never considered myself a star. I never had a full-time manager. I always took care of my own contract. Today, I take care of my business. I suppose I could have gained much more money in my career, but I cannot complain. Was Ayrton a star? He was living in a country where that decision was taken away from him. He was a star; and also, he had the entourage. In France,

Michel Platini, Yannick Noah and Bernard Hinault were not stars. We are living in a country where we do not have stars . . . well, Johnny Halliday is a star!' His point is this: the French public's affections are more easily seduced by the exploits of an ageing rock star in leather trousers than by the performance and sporting heroics of the nation's most successful sons.

All these years on, Prost regards Ron Dennis as a respected friend, having long ago repaired his differences. 'I defended Ron through last year's spying scandal with Ferrari as I did not think it was fair how he and his team were treated by the FIA,' says Prost. 'But as you saw with Fernando Alonso and Lewis Hamilton in 2007, Ron still thinks he can handle two strong personalities. But he can't. Always, he takes sides. Apart from that he is fantastic.'

Prost's world is now one without public controversy or intrusion, and he rides anonymously through the Parisian traffic on a motor scooter without worrying about a past life as one of the fastest men ever seen behind the wheel of a car. An afternoon has passed, old arguments and broken promises between himself and Senna have been relived. Two highly controversial crashes between them at Suzuka in Japan have been dissected and blame apportioned; and as you will discover these debates are not ones easily resolved. Two litres and more of water have been consumed during our rendezvous. Yet even after all that has been discussed it would have been a dereliction of a reporter's duty not to ask Prost one final time: 'Do you ever wish you had not supported Senna's appointment at McLaren?'

He looks me in the eye and, silently, begins to try to make some sense of those times. Those faraway battles that ripped at his emotions, but yet took him to a place of sustained excellence. Those fast and dangerous moments that introduced him to ecstasy and agony in extreme measures. And when he had sifted his memories, Alain Prost spoke words that must be taken for the truth. 'Maybe I am strange,' he says. 'But I never said to myself: "Shit, I have done a mistake." Never, never. Even today. I don't regret anything.

'If you ask who was the best between Ayrton and myself, I am sure there would be more people saying Ayrton. At the time, you also remember how Gilles Villeneuve was so exceptional in his attitude; and spectacular to watch at work. Keke Rosberg and Jean Alesi sometimes had this attitude, this attitude that everyone remembers in Ayrton. But Ayrton was closer to me than people think. In the way he drove, he was much more precise than people suppose. He had a charisma that attracted him to others – I was more normal. On the track, there were times when he could do something more and the people liked that. I understand. But this is also part of decision-making, part of a way of life and a way of driving.

'*I am here – and that is all I can say.*

'Many times I considered myself lucky to finish a race because it was so dangerous. There is always a story behind the story. You know, the fact that Ayrton could be considered a better driver than me is something, to be honest, I really don't care about. It is not going to change my life.'

It is an unpalatable realism, perhaps; but it is no less a reality for that. As I left Prost, smiling warmly, I returned to the street through the huge doors and in need of a taxi to take me to the Gare du Nord for the Eurostar to London. On my mind were the words he delivered almost as a postscript. 'After everything that happened, it was still a fantastic story, wasn't it?'

It was – and it is.

1

DEATH IN THE AFTERNOON

As Roland Ratzenberger feathered the throttle on his Simtek Ford and edged into the pit lane at Imola, the clock on the wall of the team garage read 1.18 p.m. How was anyone to suspect that, in reality, it was actually just minutes to midnight for Formula One?

At thirty-three, Ratzenberger was a late entrant to grand prix racing, yet from adolescence his entire life had been an apprenticeship for this moment. Probably, because most recognised the hard road he had travelled, he had been readily accepted in the pit lane after gaining his precious seat with the fledgling British Simtek team. Ratzenberger's easy manner and unpretentious attitude counted towards his popularity as well. The Simtek team had evolved from Simtek Research, a company established in 1989 by Nick Wirth and Max Mosley, later to become the president of the FIA, and a power broker with influence secondary only to that of Formula One ringmaster Bernie Ecclestone. Simtek aimed to deliver a cost-effective design, research and development service, and their clients included the FIA, the Ligier F1 team and various F3000 and IndyCar teams. In August 1993, Wirth took the decision to enter Formula One with his own team. Australia's triple world champion Sir Jack Brabham became a shareholder and his son, David, was swiftly recruited to drive. Wirth secured Ford HB V8 engines from Ford, and he enticed MTV Europe onboard as sponsors. Ratzenberger was the last piece in the jigsaw for the 1994 debut season.

Yet as the Austrian drove out of the pits on Saturday 30 April 1994 he knew success for him would be judged on a different level to most drivers fighting for grid position in that afternoon's qualifying session for the next day's San Marino Grand Prix, the third round of the world championship. For Ratzenberger, just making the twenty-six-car grid would be a triumph, as the two slowest drivers in qualifying would be eliminated from racing in the grand prix. The stakes, then, were just as high for him as championship leader Michael Schumacher and Ayrton Senna, the favourite for the title who had yet to score a point for his new team, Williams.

With Gerhard Berger, in his second spell with Ferrari, and Karl Wendlinger, driving for Sauber Mercedes, Ratzenberger's arrival meant Austria could boast three drivers in the world championship. This was a story of sufficient news value for Gerhard Kuntschik, the much-respected deputy sports editor for the *Salzburger Nachrichten* newspaper, and veteran of the Formula One paddock, to attend Ratzenberger's first test in Imola, in Italy, three weeks before the opening race in Brazil. Kuntschik drove from Salzburg to the Italian border where he met with two Austrian photographers and another writer to travel as a quartet to be at Imola, a thirty-minute drive south of Bologna, for the start of the test at 9 a.m. on 8 March.

Kuntschik recalled how the first man he encountered in the pit lane was Senna. 'The first garage belonged to Williams, as Alain Prost had won the world championship for the team the year before, and as practice hadn't started I found Senna just staring at the sun. He was obviously bored. He saw me – we knew each other as I had interviewed him on several occasions – and he came across and shook my hand. We had a five-minute-long conversation. You know the kind: "How are things, how is life?" I asked him about his car, but it was just small talk. What I wanted most at this point was to arrange for a photograph of Roland with Gerhard and Karl. The Ferrari pit and the Sauber pit were not too far apart – but the Simtek garage was all the way down the far end. Almost in another country.

'Wendlinger and Berger had private difficulties at the time, so I had to be a diplomat. Gerhard said, "No problem, the others should come to my pit." Wendlinger said, "Tell them to come to my pit." Ratzenberger simply said, "Tell me where I should go, I'll go anywhere for that picture." In the end, it took me an hour and a half to get the three Austrian drivers together for the photo we wanted.'

Austria has a proud record in Formula One: Jochen Rindt became the sport's first and, mercifully, only posthumous world champion in 1970, when he was killed in his Lotus during practice for the Italian Grand Prix at Monza four races before the end of the season; and Niki Lauda won the title three times having been given the last rites after being rescued from his blazing Ferrari at the Nürburgring in 1976.

Kuntschik – a man who easily wins friends and respect in the paddock – recalled with patriotic fervour being at Monza in 1984. 'Lauda won, on the way to his third championship, and his only one with McLaren, Jo Gartner was fifth and Berger was sixth – the best-ever result for Austria in F1,' he said. 'So, you can see that for Roland coming into Formula One was always going to be difficult. Expectations in Austria are extremely high.'

He had been closely involved with Ratzenberger's career from the beginning. 'I knew him from the age of twenty-one, but later he tried to make himself two years younger by claiming he was born in July 1962,' explained Kuntschik. 'He thought this would be better for his career opportunities as a late developer, but Roland was actually born in Salzburg in 1960, making him the same age as Damon Hill. I met Roland in 1981, when he was a spectator with a friend at a local car rally in a ski resort. He intro-duced himself to me at a service point – and asked if I was from the newspaper. The two of them asked me how they should go about becoming racing drivers.' Kuntschik advised Ratzenberger and his friend to enrol at the racing school of Walter Lechner, who had competed against Prost in Formula Three, and ran an established driving academy at the old Osterreichring in Austria. Ratzenberger clearly listened as he left technical school one year before his graduation to devote himself to racing.

'He had no sponsors, no family money,' said Kuntschik. His father, Rudolf, was a manager in the federal-administered health insurance system in Salzburg without any interest in motorsport. 'Roland managed to drive by working part-time as a mechanic with Walter Lechner. His breakthrough, as such, came in 1986 when he won the world-renowned Formula Ford Festival at Brands Hatch, in England. That led to Roland getting a works contract with BMW for the 1987 World Touring Car Championship. But Roland's only target was Formula One.'

Kuntschik kept in close contact with Ratzenberger, who had by now become a friend. After the touring car championship ended, Ratzenberger drove for two seasons in the British F3 series, and lived in rented accommodation near Silverstone. He always went to the British Grand Prix, when the paddock was on a lawn behind the pits and the smell of chicken and sausages being barbecued drifted across the old wartime airfield in the years before gourmand chefs took over the kitchens of Formula One. Kuntschik remembered his friend telling him in that same paddock, 'I will get here sometime.' Remarkably, Ratzenberger had by now acquired a cult following in Britain as a guest on breakfast television. A puppet called Roland Rat featured regularly on GMTV's morning show – and Ratzenberger's good nature meant that he was more than willing to be a foil for the rodent with the preposterous baritone laugh; and, anyway, like the man said, there's no such thing as bad publicity.

But Ratzenberger had to move to Japan to make a real impact, and a decent living, from driving in a variety of cars from 1989 until 1993. In this period, he drove in the Le Mans 24-Hour race with his mentor, Lechner. All the time, Kuntschik recorded his career in his home-town newspaper in Salzburg. 'It was in the days before mobile phones, and Roland usually called me to tell me his results, and the story of his race weekend,' said Kuntschik. 'I also had numbers for him, in England, Japan and later, Monte Carlo. One day I rang his family because I just could not get hold of Roland. One of his sisters answered the telephone and after I asked if she knew where he was, she replied: "Listen, if you don't know where he is, how should we know? We only read in the paper where he is."'

In Japan, Ratzenberger formed a kind of ex-pats' club with men like Johnny Herbert, Eddie Irvine, Heinz-Harald Frentzen and Mika Salo, who, at varying times, all made the transform-ation to Formula One. According to Kuntschik, Ratzenberger was close to getting a seat in one of Eddie Jordan's cars when the Irish entrepreneur entered F1 in 1991, but the finance fell through. Instead, he stayed in Japan and continued to be paid a high premium for his services. So much so that Ratzenberger felt a need for a home in a tax shelter.

'With his earnings, Roland bought a flat in Monte Carlo and became a resident sometime in the winter of 1991–2,' said Kuntschik. 'He also bought a luxury apartment in Salzburg, on the fifth and sixth floor of a building with enviable views, which at the time cost five or six million Austrian Schillings, I don't quite remember; but it was the equivalent of about €400,000.' Sadly, Ratzenberger would never be granted a single night's sleep in the apartment.

Women played a part in his life, as they did in the lives of all racing drivers. Ratzenberger can be said to have mixed success in romance. In 1991, he married a divorcee at a fairytale ceremony in Mirabell Castle in Salzburg, but he soon realised that they had made a mistake and they divorced within weeks. His next serious liaison was with a model from Somalia, known as Kadishya. 'She was extremely beautiful, but it turned out she was just after Roland's money,' said Kuntschik. Ratzenberger split from her in early 1994, just as he was on the brink of becoming an F1 driver.

For this development he had much to be grateful to a woman called Barbara Behlau. 'She was divorced and probably twenty years older than Roland and we never did find found out if there was a romance or not,' chuckled Kuntschik. 'But she was a wealthy woman, originally from Germany, but, like Roland, living in Monte Carlo. She ran a successful agency promoting artists, concerts and the like and had a daughter almost the same age as Roland who was an international showjumper. Barbara paid $500,000 to Simtek for the first half of the season and that was enough to get Roland into the car.' In modern times in Formula

One, talent alone has not always assured a driver access to the grand prix grid; and impoverished teams at the rear of the field have always required drivers to bring with them a bag of gold.

Ratzenberger went to the first race in Brazil, at the end of March, as a proud man, but with a precise understanding of the daunting job ahead of him in the Simtek team. The Austrian driver knew that he was being thrown into the sport at the deep end. Hardly surprisingly, Ratzenberger failed to qualify for the grid at Interlagos, a suburb of the sprawling, densely populated city of São Paulo. More surprisingly, Senna left Brazil without a point after an accident as victory fell to Schumacher's Benetton. Two weeks later, back in Japan, Ratzenberger qualified for his first-ever F1 race, the Pacific Grand Prix at Aida. For Ratzenberger the weekend improved further on race afternoon. He finished eleventh — albeit last of the cars still running. This still represented a small but significant triumph for him and his impoverished team.

For Senna, the weekend was another pointless exercise. His race ended at the first corner, when his Williams was tapped by Mika Hakkinen's McLaren, then struck more solidly by Nicola Larini, an Italian making his debut for Ferrari. Senna had climbed out of his damaged Williams, removed his helmet and walked back to the pits an angry man. En route, he visited the stewards to express his displeasure that his work, and that of the Williams team, had been destroyed within seconds of the grand prix through the negligence of others. Senna was aware, and concerned, that the average age of the drivers on the grid had never been younger in the history of the world championship.

Of course, Ratzenberger was one of the older drivers, but still inexperienced in F1 terms. At least he arrived at Imola heartened by events in Japan; Senna came to the Italian track with the cares of the world on his shoulders, according to those who knew him best. He had not settled into the Williams car, and he had made it apparent in phone calls over the winter to Alain Prost, of all people, that he had concerns over safety within the sport. His mood became more pensive when, in the first practice session on Friday, Rubens Barrichello, a twenty-one-year-old Brazilian in his second season with Jordan, lost control of his car in the 140mph fourth-gear corner, Variante Bassa.

Barrichello's car was launched by the kerbing and cleared a tyre barrier one metre high before hitting a debris fence. Barrichello was knocked unconscious by the ferocity of the impact. Jordan's chief engineer Gary Anderson said, sharply: 'The kerbing at that point acts as a launching ramp and Rubens missed the tyres, which are there to absorb an impact. He flew into the fence at an undiminished speed and it was only a matter of luck that he did not hit one of the metal retaining posts.'

Barrichello came round in the medical centre, nursing a broken nose and bruises, to find Senna at his bedside. At first Senna could not gain access to where the young Brazilian driver was being cared for as security staff had orders to block all visitors. Undeterred, Senna jumped a fence. 'The first face I saw was Ayrton's with tears in his eyes,' said Barrichello. 'I had never seen that with Ayrton before. I just had the impression that he felt as if my accident was like one of his own.' In truth, Barrichello's colossal accident shook Senna in his current state of mind. 'I thought he had been killed,' admitted Murray Walker, the voice of motorsport to millions of fans in Britain and Australia. 'It was a monumental crash. The Variante Bassa is a right-left corner, and he lost his car coming out. He went along the top of the safety barrier, and at one point was travelling upside down. It was sort of like Robert Kubica's crash in Montreal in 2007, but not quite as dramatic as Rubens' car didn't disintegrate as Kubica's did.

On the Saturday morning, I interviewed Rubens for BBC as he had come out of hospital after being kept overnight for observation. He was not allowed to drive again that weekend, though.'

Before Barrichello's accident, Senna had coincidentally bumped into Ratzenberger after they had made a visit to race headquarters at the same time. As he was a newcomer, the Brazilian deliberately engaged him in conversation, if only briefly as is the manner of racing drivers at a grand prix. A race weekend is no time for socialising. 'Roland was very unassuming and totally in awe of Ayrton, and so happy to meet him,' recalled Jo Ramirez, team coordinator for McLaren, and a man who had established a strong friendship with Senna during the Brazilian's six years with the team. 'We'd all met in the offices at the track. At Imola, they always gave the drivers a nice gift; you know, things like helmet bags, leather wallets, a Swiss knife, all personally named. Alain Prost gave me his knife – I still have it.'

Senna had another reason for wanting to establish an acquaintance with Ratzenberger. Josef Leberer, his fitness trainer, masseur, nutritionist and most trusted friend in Formula One, was Austrian. 'Ayrton said to Josef that he thought Roland seemed to be an interesting and nice guy and wanted to know him better,' explained Kuntschik, whose own friendship with Leberer cemented his good relationship with Senna.

Senna had arrived in Italy on Thursday morning to launch his own branded mountain bike – an exclusive model, naturally – in Padua. In late afternoon he travelled to the Imola circuit by helicopter with the president of Ducati, the manufacturers making a Senna-named motorbike, and the chief executive of TAG-Heuer, the company marketing a Senna-edition watch. He was becoming an ever larger corporation. Senna's plane, an eight-seat

British Aerospace HS125, had been taken by Owen O'Mahony, his personal pilot, to Forlì, a small town with an airfield closest to the circuit for ease of departure after the grand prix.

At 5 p.m., or thereabouts, Senna checked into the Castello, an intimate hotel run by Valentino Tosoni at Castel San Pietro, a spa town roughly ten kilometres west of Imola. McLaren had used the hotel as their base for years and Senna always had the same junior suite, room number 200, which cost £150 a night. He saw no reason to change habits, merely because he had transferred teams. Besides, Frank Williams, his new boss, had the room below. Senna's small band of friends at Imola included Leberer, of course. Also with him was his brother, Leonardo, his business manager, Julian Jakobi, an old friend from Brazil, Antonio Braga, the manager of Senna Licencing in Brazil, Celso Lemos, and Brazil's most cele-brated broadcaster, Galvao Bueno, from TV Globo. Senna dined in the hotel that night, and returned to his room at around ten o'clock, the time he liked to be readying for bed at a race weekend.

On Friday, Murray Walker was granted his usual time with Senna for preview material to be broadcast during the countdown to the grand prix. Walker remembers this particular interview as if it took place yesterday. 'Over the winter, I'd got out some tapes of the 1983 Formula Three duel between Senna and Martin Brundle just to amuse myself,' he said. 'And I realised as I was watching them that I had been correctly calling him I-Air-Ton Senna. And I realised that I had become sloppy and had been calling him Ayrton at the grand prix races. So, at the Brazilian Grand Prix in 1994 I started to call him I-Air-Ton again. Well, I got a torrent of abuse from the British public along the lines of who is this bloke, I-Air-Ton? Why can't you call him Ayrton like the rest of us? During the Pacific Grand Prix I reverted to calling him Ayrton and thought no more about it.

'At Imola, I sat down with him to do my usual pre-race inter-view in the Williams motorhome. "Well, Ayrton," I said. "You lost out to Schumacher in Brazil, you went off the track. You lost out to Schumacher in Aida when Larini drove you off the track. You are twenty points behind, what are your feelings?"'

Senna replied: 'What happened to I-Air-Ton?'

'How could you possibly know about that, you are in the car?' asked an incredulous Walker.

'I keep in touch, Murray.'

Walker said: 'I thought that incredible. With everything in his life, he could be troubled to raise such an insignificant detail. But, then, no detail was ever insignificant to him.'

On Saturday lunchtime Kuntschik was in the Simtek motorhome. 'I had done my story for that day and my newspaper doesn't publish on Sundays,' he said. 'I had been with Roland on Thursday afternoon and he was relaxed – but he was so ambitious. He set his targets so high, he constantly put himself under pressure. And, for sure, David Brabham had a better car than Roland. If the team had new parts, they were on David's car. Roland never complained publicly, but I knew from some remarks he was not happy. Anyhow, on Saturday I was just listening as Roland conducted an interview with a colleague from Austria. Qualifying then was between 1 and 2 p.m. At twenty to one, Roland stood up and said, "Let's finish this in the evening, I have no more time."' Kuntschik cannot forget those words: *I have no more time.*

Ratzenberger went to the Simtek garage to prepare for quali-fying. His first attempt at securing a time was without incident. Let Kuntschik take up the story: 'I was watching qualifying in the Press Room on a television in front of my desk. Someone I knew casually was in the pits and he took a picture of Roland as he put on his balaclava for his second qualifying attempt. If you look at the picture, you'd believe he was already in another world. His eyes were focused on something in the far distance. He was looking into nowhere. Right behind him was a clock. It was the last picture ever taken of him. He has this glazed look on his face. If you see it now, you would say it was destiny. It was eighteen minutes past the hour.'

Ratzenberger drove out of the pit lane and joined the circuit. On that first lap, his car rode a kerb hard, but that's what drivers did at Imola. But this generation of Formula One cars had been stripped of electronic aids, and no longer had active suspension or traction control which was meant to make them more dependent on the skills of the drivers. It definitely made them more unpredictable to drive – but none of this was to contribute to what happened to Ratzenberger as he started his second lap in search of a time to ensure him a place on the grid.

At the fastest part of the track, heading towards the right-hand curve named after the late Gilles Villeneuve – who survived an accident at this corner – Ratzenberger's car inexplicably made a ninety-degree left turn and crashed into a concrete wall. He was travelling at almost 200mph. Ferrari's Jean Alesi, not driving that weekend as he recovered from neck injuries sustained in a recent testing accident, had been a spectator at this area of the track and later said that he believed the front wing of Ratzenberger's Simtek had come off. This deprived the Simtek of downforce – and made Ratzenberger a passenger in his own car.

The left-hand side of his Simtek was ripped apart, and a wheel was sent spinning back across the circuit as Ratzenberger's car made a violent pirouette beside the perimeter wall. A hole had been gouged in his cockpit – and eventually the Simtek reversed back on to the circuit at Tosa hairpin. And as the car spun slowly, and for the last time, Ratzenberger's head slumped on to the left-hand side of his cockpit. After that, he was motionless. And an unnerving silence fell over the circuit, as it always does when a session is stopped under a red flag. All anyone can do is wait – and if so inclined pray for the man at the wheel. After all, Barrichello had escaped serious injury just the previous day and how many other drivers had walked away from huge accidents in recent years?

Damon Hill, driving an identical Williams Renault to Senna, had crossed the start-line by the time the red flags had been waved at marshal posts around the circuit to recall the cars to the pits. 'I went past Roland's car, it was a big wreck,' he recalled, when we met for coffee at a pavement table at a bistro in Godalming in the spring of 2008. 'You normally go through Tamburello at 180mph and you would be doing around 200mph when you brake for Tosa. So, that's the kind of speed Roland would have been doing when he went off the circuit. I thought Ratzenberger's accident was going to be serious, but it didn't strike me just how serious. After all, Gerhard Berger had been off at Tamburello in the past; Nelson Piquet had gone off in the air and hit the wall at Tamburello. Drivers had been walking away from big accidents for a long time. Carbon fibre [the material used to construct the monocoque] really was an amazing invention. It saved a lot of lives. But what it meant, I think, was that people felt safer. Among drivers there had grown perhaps a sense of complacency; a lot had gone through the sport without encountering a fatality.'

In Salzburg, Rudolf Ratzenberger and his wife, Margit, had just that morning returned to their home from a holiday in Mexico. Ratzenberger had not long switched on his television, tuned to Eurosport for the Formula One qualifying, when he called to Margit: 'There is a big crash in Imola.' She arrived in the room to catch the replay being shown. That was when they realised it was their son's car that had been so hideously disfigured – and that they would never see him alive again.

'I still have this vision in my eyes,' said Kuntschik. 'His car spun ten times, twenty times, I don't know. When the camera showed his head lowered and motionless, Roland looked lifeless like a dummy.' Professor Sid Watkins, the chief medical officer for Formula One, an eminent neurosurgeon, a champion of safety and a genial, wise man, arrived at the crash scene with minimal delay. 'It was clear things were pretty bad,' he said. 'There was a very good team at that corner and Roland had been already ventilated when I arrived.' Screens were erected as the medical staff went about their grim business – but not before drivers waiting to go out on the track had born witness to the terrible crash. Berger was one. 'I was in my car, watching the TV monitor when the accident happened,' he said. 'I knew how bad it was when I could see Professor Watkins doing heart massage on Roland. For the first time, I found myself shaking after an accident. I had just been with him that week on my boat in Monaco. I know you shouldn't differentiate between drivers you know, and those you don't, but this affects you in a different way. I went to the motorhome. I felt sick.'

In the Williams garage, Senna, clearly distressed, removed his distinctive yellow helmet and waited for news. Ratzenberger was brought by ambulance to the medical centre close to the paddock – but Watkins admitted: 'It was clear that he wasn't going to survive.'

Kuntschik was among the throng of journalists who converged on the building to await a bulletin. 'I feared right away Roland was dead,' he said. 'But no one confirmed this and Roland was sent to hospital in Bologna by ambulance. It would have been meaningless to use a helicopter.' Ratzenberger was brought into the anaesthesia and resuscitation unit at the Maggiore Hospital at 2.07 p.m. His death was confirmed eight minutes later.

For the first time in twelve years, Formula One had to learn how to deal with death at a race weekend. Some handled it worse than others; and Senna seemed the worst affected of all. After a decade in Formula One without intentionally yielding an inch of road; after waging a feud against Alain Prost; and after a decade of driving at breakneck speed without acknowledging a weakness in his mind, Senna was now confronted by an event beyond his experience.

Death.

He was not prepared for this moment. A man he had spoken with just twenty-four hours earlier now sat lifeless in a racing car. He had tried to convince us – himself? – through all those years that the risks of his business were something that he had considered, calculated and could be accommodated without a downturn in commitment. Had not Senna once proclaimed: 'There is a certain amount of danger in motor racing, so any time you go racing or testing you are exposed to some risks. There are calculated risks – and there are uncalculated things that can happen. And you can be gone in a fraction of a second. You realise you are nobody. And your life can have an end. You either face it in a professional, cool manner; or you just drop it and don't do it any more. I happen to like too much what I do to just drop it. I can't drop it.'

But those were words spoken before Ratzenberger's life vanished when he hit a concrete wall in front of Senna's eyes. For the first time in his adult life, Senna instinctively looked for somewhere to hide. He left the Williams garage, ignored all those who tried to catch a word, and disappeared inside the Williams motorhome with his grief. At thirty-four years old, he had met his match on a racetrack.

Betise Assumpcao, the Brazilian press attaché to Senna's Formula One ministry, recalls precisely how he went into emotional meltdown. 'After he had seen the accident, Ayrton handed me his helmet and said, "That's it, I'm leaving." He went to the Williams motorhome. I remember to this day someone from the Williams team said as he watched Ayrton disappear: "Why is he upset? Is the guy a friend of his?" I didn't even answer. You had to be a friend . . . to feel sadness about a man killed?' Perhaps people within the sport had been anaesthetised for too long to comprehend the loss of life.

The last man to die during a grand prix weekend was Riccardo Paletti in Canada in 1982. He drove from the rear of the grid headlong into the stalled Ferrari of Didier Pironi, who was stranded in the place reserved for him after claiming pole position. The last man to lose his life in a Formula One car had been Elio de Angelis, who was killed during a test at Le Castellet in the South of France in 1986.

Martin Brundle, now an award-winning broadcaster, had been driving that day in May when De Angelis' life was stolen prematurely; and he was a McLaren driver at Imola as the sport came to terms with Ratzenberger's death. 'At the test in France, there were no helicopters or sophisticated medical facilities,' he said. 'Stupidly, I suppose, we never expected it in those times. There would have been an ambulance, but you never thought about it.' De Angelis came from a wealthy family in Rome – and he was a convivial, charming and well-educated man. When the drivers staged a lightning strike without a shred of warning before the South African Grand Prix in 1982 they locked themselves into a large public room at the

Sunnyside Park Hotel, in a respectable suburb of Johannesburg, in a battle over ownership of their super licences. I remember that De Angelis, a classically trained pianist, had provided some entertainment for the drivers during the impasse that lasted almost twenty-four hours.

Ratzenberger had only his charisma as a calling card. Brundle smiled as he retraced the years. 'He came bouncing up to me at the Brazilian Grand Prix and said, "Hi, I'm Roland!" He seemed a really nice guy. We were all shocked by what happened to him, not least because of the way it happened. It wasn't driver error – it was a broken wing. And there but for the grace of God go all of us. There had been big shunts before Roland's, yet everyone kept walking away from the damned things. Don't ask me how, when you look at the cars. The side of the Tyrrell in which I had a massive shunt stopped halfway up your arm. You could see all your shoulders and upper arm outside of the car, extraordinary when you think of how the modern cars envelop all but the top of the driver's helmets.'

Outside the Williams motorhome, Betise Assumpcao stood like a sentry. 'I didn't know if I'd get in to see Ayrton,' she said. 'When someone came out, I said just let Ayrton know I am here if he wants to talk.' By then, it had become apparent he had no intention of driving again whenever qualifying resumed. And resume, it most definitely would. 'I received a message that Ayrton didn't want to talk, and that was perfectly understandable. But I had people on from his office in Brazil screaming at me to get some comments from Ayrton. They said on the phone to me, "He has to talk, a guy is dead and he is refusing to qualify . . . he has to talk!" I said to the guy on the line: "Do you want to talk to him because I am not going in there. What do you want me to write? There are three million people here who want to talk to him. The guy's very upset. I can't just write a ridiculous, fake press release. You write it – you know as much as me. I have nothing to add." We had a major fight. As you can imagine I wasn't in the best of moods.'

When the decision to restart qualifying was taken, Williams, Benetton and Sauber all withdrew their cars without fear of reprisal, and without compromising the grand prix the next day. Benetton's Flavio Briatore argued: 'Our action is taken out of respect for life. I don't care if I have one less place on the grid.' Ratzenberger had driven J.J. Lehto, the second driver to Schumacher in the Benetton team, to Imola in his Porsche.

Ms Assumpcao's afternoon, in the meantime, continued to deteriorate. 'I received a press release from the bloke in Brazil . . . in which he claims that Ratzenberger has been taken to hospital with a pulse and is still breathing,' she said. 'Ayrton went mad when I told him of what had been written. Then, he ran to the garages with every intention of running to the scene of the accident. But when he saw this would be impossible, Ayrton saw a course car parked near the pits. He asked the driver to take him out to the crash – and he got his way. Who was going to say "No" to Senna?'

He had this desire, always, to see and comprehend matters for himself. He had been talking with Alain Prost about safety issues on the telephone in the preceding weeks, and he had also had a dialogue on the subject with Berger. Senna wanted to see the track, and where Ratzenberger had crashed, for himself. He was reprimanded for commandeering the official car without permission – but this was of no consequence. Senna had never seen a man killed before. He had no experience of death – and this troubled him. What was he supposed to do now?

After he had seen the crash site, Senna had another important appointment to keep: with Professor Watkins. Again, he wanted information. 'I explained to Ayrton what had happened,' said Watkins. 'Then he put his head on my shoulder and I gave him a cuddle.' The two men had formed a bond of friendship over the years, beginning with the time Watkins first treated him after Senna had wrestled his Toleman car home in sixth place at the 1984 South African Grand Prix, in his second F1 race. 'Ayrton had spasms in his neck, something he didn't understand,' said Watkins. 'Once I explained it was muscle strain from driving that monstrous car, he realised he wasn't in imminent danger of dying! I learned then that he wanted to understand everything about himself, and about the human condition.'

And now, a decade later, Watkins offered Senna a deal on that Saturday afternoon at Imola. 'I said to him, "You're upset, you shouldn't drive tomorrow." He thought about that for a long time before he answered – which is something he normally did when you posed a serious question – and then he replied, "There's no way I can stop."'

Watkins persisted, however. 'Ayrton,' he said. 'You are the fastest man in the world, you've won the championship three times, there isn't anything more to do except to repeat yourself. It would be much better if you quit. And I'll quit, too, and we'll have more time to go fishing.'

Senna, by now calm and composed, responded: 'Sid, there are certain things over which we have no control. I cannot quit, I have to go on.' Watkins, these days living for much of the time in Florida, but still heavily involved in Formula One's ongoing campaign to improve safety, watched Senna walk away without another word.

Senna's next mission was to find Jo Ramirez, his friend from McLaren, to ask a personal favour. 'Ayrton asked for me to arrange for a helicopter to take him to his plane at Forlì after the race,' said Ramirez. 'He told me he wanted to get back to his home in Portugal as soon as possible. Ayrton said that at Williams there was no one he could count on to do this for him. To me, it was a vote of confidence. We may fly different flags at the track now, but we remained friends. I told him, "I'll do this today, and I'll do it any time you ask." I also told him that I would never lose the hope that he would one day come back to McLaren. We still saw him quite regularly. After his first two races for Williams, he would come to our garage and talk to the boys and to Ron Dennis. He knew everyone in the team. It's important. It's something Fernando Alonso never grasped at McLaren. He was in one corner, while Lewis Hamilton mingled with everybody.' Ramirez organised the helicopter, as requested.

Hill, driving in only his second season in Formula One, having spent his first year studying the methodology of Prost, may not have had the rich experiences of Senna to draw on as a racing driver. But as a man he had been called on to deal with much more in his life – and outwardly appeared better equipped to deal with Ratzenberger's fatal accident. 'I didn't appreciate at that moment that Ayrton had never encountered death,' he said. Hill is a thoughtful, decent man, who would later become a world champion, as his father had been before him. 'My dad's friends were being killed all the time,' he explained. 'I've got pictures of me playing with Jim Clark in the garden. Then one day I saw a newsflash that announced he was dead. So, it's been there all my life. Men like Jackie Stewart went into the sport knowing there was a good chance you were going to die.

'Yet I raced against drivers who had a terrifying lack of comprehension of what was involved, of what could be the consequences of what they were doing [on a racetrack]. They saw it as just a competition – and not a challenge between you and your mortality.

'I can't remember how I heard that Roland was dead; I just did. I had a team-mate, Bertrand Fabi, who was killed. I never got to race with him – we were testing at Goodwood in 1985 and he died in an accident there. He was a French-Canadian, a lovely guy. At that point, I had to rationalise my life. I had to ask myself: Why would you want to do this? I concluded that this is what I wanted to do with my life. It was what Bertrand Fabi wanted to do as well. As long as you are aware of the potential price to be paid, then you are not deluding yourself. It's a choice you have taken. So, my philosophy, if you want to call it that, was in place before Roland Ratzenberger was killed.

'I was not inured to death, though. I'd seen people I knew die, and my dad was killed, too, in an aeroplane accident. My approach was that I could see Formula One posed a risk. But I also saw how it tempted some people to play a role, to throw themselves into the death-defying element that is the worrying aspect of this sport.' His wife, Georgie, was with him this weekend. 'She was in the garage seeing what I wasn't seeing,' he said, as he rolled back through his archive of personal memories. At no stage had Georgie tried to influence him to stand down. 'We'd been through this. It wasn't like we didn't know what the possible implications were.'

More pertinently, Hill could detect an uncertainty in Senna. 'The whole weekend is a story in itself. Ayrton was considering his place in the business, in the sport. He hadn't settled into the Williams team yet. And he had this new boy suddenly arrive almost from nowhere – Michael Schumacher. The point was Alain Prost had departed and Ayrton didn't have a target any more. He's the target now and this new guy, Schumacher, had no respect, no regard for anyone.'

Senna never spoke a word to Hill that afternoon in Imola, never mentioned going out to the crash site. 'But I wasn't Ayrton Senna,' said Hill. 'He was someone who assumed a position in the world. I think he just felt he had a right to be involved. That sounds a negative thing to say – but actually what I think is that Ayrton thought keenly that people had rights. In his own way, he was a campaigner for human rights. He transcended Formula One. In the same way as Muhammad Ali transcended boxing.'

But Senna's mind was in turmoil at Imola. Not just because he had seen a man he had once raced against die in a racing car. His own life was at a crossroads. His latest girlfriend, Adriane Galisteu, a twenty-one-year-old Brazilian model, had not received a full approval rating from his entire family. Even so, Senna had invited her to join him at his home on the Algarve and she had just arrived in Portugal that weekend to begin life at his side.

According to stories later published in Brazil, Leonardo Senna had been dispatched to Imola to tell his brother that the family had an audio tape to prove Adriane was unsuitable for him. So, when Senna left the circuit, there was much on his mind: the death of Ratzenberger, Schumacher's twenty-point lead in a Benetton car that he believed was not adhering to the new regulations and his family's reservations over Adriane. Senna had always valued the opinion of his family above all else. They had wanted what was best for him and, in his mind, their sincerity and the integrity of their advice mattered. So, it would not have rested lightly with him if he heard a dissenting voice from any of them about the woman he wanted to be with. Schumacher, twenty-five, had materialised in grand prix racing as a substitute for the Jordan team at the Belgium Grand Prix in 1991 and made such an impression that Formula One ringmaster Bernie Ecclestone brokered a deal that took him to the much more competitive

Benetton team. In return, Eddie Jordan banked an estimated £3 million in compensation for surrendering his contractual hold on the German. Smiles all round. In the next two seasons, Schumacher never shied from confrontation; and that included the odd contretemps with Senna. So the Brazilian knew that he represented a real and present danger with a two-race start.

On that Saturday evening at Imola, Senna had dinner with Josef Leberer and a few close friends to celebrate his most trusted confidant's birthday. It was a sombre affair. 'It was a very sad night, and it was clear that there was a lot on Ayrton's mind after a difficult day,' said Leberer. The evening ended quite early, and Leberer asked if there was anything Senna required before he went to bed. Senna replied, 'No, not today, Josef. Go to bed.' Yet later that evening, Senna met with Frank Williams. His mind seemed to have been eased afterwards. Adriane would tell me five months later: 'I flew from Brazil to his house on the Algarve to be there when he came home on Sunday night. Ayrton telephoned me on Saturday and he was shaken. Crying, really crying. He told me Roland Ratzenberger had just been killed and that he did not want to race. He had never spoken like that and I didn't know how to react.'

We met in Rio de Janeiro where the vast beaches rimming the Atlantic Ocean run almost into the heart of the city to produce a carnival of colour and sound. Yet there was no gaiety in her voice. She explained that Senna telephoned again after his initial, disturbing call. 'By then, Ayrton had had a long discussion with Frank Williams and this time he sounded better. "I'm going to race," he said. "But I can't wait for the whole thing to be over." His last words that night were, "Come and pick me up at Faro Airport at 8.30 p.m. tomorrow. I can't wait to see you." We were going to grow old together, I was sure of it.' Behind us, Phil Collins' voice could be heard on the television in the restaurant where we had lunched. 'Ayrton listened to him all the time,' she said, and smiled as she lit another cigarette.

Adriane had opened Senna's mind to aspects of life beyond obtaining the optimum performance from his racing car. She wore her blonde hair long, and her dark eyes sparkled with life. She was girlish and uncomplicated. He felt relaxed and unworried in her company. To her he was Beco, his childhood nickname, and she was taking English lessons at his encouragement.

But there was a fundamental concern: Adriane came from an extremely humble background, which caused much of Senna's family great anxiety as they feared she looked in his eyes and saw dollar bills.

The Senna family came from the opposite end of the social spectrum. The family business required almost 1,000 staff, involved in making spares for cars and the distribution of soft drinks. His parents also farmed around 90,000 acres, on which they reared 10,000 head of cattle, and they had servants to attend to their household needs. His sister Viviane, two years older and a psychologist, came on occasions to grand prix races; they were also very close. For a time, he shared an apartment in São Paulo with his younger brother, Leonardo. These were the people Senna came home to Brazil to be with at every opportunity – the people he knew never wanted anything from him other than his presence and his love. Within his family, Senna was at peace.

Adriane Galisteu was not the *type* of woman the Sennas envisaged their son, a privileged man, rich beyond imagination and a national icon, becoming romantically involved with. Only his mother Neyde, it was said, had time for Adriane. His father Milton did not like the fact that his son was moving in a direction that was taking him outside his influence. Until this point,

Senna's character had been largely shaped by his father, a man whose wealth meant that he expected his voice to be heard without challenge. For example, Senna had posed for photographs taken with Adriane wearing a bikini. His father most definitely did not want those pictures to be published as he believed them to be harmful to his son's image. Senna listened to his father's argument – then authorised the publication in Brazil anyway. More and more, he was taking total responsibility of what he wanted from life, and that included Adriane.

Yet Senna never had any such misgivings about what motivated Adriane Galisteu to fall in love with him. He protected his privacy, so he never spoke openly of his emotional attachment to her; but his invitation to her to live with him at his home on the Algarve, in Portugal, was an illustration of his contentment and commitment to the relationship.

'Ayrton's romanticism was about taking pleasures from simple things,' said Adriane. 'At his beach house, I would often sit on his lap on the pier and marvel at the beauty all around. He would say, "Times like this make everything worthwhile." He bought me a Fiat, then called my car a "sardine can", and I'd tell him it was the "sardine can" he had given me . . . and we'd both laugh.'

Adriane had seen him off from São Paulo for the race in Aida on 11 April, with the words, 'Oh, I miss you already!' A week later was her twenty-first birthday – but Senna's call from Japan did not arrive until six the following morning. She said he apologised. 'Ayrton told me, "I'm really sorry, but I'll give you all the caresses and presents when you come to Portugal."'

Ramirez felt sure she was *the one* for Senna. 'Adriane was the love of his life, one hundred per cent,' he said. 'But he was conscious the family did not accept her. It was a battle.' Leberer was less certain about the mindset of his friend, who showed himself more intimately to him than most others. 'It is not for me to say,' said Leberer, 'but there were reservations in my eyes over Adriane, yes.' But what is not in any doubt is that Senna could not wait to be reunited with Adriane in Portugal.

Prost had taken his own calls from Senna over the winter, calls in which the Brazilian pleaded for him to come out of retirement and race again. Calls in which he expressed his growing concern over safety issues, matters that had never troubled him greatly before. 'Ayrton was a different man,' said Prost. And he was there at Imola, for French television, and for Renault, waiting to meet with his nemesis on much improved terms.

In Austria the next day's news bulletins were naturally dominated by the death of Roland Ratzenberger, the second internationally renowned Austrian sports personality to die in a matter of three months. In January, world champion skier Ulrike Maier, also from Salzburg, had been killed in an accident at Garmisch Partenkirchen. 'These were shocking times for us in Austria,' said Gerhard Kuntschik, a man still mourning a friend and someone, who, after all these years, still visits Ratzenberger's beautifully kept grave at least twice a year. Rudolf Ratzenberger came to Imola in a friend's car in order to drive his son's Porsche back to Salzburg. He can never have made a more harrowing journey.

But that weekend held still more tragedy. On Saturday evening, Martin Brundle had chanced upon Senna. 'I met him in the lift at the hotel where we were both staying,' he recalled. 'It was quite late at night. He was very emotional.'

With the new dawn, Formula One would be nudged ever closer to midnight.

2

LITTLE NAPPER

To begin this story it is necessary to travel back three decades. In the midst of the 1979 world championship, McLaren's title sponsors, Marlboro, were growing impatient with a lack of success. Emerson Fittipaldi, in 1974, and James Hunt, in 1976, had been world champions with Marlboro McLaren; and with support from second driver Denny Hulme, the team had also won the constructors' world championship in '74. But the glory days were fading into distant memory and those responsible for distributing Marlboro's largesse to the team were becoming unamused by the stagnation.

John Hogan ran the Marlboro budget for Philip Morris, the American tobacco giant, from a fifth-floor office in a building on the outskirts of Lausanne, Switzerland. 'In those days sponsors had a huge influence,' explained Hogan. 'We essentially agreed with the team which drivers we would have. We negotiated and paid the drivers' salaries.' Marlboro had started funding McLaren in 1974, a deal pieced together by Hogan who was promotions' coordinator at that time. Initially, the arrangement was a runaway success. 'After winning the world championship Emerson left at the end of 1975 and James brought a freshness and vitality and enthusiasm, which, in a funny way, Emerson had drained out of the team,' said Hogan. 'Emerson was a hard taskmaster. He'd really given the team a hard time to get up to speed. In a strange way, they were quite knackered. Then James came along with his boyish enthusiasm, not really caring how the car was set up or anything like that.' As an illustration, Hogan recounts one incident: 'At Watkins Glen in 1977, James had thrown the car into the Armco on the last lap of qualifying and marched back down the pit lane smoking a cigarette to announce, "The car's up there in the barrier". And it was – totally rooted.'

Hunt had been to school at Wellington College, in Berkshire, and first drove in Formula One for Lord Hesketh, whose family pile was in Towcester, not far from Silverstone. Hunt and Hesketh were made for one another: unconventional, cavalier and with a predominant desire to have a good time while still bringing a competitive instinct to the paddock. Hunt is the only Formula One world champion to have dressed in a T-shirt bearing the legend: Sex – the breakfast of champions. His closest friend, and fierce rival, Niki Lauda, who would one day win a world championship driving a McLaren, received the news of Hunt's sudden death after a heart attack in the summer of 1993 as badly as anyone.

Yet Lauda could put in perspective Hunt's death, at the age of just forty-five. 'James saw more of life than most men who live to be ninety,' he said when we spoke in the days before his friend's funeral. In their formative years, Lauda and Hunt had shared a flat in London. At the peak of their lives, they had duelled for the world crown. Lauda had been given the last rites in the summer of 1976, having been rescued from his blazing Ferrari at the Nürburgring, the notorious German motor racing circuit in the shadow of the Eiffel Mountains. Yet within weeks he had returned to the track to hound Hunt before, finally, he accepted defeat on a rain-drenched circuit at Fuji and the Englishman was acclaimed champion.

'We had so many good times, James and me,' recalled Lauda. They were like-minded men. Lauda – who abruptly retired from the sport during the penultimate grand prix of 1979 in Canada, only to make a comeback with McLaren two years later – offered a flavour of their friendship when he divulged: 'On one occasion, we went to a party together in Vienna. The next day we had to fly to a test at Paul Ricard, in the South of France, with me driving for Ferrari and James for McLaren. I was giving James a lift on my plane and told him that I would be leaving at 8 a.m. sharp. He was still at the party when I left – and that was not very early! James came to the plane the next morning just minutes before we were ready to take off and we hardly spoke as we both rested. At the circuit, I got lucky. My car was shit and I could not drive. I went for a sleep in the team's motorhome.

'But I was suddenly woken up as there was a lot of activity outside . . . James was the only other driver on the circuit and his car had not come round. Everyone feared the worst. I jumped in one of the cars that rushed out on to the circuit. Eventually, we came across his McLaren parked off the track. Inside, James was asleep.' His affection for his old friend and foe was audible. 'That was James,' said Lauda.

By 1979, Hunt was no longer a McLaren driver. Team principal Teddy Mayer, an American lawyer, had not renewed his contract.

The quintessential Englishman's racing career came to a miserable conclusion before the end of that year when he gave up on the uncompetitive Wolf team. Yet the McLaren team that he had left behind, with John Watson and Patrick Tambay at the wheel of their cars, remained in a rut. Hogan understood action had to be taken. He formulated a plan that would take some months to execute, but his forward thinking was to radically reform McLaren, and ultimately lead to them becoming a potent force in the sport.

Marlboro, you see, also backed a BMW M1. That car was prepared and operated by Ron Dennis, who owned a company called Project Four. Dennis had eight years earlier established Rondel Racing with his friend Neil Trundle, a colleague from times spent together with the Brabham Formula One team. Dennis rose to become Brabham's chief mechanic before he branched out on his own to make a reputation with his Rondel cars in Formula Two. Pertinently, Lauda drove the car in this one make Procar series that was staged as a support race at key European grands prix in 1979. Hogan began in that year of 1979 to edge Mayer towards an amalgamation with Dennis's Project Four organisation. For Hogan knew that Dennis was driven to getting himself, and his company, into Formula One and the current McLaren management in his estimate had become stale.

But with such a political minefield to negotiate, Hogan had to move slowly. 'I'd worked with Ron in his Rondel days and knew what he was capable of, but it was still a bit of a gamble,' he admitted. 'As a company, we were committed to Formula One, but if you took a look around the pit lane you thought to yourself: "Where else can we go?" Lotus was iffy, if you studied the financial structure. Williams was the same. Brabham had Parmalat. One way or another, we came to realise we'll stay with what we've got, but with significant changes.'

Those changes in full would not materialise until the following year. However, Hogan was able to insist on one immediate recommendation to McLaren. In the early summer of 1979, Hogan watched a Frenchman called Alain Prost win the prestigious Monaco F3 race, staged on the unforgiving streets of the Principality as a support act to the world's most famous grand prix. All the Formula One team managers scouted this race – but Hogan acted promptly and instructed Mayer to provide Prost with a test drive in a McLaren at the end of the season. Prost, already twenty-four, had four years of karting under his belt, and had been champion of Formula Renault France, then Formula Renault Europe. In 1978, he won the French F3 title and at Monaco, in '79, he was en route to becoming runaway European F3 champion. 'Winning that race in Monaco was one of the greatest days of my driving career,' said Prost. 'It was absolutely necessary that I won to have any chance of being in Formula One and I came to understand long afterwards that the contacts I had in Formula One towards the end of the season came exclusively from this result in Monaco.'

Prost announced himself in that season as a man with a rare gift, one that would be a passport to riches and success beyond his boyhood imagination. As a teenager, he preferred to play football rather than fantasise about motor racing. In contrast his older brother Daniel – whose life was to be so tragically cut short by cancer – decorated his bedroom walls with posters of Jim Clark and Jackie Stewart at the family's modest home in Saint Chamond in the *département* of the Loire. His father, André, had a basement workshop where he manufactured, among other things, kitchen furniture. Crucially, it was his father who introduced Prost to karting while on holiday in the South of France when he was fifteen. He was addicted from his first drive.

Nine years after that humble introduction to karting at a venue called Siesta, on the coast road between Antibes and Cannes, Prost received his invitation to drive a McLaren at a specially convened test at the Circuit Paul Ricard, at Le Castellet, not far from Marseilles. In all likelihood, McLaren would have a vacancy for the 1980 season. In November 1979, Mayer arranged for Prost, along with an American named Kevin Cogan, to audition for the team. Legend has it that, after watching Prost for ten laps, Mayer jogged to his car to retrieve a draft contract for him to sign on the spot. Whatever the truth, Prost soon afterwards accepted a one-year contract with McLaren holding a further one-year option on his services. With Frenchmen Jacques Laffite, René Arnoux and Didier Pironi already on the grid, F1 attained a strong Gallic flavour. Yet the team Prost joined would be unrecognisable to the one that Lewis Hamilton has known his entire life. Tony Jardine was integral to McLaren at the time. 'Our factory was on a trading estate near Slough, not far from Heathrow Airport,' said Jardine. 'People used to joke we had tyre tracks from planes on the roof of our building. This was where Bruce McLaren had started. When Concorde flew over my office shook.'

Jardine met me during the Monaco Grand Prix in the summer of 2008 at the Bridgestone Motorhome parked on the harbourside. Not many roles in Formula One have eluded Jardine, known throughout the paddock as Teach. He has been a draughtsman in the Brabham drawing office; team manager; an analyst on the ITV's Formula One show and a businessman with his own marketing and public relations company, which operates these days as Jardine International. 'Before I joined McLaren I got a job in the Brabham drawing office of chief designer Gordon Murray simply because I'd been an art teacher in Kuwait,' he said.

'When the designs were done, I'd draw the components together in an exploded view diagram, if you like. The first day I was at work I remember Bernie Ecclestone [then Brabham team owner] coming into the office and taking one look at me before exclaiming: "That's just what we need, isn't it – another fucking designer".' Jardine's penchant for mimicry – his repertoire includes Prince Charles and Sir Jackie Stewart – coupled with his quick wit led him to entertain the notion he could cut it as a professional comic. 'In the Brabham days I was appearing at the Comedy Store with Alexei Sayle,' he explained. 'Only Alexei and me got paid. We received a tenner a night, the others just got booed off; but then so did we, usually. Whatever did happen to Alexei Sayle?'

When Prost signed for McLaren, the entire workforce barely totalled thirty people, the norm in most teams with perhaps the exception of Ferrari. In contrast, almost 1,000 people are employed these days at the McLaren Technology Centre, a £250 million confection of glass and steel, designed by Sir Norman Foster, standing in immaculate isolation on the edge of Woking, Surrey, where the cars are designed and built for Formula One in the twenty-first century. Jardine, an affable man, but with a hard-nosed business sense, recalled: 'Although I managed the team, I was called assistant team manager. I used to be involved with most things: sponsorship, running the team flights, freight and, if an engine needed changing at 3 a.m., you helped out. I tended to pick up Alain from Heathrow in my wife Jeanette's Citroën 2CV, I thought he'd like that.'

Mayer offered to host Prost on his visits to England, but more often than not he would ask to stay with Jardine. Prost preferred the informality of the Jardine household. 'Alain used to duck out of heavy team things whenever he could, and that included opting to stay with me rather than Teddy,' said Jardine.

Two factors about Prost instantly caught the eye of Jardine the artist. 'We'd never had such a diminutive driver as Alain,' he said. 'And we'd never had one with a conk the size of his!' Jardine liked to greet Prost with the cry: 'Get the oxygen out.' The first time this happened Prost looked puzzled. 'What do you mean?' he asked. Jardine replied, 'With the size of your nose, mate, we're all fighting for air.'

Prost had come to an ailing team. In 1979, McLaren finished seventh in the constructors' championship with a meagre fifteen points – almost one hundred fewer than champions Ferrari whose South African driver Jody Scheckter was world champion with his team-mate Gilles Villeneuve runner-up. No one would have believed then that Ferrari would have to wait for twenty-one years before Michael Schumacher next won the world title in a Ferrari.

'We'd gone back to basics for 1980 after the disaster of the 1979 season,' explained Jardine. 'The impressive thing about Prost from his start in Formula One was he never looked fast. He looked like he was on rails, no fuss. It was unreal. The appliance of science taken for granted nowadays wasn't around back then. The design guys would work on big drawing boards like draughtsmen. Some got it right, some got it wrong. In 1978 Colin Chapman, then considered a genius, got it absolutely right for Lotus, winning the constructors' championship with his drivers Mario Andretti and Ronnie Peterson taking the first two places in the drivers' world championship. Of course, there was a heck of a lot of copying. We caught people underneath other teams' cars trying to take measurements.

'My counterpart at Lotus was discovered lying beneath a Williams in the 1980 season. All you could see were his feet – when he was pulled out he had a tape measure in his hands!

You'd get photographers to take pictures of rival cars, to look at the aerodynamics, anything to give you a clue what was going on.' Perhaps this means of espionage was naive in the extreme, tinged with the slapstick of an Ealing Comedy. But was it really that much different in complexion from the 'Spygate' scandal that cost McLaren a fine of $100 million from the sport's governing body, the FIA, in the autumn of 2007? McLaren were punished for being in possession of drawings and data that were adjudged to be the intellectual property of Ferrari – a storm that erupted only because a disenchanted Ferrari employee called Nigel Stepney broke ranks.

But the harsh reality was that in 1980 no one was interested in the McLaren cars. Even so, Prost commemorated his debut in Formula One at the Argentine Grand Prix by finishing sixth, and scoring his first point in the world championship. Only seven of the twenty-four cars that started were classified at the end. 'Of course, I was happy to have a point, but I was not proud of it,' commented Prost later. Prost underplayed his accomplishment as no driver had finished in the points in his first grand prix since American George Follmer, driving a Shadow Ford, seven years earlier in South Africa. Another nine years would elapse before the next driver scored on his debut: Johnny Herbert for Lotus in Brazil, and Jean Alesi for Tyrrell in France, both in 1989.

In the next race in Brazil, on a notoriously bumpy track at Interlagos, Prost came fifth. For the second weekend, his long-established team-mate John Watson was nowhere. Jardine, an accomplished caricaturist, went to work on the large chalkboard in the team's garage. He drew Prost looking up at Wattie who had a tennis racket in his hand, with the caption: 'Now I'll teach you to play tennis, that's easy as well.' In another caricature,

Jardine portrayed Prost as Napoleon, arm tucked in his tunic with one foot in the car. 'We called him Little Napper in those days,' said Jardine. 'Alain told me he still has that particular cartoon hung in a toilet in one of his homes.' Watson felt the cartoons mocked him unfairly – and Prost felt them to be 'cruel but funny', according to Jardine.

'At McLaren today, Ron Dennis would have a cartoon like that off the wall in one second,' said Watson years later. Team principal Teddy Mayer felt Watson had no grounds for complaint. 'Did we focus on Prost even though he was a rookie?' he asked. 'That's true and the cartoons did demonstrate that, of course they did.' Mayer offered his remarks to Christopher Hilton, an old colleague and friend of mine from the *Daily Express*, who wrote a biography of Prost seventeen years ago. Tellingly, Mayer also said: 'It's every man for himself, it's crazy, yes, but the way it is. We were under pressure from Marlboro, we had been for some time . . .'

Even with his halting English, Prost had been able to swing critical elements of the McLaren team behind him. Watson explained this in succinct terms: 'Alain didn't have any experience of Formula One cars or ground-effect cars, he was just very good. Anyway, the emphasis was quickly focused on Prost and I got left behind. They looked to Alain to be the cure to the car's problems rather than the problems being with the car itself. Fundamentally, the team had not recognised the importance of certain aspects of ground effects in detailing the underbody, the importance of the aerodynamic side of racing cars. In hindsight, these things were more important than mechanical considerations. This was certainly within the knowledge of Williams, Brabham and Ligier, and it outweighed the traditional way of making a car handle, which was springs, roll bars, wings front and rear. Now you had underbodies that brought the car down and the team did not fully understand how that worked, how you could control and what you needed to do. In reality, it was something a driver could not do either because the information was orientated around a wind tunnel. You had to get it right in a wind tunnel. What the driver can do is say, "At this particular corner the car is doing this, at that particular corner the car is doing that", and I know Alain is very good, no, he's outstanding at it. As part of his character, Alain is very, very singularly minded and ambitious. Quite right, too. Or what are you about in motor racing? That is a strength, not a weakness.'

Prost had settled easily into the team, no question. He told me: 'It was important to me to know everybody from the boss to the secretary, from the engineers to the mechanics. I found this easy.' From the beginning in Formula One he adopted this philosophy of bringing the team onside. Without total cooperation from your team even the fastest of men can find themselves disadvantaged. But the McLaren car itself was another matter: at the next race in South Africa he had two accidents. In the first one during an unofficial session something went wrong at the front of the brand new McLaren M29C and Prost hit a wall. The following day, he experienced a rear suspension failure in the spare car and crashed even more heavily. Prost's weekend was at an abrupt end: he had broken a bone in his left wrist and could not drive in the grand prix. This was an ominous insight into the remainder of the season. Prost missed the next race, the United States Grand Prix West on the streets of Long Beach, California, and his return at the Belgium Grand Prix was another debacle with a transmission failure. At Monaco, the McLaren team plunged to rock bottom. Watson, attempting to qualify for his 100th grand prix, was one of three men who failed to make

51

the grid that is limited to twenty drivers. Prost began from tenth position – but for Watson the party was over before it began. He was stripped naked of his pride in the most public of motor racing auditoriums. If there is one race that gains the attention of the world, if there is one race where celebrities come to play under the intoxication of high-octane fuel and lavish cocktail parties, this is the race. Jardine recalled his own displeasure at having to accompany Watson from the pits. 'I am not walking back with you – you're a failure!' said Jardine, his humour as hard edged as his artwork. 'On race morning, Wattie came to the pits on a scooter, hit a kerb and fell. I said: "Wattie, you can't even drive a bloody moped!"'

A few days after he had failed to get on the grid at Monaco, I went to see Watson at his picture-postcard cottage, close to the sea at Bognor, in Sussex, to hear his story for the *Daily Express*. 'I felt ashamed of myself,' he admitted. 'It was as if I'd done something dirty, like being caught as a neighbourhood Peeping Tom.' Watson, thirty-four, contradicted the popular iden-tikit picture of a grand prix driver. He might easily have been mistaken for an accountant. A fastidious man, he kept his home spotless. Mostly, he took care of his own laundry and no one could remember the last time he was photographed in a nightclub. The sleepy pace of Bognor suited him just fine. Only the pres-ence in his garage of a low-mileage Porsche – in pristine condition, of course – offered any indication that he was a man who drove cars fast for a living.

But Watson, who began his Formula One career in 1973, had already won the Austrian Grand Prix four years earlier for the Penske team which ran just one car. In time, he would claim four further victories for McLaren, but on this afternoon on the south coast his disappointment cut deep. 'I had been robbed of my pride,' he argued. 'It was so bad I was even afraid to walk down the pit lane.' Just two-tenths of a second had been the difference between racing on the streets of Monaco and having to make an igno-minious retreat. After the retirement of James Hunt, Watson was now Britain's senior ambassador on the world's racetracks. It had become a hard, lonely job for the eloquent Ulsterman.

Watson's job was his passion as well as his livelihood. 'I still enjoy motor racing, the competitive element and the lifestyle,' he explained. 'It's a violent sport – not just because of the danger – but because of the power of the machinery involved. I get satisfaction out of taming that power and making it look non-violent. To me, driving is an art form. A painter uses a brush to create something beautiful, my brush is my car. I like my driving to be graceful, beautiful to watch. I believe I was born with a God-given ability to drive. It's like being born with a silver spoon. Other drivers have to adapt and dedicate themselves to a much greater extent than me. Material wealth doesn't motivate me. I want to be world champion not for the things it would give me, but because I want the championship to satisfy something inside me.'

If Watson was inconsolable, Prost, as it transpired, was to leave Monaco almost as downhearted. The Frenchman's race did not last beyond the first corner, Ste Devote, as he was a victim of a spectacular shunt, which began with Irishman Derek Daly's Tyrrell cartwheeling two and a half times through the air. Daly flew over the top of his team-mate Jean-Pierre Jarier, who was instantly excluded, while Bruno Giacomelli was also eliminated in the mayhem along with Prost. Mercifully, all four drivers escaped uninjured. Later, when asked about the accident, Daly said: 'I remember my flight plan very clearly!' Sometimes it is easier to laugh than cry.

Prost claimed further points in the British Grand Prix and also at the Dutch race in Zandvoort to take his aggregate total in the world championship to five. McLaren had now come under the influence of Project Four designer, John Barnard, who, in time, would play a huge role with Dennis in turning around the fortune of the team. But Prost was not destined to score any further points in his debut season, although Watson finished strongly once he had regained confidence in his car after a design flaw had been corrected in Holland in late summer. In the countdown to that grand prix, dear old Wattie, as he was affectionately known, had chosen to rail against the British media in an interview with *Motoring News*. Watson argued that he had been largely ignored, and, when he was not ignored, he had been misunderstood by those writing despatches for the Fourth Estate. He accused journalists of 'spending too much time enjoying sponsors' free food and booze rather than doing what they're paid for.' Not a sure-fire way of gaining sympathy in the popular prints, perhaps, yet Watson had a great deal of goodwill in the bank with the press. He also had journalists' full attention when he crashed heavily as a result of brake failure at Tarzan, the hairpin at the end of the pits straight in Zandvoort during practice for the Dutch Grand Prix. Thankfully, he escaped with just muscular pains and the next day, with the underbody of his car properly relocated, he qualified to start the race from the fifth row of the grid, his best performance for more than a year.

Maurice Hamilton, these days the much respected analyst for BBC Radio Five Live's Formula One race team, wrote in the *Autocourse* annual he edited at the time: 'For seventeen laps Watson was up there with Arnoux, Reutemann and Andretti, driving with the skill and experience that somehow had been misdirected during the previous few races. The fact that he scarcely had brakes to speak of did not deter him from getting on with the job *he* was paid to do and members of the over-nourished Press were quick to congratulate John on an excellent showing which, sadly, had been halted by engine trouble.' On a scale of one to ten of spats we have known between a sportsman and the media, this registered below one on the Aggravation Scale. Watson's inherent good nature would never have allowed it to be otherwise.

Prost and Watson never had a problem with one another. Indeed, Prost is extremely grateful to the generosity of spirit the Ulsterman always showed him. 'John was like a big brother to me,' he said. Even when Prost demonstrated a swift turn of speed, and an equally fast mind, Watson never sulked or withheld his cooperation. This is rarely the way of the world in Formula One.

But Watson's exposure to Prost would not last. The Frenchman had become disillusioned with the car he was driving, and when his season plunged downhill at the last two races he was vulnerable to the approaches being made to him from Renault's management. Representatives of the state-owned car company wanted to bring his talent back to the French side of *La Manche*. This was probably the worst kept secret in the paddock.

McLaren's dwindling hopes of keeping Prost – in spite of his instant appreciation that the arrival of Ron Dennis would lead to better times – vanished in the twilight of the season. In the last two races in North America, Prost was involved in accidents that shook him to the core. At the Canadian Grand Prix – where Alan Jones became world champion for Williams – Prost's McLaren turned sharp left and hit a barrier. This was a consequence of suspension failure, a legacy of an earlier joust with Riccardo Patrese's Arrows as the Frenchman again illustrated his natural ability at the wheel. 'It was a shame because this race, honestly, I could have won it,' said Prost, remembering the incident twenty-eight years later. 'The shunt with Riccardo at the hairpin must have done the damage.'

At least Prost was unhurt, unlike his compatriot Jean-Pierre Jabouille who sustained a broken leg when his Renault crashed. Jabouille had won the Austrian Grand Prix and was leaving the team for 1981 to accept an offer he could not refuse from Talbot Ligier. His team-mate René Arnoux had taken two victories, at the start of the year in Brazil and South Africa, but in most eyes the turbo-charged Renault had flattered to deceive. This was a team on a state-funded budget, after all. There was just one man they wanted to fill their vacancy – Prost. One of those to visit Jabouille in hospital in Montreal was Jones, the first Australian to take the title since Sir Jack Brabham, who won the crown for a third and final time in 1966. I had breakfast with Jones at his hotel in Montreal – after midday. He had black coffee with a Vichy water chaser. The party the night before had been a good one, clearly. 'When Jack heard that I'd won, he apparently said that I'd drink more Foster's in a month than he drank throughout his career!' laughed Jones, a man's man and held in eternal affection by Sir Frank Williams and his partner, Patrick Head. Jones's triumph was a reward for the stoicism of Williams. At one stage, not that many years earlier, he was so impoverished that he used to conduct his business from a public telephone box after his phone line had been disconnected.

Rival team owner Ken Tyrrell, who ran Jackie Stewart in his halcyon, championship-winning years, had fallen on hard times himself as Williams celebrated. Before Christmas, Tyrrell reduced his payroll from thirty-eight staff to thirty-two. It was, he knew, a retrograde step forced upon him by simple economics. 'Frank Williams employs somewhere between sixty-five and seventy people at his factory; you need that amount if you want to progress,' said Tyrrell, who died in 2001 after selling his beloved team that evolved from British American Racing to BAR Honda into plain Honda before being unexpectedly withdrawn from the sport as a response by the Japanese manufacturers to the economic crisis that enveloped the motor industry at the end of 2008. 'When Frank was down, really down, and not deserving to be running an F1 team, he got off his backside and found the money he needed. He's done an incredible job when you think of the old bangers he used to run. Now he's got the world champion – Alan Jones – and is the constructors' champion, too,' added Tyrrell.

Jones, whose uncompromising duel with Brazilian Nelson Piquet brought the championship to a red-blooded climax in Canada, with the two men colliding at the first corner, requiring the race to be restarted, was a deserving champion. While Jones headed in good heart for the last race at Watkins Glen, in upstate New York, Prost had much on his mind. Hogan, the man directing Marlboro's resources, recalled: 'Ask anyone involved in that McLaren and they will tell you it was awful. There wasn't one thing on it that was commendable.'

In practice at Watkins Glen, Prost's car went straight on at a fourth-gear left-hander. 'I had a suspension failure,' he said. His humour and patience were now exhausted. 'Of all the crashes that year this was the most impressive. I was hurting a lot. I took a fence post on my head, I think. I went to hospital and nothing was broken – but I had a big problem with my neck and my head.'

Ron Dennis was in the United States and clearly wanted to keep Prost for 1981 as his company, Project Four, readied them-selves for joining forces with McLaren. Everyone understood what that meant in real terms – Dennis and Barnard were about to take the reins in the deal Hogan had brokered on behalf of Marlboro. Dennis visited Prost in hospital – as did Jardine. It was Jardine who received the unwanted news from the Frenchman. 'Alain said to me, "I'll never drive a McLaren again",' said Jardine. In fact, Prost, drove in the warm-up on race morning, but felt too unwell to drive a grand prix distance on a track renowned for taking a heavy toll on the body.

In Paris, all these years later, Prost tried to rationalise the complexities and consequences of that particular crash. 'It's difficult to talk about the speed of the accident. When people say they crashed at 300kph, it doesn't mean anything because as soon as you brake you lose speed. So, I can't tell you the speed of this crash except that it was very fast. It happened at the last left-hander, a really fast corner. I just had time to brake, but I went straight on. I didn't lose too much speed. That was a really big accident.' His body and his mind were jarred. 'I almost could not walk, I'd lost balance. I had to stay almost two weeks at home. Afterwards, my back was always a weak point.'

Pertinently, the crash had broken any slender resistance he might have felt to switching allegiance to Renault. 'I met Ron [Dennis] and John [Barnard] in Canada and I knew they were coming into McLaren,' said Prost. 'With Ron and John coming I was tempted to stay. But this crash at the last race was too much. I lost all confidence. Maybe without this crash I am not sure I would have gone to Renault. For me, even at the time, I did not care whether I drove for a French team or not. I just wanted the best car.'

Hogan had flown to Watkins Glen to try to thwart the Renault management from poaching Prost, regardless of the fact that he knew he was almost certainly on a fool's errand. Prost's decision had been made – Renault had their man even though McLaren had him signed to a contract for the following season. Hogan remembered the contact he had at the race circuit with a member of Renault's senior management. He said: 'I was told in that wonderful French arrogant way, "I'll put a letter in the post". I told him he could stick it up his arse. Prost was not for sale.' But Hogan realised, as did Renault, that recourse to the courtroom was not an option. 'This was the downside of the sponsor being responsible, or partly responsible, for hiring and firing drivers,' he said. 'Are you, Philip Morris, going to take Alain Prost to court in France? The answer was: "No way, in the world". In a funny way, we'd seen the error of our ways. We'd got ourselves into a situation where we couldn't enforce a contract. We realised there had to be a different way to do this, giving authority, power, whatever you want to call it, back to the teams.'

Dennis and Barnard duly amalgamated Project Four with McLaren Racing to form McLaren International, a liaison that would in future years profoundly redefine the balance of power in Formula One. Prost went ahead and bailed out for Renault, insisting that money was not at the root of his decision: 'They paid me about half what I could have got if I had stayed with McLaren.' Prost's motivation was simple: he wanted to get behind the wheel of a winning car for 1981.

If that meant breaking the contract he had signed with McLaren, that was the way it would have to be. Others had done so before him, and others would do so afterwards as that is the manner of business in Formula One. Besides, Prost was a relatively small-time player in the game at this point. Much bigger controversies lay ahead.

3

BOY FROM BRAZIL

Just a fortnight before Prost made his debut for Renault in the United States Grand Prix West in March 1981, a young Brazilian sat on the start-line at Brands Hatch for the opening round of the Formula Ford 1600 season.

Ayrton Senna da Silva, not yet twenty-one, was thousands of miles from his home in São Paulo, Brazil. Da Silva – and he would not reduce his name to Senna for another couple of years – had come to England to learn to be a motor racing driver. He had been introduced by Brazilian racing driver Chico Serra to Ralph Firmin, an Englishman renowned for running cars in junior formulae from his base in Norfolk. Senna was entered in all three Formula Ford 1600 (FF 1600) championships that existed for that season; and, in effect, he was placing himself in the shop window of motorsport as England was widely recognised as a training ground for bigger and better things.

He had been living in a rented bungalow in Norfolk for weeks preparing for this moment. Firmin had given opportunities to other South Americans – Carlos Pace, Roberto Moreno, Raul Boesel as well as Senna – and all of them moved into Formula One. Senna – and we shall call him that to avoid confusion – wore his dark-brown hair over his collar and spoke little English when he arrived from São Paulo. But there was already an intensity in his eyes, something that would never leave him. Even then, Senna appeared to look into the middle distance, surveying all in his vision. No detail wittingly evaded his attention.

He had driven karts since he was four, when his father Milton da Silva made his son his first hand-built model driven by a one-horsepower engine. His father owned metalworks that specialised in manufacturing car components, and then became an immensely successful cattle rancher. Senna had an older sister, Viviane, and the family would be completed by the arrival of a son, Leonardo. Milton and his wife, Neyde, provided a home full of warmth and love; and in a country where millions lived in poverty – and still do – Senna's childhood was a privileged one. Inside the family home he was known as 'Beco'. Senna excelled in domestic kart racing. His path had been decided on from an early age; and he made his intentions clear to his family when he informed them that he would like to quit business studies at college in an attempt to become a professional racing driver. His father accommodated his son's wish by providing Firmin with the financial incentive to put Senna in his car.

When Senna came to England, he was already married. Liliane Vasconcelos Souza, a blonde woman of enchanting beauty, from a similar social background in São Paulo as the Da Silvas, had become his bride when he was nineteen. After dedicating himself for weeks in preparation for his first race in England at Brands Hatch, Senna finished fifth. His two team-mates, Enrique Mansilla from Argentina and Mexican Alfonso Toledano, came home first and fourth respectively. It was an honourable debut from Senna.

His next race was at Thruxton in south-west England. On that afternoon, he found himself continuously staring into the lens of the camera of one particular photographer. Like Senna, Keith Sutton was a novice attempting to make a name for himself. Sutton, from a comfortable family home in Cheshire, had been taken motor racing at their local circuit at Oulton Park at an early age by his father, Maurice. For the past three years he had become fascinated by photographing the cars and drivers. He had become so engrossed with his hobby that he decided to make it his career. At Thruxton he was embarking on the earliest days of a journey that would one day make him an immensely wealthy man with an agency of his own, Sutton Motorsport Images. But Sutton, neither then nor now, professed to having a crystal ball in the early spring of 1981. Nor did he pretend that he recognised within the young Brazilian a latent brilliance. Less romantically, Sutton understood that Senna might provide him with the money to pay for a meal at a cheap'n' cheerful roadside café on his way home if he could take a saleable photograph of him.

Sutton had ventured into professional photography as a free-lance without any significant clients or finance. He had a scattergun approach with the camera; any driver from overseas was a target, but Sutton's good fortune was to be in the right place at the right time. He did not know it then, but he was about to gain access that would allow him to create a photographic archive that will be in demand for eternity. He explained: 'At the end of 1980 someone asked me if I had seen the FIA Yellow Book with the rules and regulations. In the back was a list of all the motorsport magazines around the world. I just wrote to them all. I suppose I got a response from almost twenty-five per cent of them – I was delighted. Typically, I was told by editors that they had Formula One covered, but that they were always on the lookout for pictures of drivers from their country who were competing in F2, or other junior competitions.'

Those countries where magazines showed an interest in his work included Japan, Italy, France, Switzerland, Germany, America, Argentina and Brazil. Sutton selected a race schedule around the interest he had solicited from across the globe, and slotted a handful of Formula One races into his diary as well. At Thruxton, he had seen the initials 'BR' – shorthand for Brazil – behind the name of Ayrton Senna da Silva. 'I never introduced myself – I was shy – but I followed him all that day,' said Sutton. Senna came third. 'I got loads of shots of him. I also noticed this very attractive Brazilian girl, who I hadn't realised was his wife, Liliane. As she wandered through the paddock, a lot of the mechanics would put their tools down just to stop and ogle her. They'd never quite seen anything like it; a woman in very tight trousers with that Brazilian arse we all love. It was a treat. You could tell she was absolutely frozen and hated being there – but of course I photographed her as well!'

After Thruxton, the drivers returned again to Brands Hatch. Sutton had to use his imagination to get from his home in Cheshire to the circuit in Kent. In the weeks beforehand he had collected tokens from a brand of cereal to qualify for a free train ticket to anywhere in the country. 'I was on a very tight budget,' he remembered. 'My plan for the year was to get lifts where I could, hitch-hike or scrounge a ride with a motor racing truck as I later did with McLaren to get down to the grand prix at Monza. Basically, I'd travel by any means where I didn't have to pay. So, the train ticket from the Corn Flakes promotion was a bonus. I was wandering around the paddock at Brands Hatch, looking for likely drivers to photograph, when Senna came up to me. In broken English, he said that he had noticed me taking pictures of him at Thruxton the week before and wanted to know why. I told him I was working for a Brazilian magazine.'

Senna responded with another question:'Are you professional?'

Sutton told him that he was, but perhaps failed to mention that he had only just left the amateur ranks. Senna revealed that he was in need of a photographer to send pictures back to Brazil in order to promote himself. He asked Sutton if he would be willing to undertake the assignment.'Not a problem,' said Sutton, like Senna just twenty years old. 'As long as you pay me.' The two young men struck a deal. It rained that day, but Senna, in a new Van Diemen RF81, won his heat, and then the final. Senna's gift behind the wheel looked even more spectacular when he was driving in the wet and here, on a soggy afternoon in Kent, was the first glimpse into the future.

'The podium at Brands is high and, as a photographer, you stand opposite on the pit wall with a big, long lens,' said Sutton. 'But as I now felt that I was *Senna's* photographer I went up on the podium with him. Liliane was up there as well. It was late in the afternoon and the sun was shining right into their faces. I got some lovely pictures of them together. That was the start of my relationship. Through that year I tried to attend as many races as I could. If I didn't go, I'd send my dad, who ended up taking more pictures of Liliane than Ayrton!' The date of Senna's mastery of Brands Hatch in the rain was 15 March 1981.

On that same day 6,000 miles away, Prost started life as a Renault *pilote* at Long Beach, a street circuit in a city suburb twenty miles from downtown Los Angeles. The new season was already mired in controversy – over the legality, or otherwise, of Colin Chapman's latest Lotus.

Under new regulations the aerodynamic skirts that adorned the last generation of F1 cars (providing them with sliding body-work that, when lowered, created greater downforce) had been condemned to the scrap heap of history. Chapman's response was to design his T-88 with two chassis. This was meant to circumvent the ban on sliding skirts. The primary chassis carried the driver, fuel tanks and drive train, all relatively softly suspended. A second chassis carried the bodywork, side pods, wings and radiators and transmitted the downforce to the unsprung portion of the primary chassis. Chapman's critics, like Frank Williams, argued that the outer body – Chapman called that the primary chassis – was simply a moveable aerodynamic device. And they had been outlawed. Williams threatened: 'If the new Lotus is allowed to race, I'll just pack everything up and go home.' Ron Dennis, now joint boss of Marlboro McLaren, was believed to be just as incensed.

For race promoter Chris Pook this was just another headache to deal with. Pook packaged the only street race for Formula One cars outside Monaco. Until he brought grand prix racing to Long Beach five years earlier, the city had hardly been gyrating. It had an average temperature of 70 degrees Fahrenheit and an average age of ninety, so the story went. At thirty-nine, he looked a dead ringer for country singer Kenny Rogers. I met him in his ninth-floor office on Ocean Boulevard with a panoramic view of the city. For the next ninety-six hours, the voice of a man educated at a Dorset public school, the Sorbonne and London University, was law around this town.

'Last night the city turned everything over to us,' he said. 'The streets became our property; we police the area and insure the whole works for £4.5 million.' Four thousand people had been involved in the construction of grandstands and five miles of pre-cast concrete safety barriers. Two hundred off-duty policemen were hired each day – and Pook estimated the grand prix cost £1.3 million to stage. As a neat gesture to 150 old-age pensioners, whose apartments overlooked the track, Pook arranged for transport to bus them out of town on race day. 'We give them five bucks each for lunch,' he said. 'And indigestion tablets!' His English sense of humour had withstood the transatlantic flight, clearly.

He had braced himself for the storm developing around the presence of Lotus and their controversial new car. 'It's all a matter of interpretation of the new rules,' said Pook. 'The pressure is really on us on the technical side. Has the manure throwing of the past year stopped [1980 was punctuated with political fallout] – or is it about to break out again?' Chapman, an innovator throughout his life in F1, who provided championship-winning cars for Jim Clark, twice, Graham Hill, Jochen Rindt, Emerson Fittipaldi and, most recently Mario Andretti in 1978, admitted: 'I knew the car would cause a fuss. But I've always believed it to be legal and I hope it is the car to take us back to the front of the grid.' In the event, the stewards ruled the car illegal.

Against this backdrop, Prost's first race in a Renault caused little more than a ripple of interest outside France, and perhaps not much more inside the country either. Just as well in the circumstances, he must have thought.

Andrea de Cesaris, his replacement at McLaren, ensured he had a miserable afternoon. De Cesaris, driving in just his third grand prix, and a man who would through his early excitable years become known as De Crasheris, struck Prost's car at the start and spun him out of the race. Williams took first and second places through Jones and Carlos Reutemann to announce that the team had lost none of its competitiveness over the winter break. Only eight of the twenty-four cars that started the race were still running at the end.

Jones's speed at the start of the weekend had, however, brought him trouble on a California freeway. He received a ticket for driving at 85mph in a country where the speed limit was 55mph. 'Did the police recognise me? You must be kidding,' said the world champion in a self-mocking tone. 'Over here they are so insular that they congratulate me for speaking such good English for an Australian! And the trouble with the police is that they watch too much *Starsky and Hutch.*'

Prost scored his first points for Renault at the third race, the Argentine Grand Prix in Buenos Aires, with a third-placed podium finish. His team-mate René Arnoux came home fifth. Back in Europe, the next four races at Imola (San Marino Grand Prix), Belgium, Monaco and Spain brought Prost no reward. But then he hit the jackpot – at his home grand prix in Dijon. Arnoux won pole position with Watson alongside him in the McLaren MP4-1 carbon-fibre composite challenger designed by John Barnard, an integral part of the management structure composed by Dennis. The materials for this car had been supplied in a deal with a company called Hercules Aerospace in Salt Lake City, Idaho, USA. According to the team, the car was 'stiffer, lighter and safer' than a conventional aluminium honeycomb chassis. Barnard also estimated that around fifty sections of aluminium had been required on the M29 chassis, whereas his car had just five CFC panels in addition to its outer shell.

Prost was third on the grid. At the outset, Arnoux made a blunder and he was swallowed by the pack. Nelson Piquet opened up a formidable lead over Prost, in this season when the Brazilian was to win the world championship by the narrowest of margins after a shoot-out in Las Vegas. But the heavens opened after fifty-eight of the eighty scheduled laps, causing the race to be stopped. Under the rules, a grand prix has to be 75 per cent complete for the result to count. So, had he driven for another two laps Piquet would have been home and (even in the circumstances) dry, a winner. Prost had no chance of catching him until the storm blew in as his Renault had lost fourth gear. But a fifty-five-minute delay enabled mechanics to repair his gearbox. Prost and Watson had another advantage for the restart. With only twenty-two laps left, they were able to use intermediate Michelin tyres offering greater traction in the conditions. That type of tyre was too soft for full-race distances – and this was an era when pit stops were not part of a race strategy as they are in contemporary grand prix racing – because it wore out too quickly. The Brabham team was contracted to run Goodyear tyres and they did not have comparable rubber.

At the second start Watson passed Prost on the first lap, but he overcooked the manoeuvre and caught a kerb. Prost seized the moment to drive back into the lead, a lead he would never relinquish as he claimed his maiden grand prix victory on home soil. Prost's winning margin was 2.29 seconds on aggregate. Critically, Prost had completed an important voyage of self-discovery. 'After this first one, I knew I could do it again,' he said. 'My mentality changed and from that day every start was taken with the object-ive of winning.' Prost was true to his word. He led races in Britain, Germany and Austria, then won back-to-back grands prix in Holland and Italy. His credentials as a man with a golden future were now undeniable.

Yet, as he prospered, so did the McLaren team that he had abandoned. After being edged out by Prost in Dijon, Watson had said: 'I was third at the last race in Spain, second here, so it looks like first place for me at Silverstone in the British Grand Prix in a fortnight.' Two weeks later, Watson duly delivered before an ecstatic British crowd at the circuit on the old wartime airfield in Northamptonshire. 'After so many races, so many disappointments, I was beyond the point of picking and choosing what grand prix I'd like to win,' Watson told me for the column I ghosted for him for the *Daily Express*. 'I've not had too much success and I appreciate that winning is a special thing. Saturday was very special for British racing enthusiasts. At last, a British driver had won a British Grand Prix in a British car for a British team. It seemed as if the 80,000 people at Silverstone were alongside me driving the car. It was marvellous. Thank you.'

The development of McLaren, under new management, would not have escaped Prost's notice. Little did. Ten days after Watson's triumph at Silverstone, Ron Dennis introduced the team's new premises. The factory, on the fringe of Woking, Surrey, was a warren of spotless, carefully planned workshops housing around £1.5 million worth of sophisticated machine plant. The offices had wall-to-wall carpeting, air conditioning and push-button telephone consuls. Teddy Mayer said with mock seriousness: 'All this and sixty-five people to keep two drivers in toys for the weekend.'

At thirty-four, Dennis was consumed by the idea of broadening the frontiers of Formula One expertise, organisation and presentation. McLaren was already becoming a brand. I remember him telling me: 'I can visualise something bigger, better, than anything that has existed in Formula One. The ultimate team hasn't existed. It's not the desire or the ability that has hindered people – but money. We are trying to evolve something at McLaren International where there is no figurehead. We want the team to portray character and style. The closest example I can give is Ferrari. Any driver would want to drive for them yet they know that if they fall out they become immediate history. It's that sort of mystique, that intangible thing that we want at McLaren.' In that brief speech, he had envisaged the blueprint that would one day profit not only McLaren, but also Prost and Senna.

While McLaren were taking positive shape, Prost's inaugural season with Renault had been far from a failure. After taking second place in the final race in Las Vegas, which was staged, believe it or not, in the car park of Caesars Palace Hotel, Prost finished fourth in the world championship. Jones won the race, which he claimed would be his last. Piquet's fifth place was enough to win him the title from Carlos Reutemann by one point. Piquet experienced motion sickness and fatigue after driving between concrete pillars all afternoon. And the man who designed Piquet's championship-winning Brabham, Gordon Murray, was already at the airport waiting to leave before the flag dropped. Las Vegas was an affront to his senses. Yet to those with a fast buck in mind, the apparent madness of running a Formula One race in a car park made sense. In a town where people are willing to wager a fortune on the turn of a roulette wheel; in a town where clocks are banned; and where hotel room windows are locked to remove the temptation for down-at-heel gamblers to leave the premises other than through the front door, wasn't an F1 race just another vehicle to bet on? For Prost, his result in Vegas meant that in the final eight races he had claimed three victories and two seconds. Pertinently, he scored thirty-two more points than Arnoux in the season. There was no one betting against him starting the following year as the man holding the aces within Renault.

Back in Britain, Ayrton Senna had been making tremendous inroads that would bring him victory in two of the three FF1600 series, the RAC and Townsend Thoresen Championships. He encountered an occasional bump in the road. At Silverstone, Senna's four-race winning sequence came to an abrupt end when rival Rick Morris skipped over the kerbs at the Woodcote Chicane to steal victory in the final few hundred yards. 'Ayrton was furious,' recalled Sutton. 'Really mad . . . I'd not seen him like this before.' Initially Senna talked about making a protest, but, instead, walked back to inspect the chicane with Sutton, his chief mechanic Malcolm 'Pudding' Pullin and Liliane. Morris would later claim his move was legitimate – and there had been room for his Royale to squeeze through – and he would testify that during the final lap he had been edged by Senna on to the grass at full speed, at around 125mph. Sutton remembers most vividly of all: 'I suddenly noticed how Liliane was very nervous. She wasn't very comfortable with Ayrton being a race driver. She worried a lot. Also, she hated how cold it was in England.' From twenty starts, Senna's record in FF1600 was: twelve wins, five second places, one third, one fourth and one fifth. And for one, stunning moment at Brands Hatch in October this looked like it would be the only record he would leave behind in Britain. As Senna stood on the podium, Brian Jones, the voice of Brands Hatch, innocently asked him what plans he had for 1982.

Sutton looked on transfixed as Senna replied. 'Ayrton told Brian, "I'm finished with racing",' recalled Sutton. 'He said, "I am retiring and going back to Brazil". I couldn't believe it. I had no idea this was coming.' Senna had been massively disappointed not to make any kind of impact in Brazil. Piquet's drive to the Formula One world championship had been a headline-making story all year, of course; but in addition Brazilians Roberto Moreno and Raul Boesel had been wining in F3. Sutton explained: 'Ayrton was dispirited that as a Formula Ford driver he had not registered with the Brazilian public. He said that he was going home to work with his father, as had been the original plan when he went to college on a business studies course. I said goodbye to him.

'Ayrton wrote me a lovely letter, which I have on the wall of my office in Towcester. It reads: "To Keith and all the family, thank you for all your help and support this year. I hope to see you again one day." That was it – and I never thought any more of it. I had loads of drivers to photograph, he was just one of them. It never dawned on me how great he was to become . . .' But, truthfully, no one could have known that.

Not too long after Senna had flown home to Brazil, one man whose greatness was a known quantity made a reappearance. In November, Niki Lauda ended the speculation of Formula One's chattering classes by announcing his comeback to grand prix racing with McLaren. Ron Dennis had acquired the signature of the man he felt was a proven winner. John Hogan, from Marlboro, had been part of the decision-making process.

Lauda had abruptly quit grand prix racing during practice at the Canadian Grand Prix in late September 1979, when he was driving for Bernie Ecclestone's Brabham team. He had tired of driving round in circles, he said. Being Lauda, he just stopped. He wished to devote himself to the expansion of his airline, Lauda Air. Of course, he had nothing more to prove in a racing car.

He had twice been world champion for Ferrari, in 1975 and 1977. Lauda had the T-shirt, all right.

But Dennis had established a relationship with the enigmatic Austrian when he ran him in the Procar series. Dennis's would have been a persuasive voice in Lauda's ear to tempt him from retirement – and Hogan would have increased the pressure by reminding him how much he could earn. James Hunt would also play a prominent role in Lauda's recruitment. Hogan explained: 'Ron and I talked through the idea of getting Niki into the team. Then I asked James about how the lay-off could have affected Niki. James replied that it was self-motivation that mattered most. James said that if you were a first-class tennis player, or a golfer, you would always be able to hit the ball, or swing the club. The same applied to drivers; Niki wouldn't have become a bad driver because he had been out of the car for a time. The point James was making was this: We had to find out if Niki still wanted to drive a Formula One car in a competitive manner.' Quite clearly, Hunt did not. In late autumn 1981, it had been reported in the British media that he had been offered £2,600,000 to make a comeback with Brabham. He rejected it flat, when he said: 'There's no point risking your neck for money you don't need. You can't spend a fortune if you are dead.'

Hogan and Dennis found Lauda more receptive to their overtures. 'So Ron put him in a car, at Donington, I think,' said Hogan. 'I heard that Niki was knackered after twenty laps or so. But Ron saw enough . . . he saw that Niki still wanted to do it.' Lauda's scars from the Nürburgring might have disfigured him for life, and he is never seen without a baseball cap, but his sabbatical from frontline motor racing had restored his appetite for Formula One. 'You can't go back to a dangerous sport like motor racing for any other reason than ambition,' said Lauda, at the press briefing called in London to announce his comeback on a £1.5 million a year (plus bonuses) contract. Those of us present heard Lauda add: 'My heart was always beating for motor racing. It just started beating heavier and heavier so I decided to give it a go. No racing driver's wife would support a decision like this, but I think my wife is clever enough to understand that if I really want to do something there is no way she can stop it. Fear is something you have to live with.'

4

JOYLESS SUMMER

Niki Lauda had a minimal amount of time to prepare for his return over the winter. By mid-January drivers and teams had assembled in South Africa for the first grand prix of the 1982 world championship. In many eyes, Alain Prost was favourite for the title.

Lauda, however, had readied himself with due diligence. Some said he was driving again because both his airline and his marriage were in difficulties. He denied this, in that staccato manner that is the man's hallmark. 'I am here because my heart still beats for racing,' he said. 'No other reason.' Lauda had not returned merely to collect a pay packet, no matter how large that might be. He came back for one principle reason – to be the best all over again. Other drivers frolicked around the pool at the Kyalami Ranch, a rich man's playground of thatched huts and chalets. Lauda could be found in mid-afternoon in his room receiving a punishing massage from his personal trainer Willie Dungl – the mentor of Josef Leberer, a man who would later feature in the lives of Senna and Prost, most specifically that of Senna. As Dungl plunged his hands into Lauda's back, the twice world champion told his small audience: 'I am in the best shape of my life.' Running, cycling, cross-country ski-ing and vigorous exercises had combined to dust away the cobwebs that had formed during his retirement years. His speed in the car had already caught the attention of Ferrari's Gilles Villeneuve. 'Niki is making everyone else look silly,' he said.

Importantly, Lauda had cleared his mind for what lay ahead, the risk of doing himself further harm; or worse. 'When I was thinking about coming back, I wondered how I would handle the fear,' he admitted. 'Then I thought about the crash in which I almost died. I made it back after that, so I told myself I can make it now.' Lauda was the story of this opening race – and not all thought he had made a wise decision.

Gordon Murray, the designer of the Brabham, which Lauda walked away from so suddenly, declared serious misgivings. 'I think he's making a mistake,' said Murray. 'I believe part of his come-back concerns money, and that's the wrong reason to go racing.' Yet Murray conceded that now that Lauda had committed to driving in Formula One again, the Austrian would do more than bank his cash. 'Now he's in the car again, he won't shirk,' said Murray. 'The sport needs characters like him.' Then – and always.

The Austrian's team-mate John Watson viewed Prost as 'the closest I have seen to a Lauda clone'. Watson had driven with Lauda in their time together at Brabham – and was about to compete with him again, this time in identical McLaren cars. 'Alain is single-minded, determined and self-confident,' said Watson. 'He knows what he wants and he knows how to get it.' Renault chief Gérard Larousse also felt he understood the measure of the man he had played a part in poaching from McLaren. 'Prost is not the type of driver to be affected by pressure,' argued

Larousse. 'Whenever he has been under pressure in the past, he has responded by being very fast. We started last season in a fog at Renault, but the team never became depressed as Alain always inspired confidence. He drives with a pure, clean style reminiscent of [Jackie] Stewart.'

There was a strong sense of anticipation within the team as the high-altitude track – 6,000 feet above sea level – on the outskirts of Johannesburg was known to favour their turbocharged engine. Larousse suggested: 'We race without thinking about the championship, but we aim to put one of our drivers on the podium at every race. Ferrari could be our most dangerous rivals, while the British teams, Brabham, Williams and McLaren, will be competitive once again.' Yet, despite his admiration for Prost, Watson voiced an air of caution before a wheel had been turned in anger. 'Prost is such a strong favourite that it makes me believe he will not win the championship,' he said. 'Strong favourites have a habit of going down.' Watson had covered all the bases: Prost was fast, seriously motivated, intelligent and, he might have added, politically streetwise; but he would not be world champion. Not this season, at least.

Once down to work in high summer in South Africa, the awesome speed of the cars lapping the Kyalami circuit in practice was captured in one graphic statement from reigning world champion Nelson Piquet, whose Brabham was powered by a BMW-turbocharged engine. 'There should be a sharpshooter at the end of the straight,' said the twenty-nine-year-old Brazilian. 'If anything goes wrong, it would be kinder to get a bullet between the eyes rather than risk hitting the barriers at these speeds.' McLaren designer John Barnard estimated that those cars without turbos – and that included all but the Renault, Brabham and Ferrari teams – were in for a rough time. 'I'm not happy to be fighting for seventh place on the grid, but there's nothing else we can hope for as we are giving away 150 horsepower to the turbo teams,' said Barnard.

But this discontent in the paddock soon gave way to a grievance of another more militant kind. On the eve of the first practice for the South African Grand Prix the drivers – led by Lauda – took what can be only described as industrial action. The wording of the 'super licence' each man needed to possess in order to race in Formula One had appalled Lauda. When the drivers arrived at the circuit, they were met by Lauda and Didier Pironi, president of the Grand Prix Drivers' Association (GPDA), who invited them to join a coach that they had arranged to be parked close by. To our astonishment, the best, and highest paid drivers in the world, all climbed aboard with the exception of Jochen Mass, a driver for the impoverished March Rothmans team, and Pironi. Mass refused to join the strike, while Pironi had been deputed to stay at the track to negotiate with Jean-Marie Balestre, the president of FISA (then the motorsport arm of the FIA, the governing body), and Bernie Ecclestone, the president of the Formula One Constructors' Association (FOCA). For once Balestre and Ecclestone were on the same side of the argument.

The other drivers were chauffeured to the Sunnyside Park Hotel, in a suburb of Johannesburg, where they barricaded themselves into a banqueting suite. Lauda had wanted the drivers to be together to make them less vulnerable to communication or coercion from disgruntled team owners or their management. Once it was apparent there would be no swift resolution to the dispute Lauda requested a bulk delivery of mattresses to the suite. This was militancy of the old school, action that the TUC would have approved, but a shock to the senses of all those involved in keeping the wheels spinning in the multi-million pound business of Formula One.

Lauda was unrepentant. He had seen that the 'super licence' he had been asked to sign required him – and all his rivals – to commit himself to the team that presently paid them. Lauda interpreted this to be a potentially restrictive contract that would limit movement and damage a driver's negotiating position. Lauda informed Pironi – and strike action was secretively planned and executed without the paddock grapevine hearing a whisper of the drivers' intentions. Yet the success of the drivers' stand depended on them maintaining solidarity, not an easy task when the first instinct of a driver is to attempt to gain an advantage over a rival at the earliest opportunity. But Lauda seemed to have a galvanising effect on them.

The atmosphere at Sunnyside Park Hotel was good-natured, like that of a senior dormitory at a boys' school. A piano in the suite was put to good use. Gilles Villeneuve played some Scott Joplin ragtime numbers, then Italian Elio de Angelis, a classically trained pianist, silenced the room with a beautiful rendition of Mozart. The piano proved to be of immense value and not just for the drivers' entertainment. When Arrows owner Jackie Oliver tried, with the help of local muscle, to make a forced entry the piano was pushed against the door to repel the intruders.

The strike was worldwide news, of course. Miners took industrial action – but pampered Formula One stars? Predictably, Balestre tried to threaten the drivers into submission. He would suspend them all, he said. The race would be deferred for a week, and he implied that a wholesale recruitment of replacements would be rounded up across Europe and flown to Johannesburg over the next few days. Balestre, a hard-headed man at the best of times, growled: 'Lauda would be better off at home running his airline instead of stirring up trouble among the drivers.'

Yet when news of their suspension reached their hotel head-quarters, the drivers responded with a round of applause. Pironi insisted: 'We are determined to stay together to resist any pressures that the team managers might try to exert to make us drive. There's no need for a vote. We are completely united. We are not going to drive unless the conditions are changed.'

Several team owners tried to reach their own drivers – and, remember, this was an age before mobile phones had become commonplace – but they were refused entry. But not all owners subscribed to the notion that substitutes could be employed to salvage the South African Grand Prix – and by common consent the prestige of Formula One. Dennis said, plainly: 'No one but Niki Lauda and John Watson will be driving our cars.' One driver did break ranks – Toleman Hart's Teo Fabi. Nigel Roebuck, an esteemed columnist for *Autosport*, reported how Williams' Keke Rosberg had reacted to the Italian's desertion with contempt. 'Fabi ran like a chicken – and lost our respect forever,' said Rosberg. 'Not because he decided to leave, but because he betrayed us. He went straight to Ecclestone and Balestre and related everything we had discussed.'

After a night at the barricades, Pironi rang Lauda the next morning to tell him the drivers had won the day and that they should all return to Kyalami to practise and race. They did – but there was an air of confusion hanging over Kyalami. Roebuck again: 'After a night of indifferent sleep, and not really sure what had been agreed, they complied. A brief practice session, then an hour of qualifying, and that was it as far as race preparation was concerned. The following day, Alain Prost drove one of his greatest races, puncturing a rear tyre while leading, then crawling back to the pits, rejoining in eighth place, and then taking the lead again nine laps from the flag. There weren't too many smiles on the podium, though, for, during the race – *during the race* – a statement was issued by the stewards: "For the purpose of running a race, a temporary truce was called in the disagreement between the drivers and officials. The truce lasted until the end of the race. At the end of the race, the truce was terminated. This means that the position that existed prior to the agreement is effectively reinstated. All the drivers named are suspended indefinitely."

'Duplicitous this may have been, but it was all hot air. When they got to Rio, for the next grand prix, it was still Lauda in a McLaren, Rosberg in a Williams, Prost in a Renault, Villeneuve in a Ferrari and Piquet in a Brabham. And while most of the FOCA team owners may have been livid about the drivers' behaviour, within a few weeks they went on strike at Imola.' The fallout from that action would become apparent soon enough.

Prost's jubilation in Kyalami was evident to all present. 'I just can't believe it,' he said in the post-race celebrations at Renault. 'When I went into the pits after stripping my back left tyre on lap sixty-nine, I thought it was all over.' But on this afternoon in South Africa, after the most extraordinary countdown to a grand prix in Formula One history, Prost provided an exhibition of car control, speed and intelligence to snatch an improbable victory. This would not be an isolated incident, of course.

Lauda commemorated his comeback with fourth place, prompting Dennis to comment: 'Niki was just fantastic, so fit. It all went better than we dared hope. We know we can get the car better than this.' One man not the least surprised by the impact of Lauda's return – inside and outside the car – was Tony Jardine. 'Niki was known to us at Brabham as The Rat,' smiled Jardine. 'That's what he was, in all senses of the word.' The nickname has stuck with Lauda, and in all honesty it is a term of endearment. But Jardine saw The Rat at work at his devious best during his partnership with John Watson at Brabham. 'We took two cars to Long Beach, and Niki came into the pits and demanded more tyres, pointing to some that had been allocated to Wattie,' said Jardine. 'C'mon, I vont zose,' said Jardine, offering a passable impersonation of Lauda's clipped English. 'Wattie came in afterwards and there were no tyres for him; meanwhile, Lauda is setting pole. Then he comes in and hands the tyres back, knackered. That was The Rat.

'Another time we were tyre testing in Brazil. In those days we had five or six qualifying tyres [constructed from an ultra-soft compound with, at most, a life of two laps] to choose from. We had a humungous amount of tyres at the old Interlagos Circuit, where there was a bog in the middle and it was believed to be full of snakes. Niki went out on a set of tyres and the guys from Goodyear [an American tyre company] would go to the pit wall to wait for him to come round. Instead, Lauda reappeared in the pits. Someone ventured, "Hey, Niki, what do you think?" Lauda looked hard at him and said, "Those tyres no good, next!"'

This was a routine repeated a couple of more times, until the guy from Goodyear played what he thought was his ace. 'These tyres are real special, Niki, super soft,' he insisted. Again Lauda drove straight back to the pits and said, sternly: 'Those were joke tyres, give me some decent ones.' On his next run, Lauda lost control of his Brabham and went through some catch fencing out the back of the circuit. Jardine recalled: 'There was one ambulance somewhere, which probably had two Brazilians asleep inside. Niki had gone off down by the lake that had drained in the middle of the track. Then the debate began as to who would go to rescue him – we were all afraid of snakes! Anyway, when we got to him, his helmet was damaged, the back of his hands were ripped open and there was blood everywhere. I am not saying his life was in danger, but he was very white. He had his wits about him, though. "Don't take me to any fucking hospital in Brazil, I go home," he ordered. And that's what he did. We had four more days of testing and no driver. It was one hundred per cent a different era.'

Over time, Jardine watched Prost mature in a not dissimilar vein. 'What I am saying is that Prost developed that same cunning and guile that Niki had,' explained Jardine. 'The Professor and The Rat, what a thinking combination.'

Prost's start to the 1982 world championship continued to gain momentum at the next grand prix in Brazil, but only after a further controversy that was to spark civil war within Formula One. Prost was awarded victory only after Nelson Piquet, first past the chequered flag, and Keke Rosberg, second on the track, had been disqualified when their cars were found to be under the minimum weight of 580kg. Renault had successfully challenged the legality of Piquet's Brabham and Rosberg's Williams.

In brief, the FOCA teams, which comprised all but Ferrari, Renault and Alfa Romeo, the major manufacturer entrants aligned to FISA, the sporting arm of the governing body, had found a loophole in the weighing procedure. They felt disadvantaged by the greater horsepower being generated by the turbocharged engines being used by the manufacturers. The rules stated that a car would be weighted with all coolants and lubricants on board, and said nothing about whether they needed to be in the car when the race finished. FOCA teams claimed this meant that all coolants and lubricants could be 'topped up' after the race. At Brazil, the FOCA teams arrived with 'water cooled' brakes. They were also fitted with large water tanks, which it was claimed were needed to hold the water to cool the brakes. In reality, the water was released in the early laps of the race, which resulted in the cars running most of the grand prix significantly under weight. In motor racing less weight equals more speed. Renault only protested the two cars that finished ahead of Prost – driven by Piquet and Rosberg. But battle lines had been drawn, and after the United States Grand Prix West at Long Beach there was to be a boycott of the San Marino Grand Prix.

It was anticipated that all FOCA teams would boycott this race as a show of solidarity against the handling of the regulations and financial compensation, as well as being a resounding vote of no confidence in Balestre's ability to hold office. But citing 'sponsorship' obligations four teams broke ranks: Tyrrell, Toleman, Osella and ATS all turned up at the Imola circuit, some thirty minutes south of Bologna. In all, fourteen cars formed the grid on 25 April. Arnoux and Prost annexed the front row for Renault – but this was to be an afternoon that would have the most painful consequences for Ferrari drivers Gilles Villeneuve and Didier Pironi.

Prost knew them both exceptionally well. He kept a boat at St Tropez, which was not far from where Villeneuve lived. 'We were having a lot of fun,' said Prost. The three men also shared a game peculiar to them when testing demanded that they should be at Circuit Paul Ricard at Le Castellet. 'I had my best experiences with Gilles and Didier when we were at Le Castellet,' he explained. 'They had a funny game I was involved in, but only at the beginning because this game was too much for me. It was unbelievable what was happening in those days with road cars, the speed we went; making races, doing stupid things. There was a corner going down to Le Castellet and they were seeing who could crash at the highest speed. This meant the car going off the road into a vineyard. I won. once – putting my rental car off the road as fast as I dared. The car was in the middle of the vineyards and completely destroyed. At the end this was not too funny to me; it was too much. Didier was winning all the time because he was much worse than Gilles at this game. He was unbelievable. We were banned from hiring rental cars in Marseilles for a long time!'

Another story of the time involved Villeneuve and Pironi racing each other in Ferrari road cars from Monte Carlo to Maranello outside Modena, the headquarters of the Scuderia Ferrari Formula One racing team. With some inevitability, they attracted the attention of the Italian police who were amazed at the speeds these cars were maintaining on tight, twisting public roads. The two Ferraris were eventually flagged down – with the police waiting to throw the book at them. But once the policemen established the identity of the drivers – Villeneuve and Pironi were considered as nothing less than legends in Italy – the attitude of the officers instantly changed. Instead of writing out tickets, they politely asked if Villeneuve and Pironi would re-enact their race for their private benefit. An apocryphal tale? Maybe. Plausible? Most definitely.

Villeneuve and Pironi had travelled to compete in the San Marino Grand Prix as friends; they would leave with Villeneuve vowing never to speak to his French team-mate again. Prost described the mood in the paddock before the race, when so many teams like McLaren, Williams and Lotus were absent. 'You know, because we had so few cars we had a meeting before the grand prix,' he revealed. 'That was the only race in my life where we had a kind of arrangement, let's say, for the show.' In spite of the boycott, a sizeable and enthusiastic crowd had converged on Imola; after all, with fewer cars the prospects of Ferrari ending the day triumphant had been improved.

The odds on a Ferrari win improved almost instantly. Prost's participation in the race lasted barely six laps before he retired with mechanical failure. After Arnoux's Renault also broke down, on the forty-fourth of the sixty-lap race, Villeneuve and Pironi had no one else to trouble them as they toured the 5.040-kilo-metre circuit in close order. Team orders from the pit wall told both drivers to ease back; a one-two was assured. Villeneuve had survived a heavy crash the previous year at a corner that now bears his name at Imola, so this was to be a moment to savour in front of the *tifosi* who so adored the French-Canadian's fearless and flamboyant driving. This was a man who once brought his Ferrari back to the pits on three wheels, having lost the other one at racing speed. This was a man who the previous summer had won the Monaco Grand Prix, then in the next race kept a train of four cars behind him to win the Spanish Grand Prix at Jarama. This was a man who had been given his drive by Enzo Ferrari, *il Commendatore* of Scuderia Ferrari, who was offered him by Marlboro after McLaren chose not to sign him following a trial in the 1977 British Grand Prix.

According to Brock Yates in his book *Enzo Ferrari: The Man, the Cars, the Races*, the old man looked at Villeneuve and said to colleagues afterward: 'When they presented me with this tiny Canadian, this minuscule bundle of nerves, I instantly recognised in him the physique of the great Nuvolari and I said to myself, "Let's give him a try."'

Pironi, thirty, was not interested in history or team orders on this day at Imola when only one car stood between him and victory. His only grand prix success had been claimed in a Ligier Ford and now he had a Ferrari capable of winning, in Italy. The temptation overcame friendship and loyalty – and team instruc-tions. He simply passed Villeneuve. But at this point, Villeneuve was untroubled. He thought Pironi was providing some theatre, and he knew that a friend would not behave in an underhand manner. So, Villeneuve joined in. His response was to attack and he duly regained his place in the lead. The crowd loved every second. But with the ascendancy properly his once more, Villeneuve assumed that Pironi would now obey team orders and maintain station. On the last lap, Villeneuve never bothered to defend the racing line on the entrance to Tosa, the hairpin not quite the midpoint of the circuit. To his horror, Pironi swept past and with no time for Villeneuve to respond the Frenchman took the flag.

Briefly, Villeneuve attended the podium ceremony, but he was present under sufferance. He felt he had been betrayed by a man that he had considered to be a friend. To further infuriate him, Ferrari's management never scolded Pironi or accused him of ignoring orders. Villeneuve was cut adrift. Before he left the circuit, he vowed: 'I'll never speak to Pironi again in my life.' It was a promise he would keep.

Prost was not the least surprised, as he explained: 'After Imola Gilles was calling me every day. Every day he was talking to me about how angry he was with Pironi and Ferrari. He was so angry against Didier and so disappointed by his situation with Ferrari. He was so close to the team – I don't know if the *Old Man* was aware – but he felt they had betrayed him as well.'

As Prost recounted the bitterness Villeneuve experienced, the irony was not lost on him. Seven years later, he would feel similar disgust towards Ayrton Senna at the same racetrack for an identical reason: betrayal.

But in 1982 the anger was confined to Villeneuve. According to Prost, it was eating him from the inside. 'Didier did not play the rules and Gilles was still absolutely furious when we all got to Zolder,' said Prost. 'If you talked to Gilles all week, as I had, you would understand that he was in a completely different situation in his mind when he came to this race. He was absolutely out of control.' Pironi was ahead of Villeneuve in qualifying when the Canadian drove out on to the circuit determined to record a faster time. He was living the final minutes of his life.

On the track, Villeneuve came at full speed upon the March Rothmans of German driver Jochen Mass. Somehow, the left front wheel of the Ferrari touched the right rear wheel of the March and Villeneuve's car flew into the air. The force of the landing, nose down, tore the seat from the Ferrari with Villeneuve still strapped inside it. 'I came on this accident about ten seconds after it happened,' explained Prost. 'Gilles was still in the seat, close to the catch fencing. Derek Warwick [driving for Toleman Hart] was already there and he came to me and said, "Don't go any closer, Alain." I was about ten metres away.' Villeneuve was pronounced dead in hospital. Prost had no doubts about the cause of death. 'Gilles had killed himself because of his dispute with Didier – he went too far,' he said.

Pironi's Ferrari was withdrawn from the grand prix out of respect for Villeneuve, and no matter the mournful mood of the Zolder paddock the show still went on. The next day Watson won the Belgium Grand Prix – but I remember it more for the lunch we had together a week later in London than for his drive in the most difficult of circumstances. He had been in the business sufficiently long to appreciate some hard truths. 'I'm sure Ferrari's telephone hasn't stopped ringing since last Saturday night with drivers offering their services,' he said. 'Motor racing is a hard, cold business and the people within it have to be like that to exist. When it comes to grasping an opportunity, self-interest comes first.' Watson looked neither hard, nor cold. He is a sensitive man – some would say too soft for the game – who had lived within the boundaries of Formula One for nine years. Villeneuve was the eighth driver he had seen killed on the track. Who could name them, you ask? 'Me, but motor racing memories are short,' he agreed.

'I've no wish to end my life in a racing car, but should it happen it's not going to be me who suffers. For me, it's over. Finished. It's friends and family who suffer.' Some pictures cannot be erased from your mind, no matter how detached you think you are. For Watson, it was the sight of Villeneuve's helicopter standing un-attended that remains clearest. 'Your emotions and feelings have to be suppressed, you're just there to do a job and you must do your best on the day whatever state of mind you're in. But some things strike you like Gilles' helicopter standing at Zolder. It's the personal things that have to be tidied up afterwards, that's the hurtful part.'

Some drivers were disgruntled by the cornering speeds of the cars and the rules that allowed them only two sets of qualifying tyres to fight for their grid positions. The tyres have a life expectancy of one flying lap. 'It means you've got two banzai laps in a session, where you throw caution to the wind,' said Derek Daly, an Irishman driving for Williams. 'You commit your car a hundred yards from a corner and just pray there's no one there when you arrive.' A sport bitterly divided by politics was unlikely to reach any work-able conclusions from any inquiry into Villeneuve's accident. Ron Dennis could not subscribe to the theory that unlimited numbers of tyres in qualifying would lift the pressure. 'Most drivers turn their brains off during qualifying,' he ventured. 'If they could get through twelve sets of tyres, rather than two, it would just give them another ten chances of having an accident.'

There was an apparent desire within the sport to slow cornering speeds, but not for the first time in history, nor for the last, rival teams could not agree on a formula. Perhaps the real clue to the continuing disruptions was held in the competitive nature of those involved. 'I'm not in racing to compete, I'm there to win,' said Dennis. That was the code under which Villeneuve lived – and died.

The misery in that summer of '82 was seemingly endless. At the Canadian Grand Prix in June, Pironi took pole position, but as the cars were released from the grid his Ferrari remained motionless. Young Italian Riccardo Paletti came thundering from the rear of the field and ploughed straight into Pironi's stationary car. Paletti, two days from his twenty-fourth birthday, died from the injuries he sustained at the newly renamed track in Montreal, the Circuit Gilles Villeneuve.

Pironi rebounded from this latest tragedy to win in Holland, then came second at Silverstone. Prost won a solitary point at these two races with a sixth-placed finish at the British Grand Prix. But a row on the same level as the one that divided Villeneuve and Pironi awaited Prost a week later at home at the French Grand Prix; a controversy that drove him and Arnoux apart and split Renault down the middle as though cut with an axe. What happened at Le Castellet on 25 July is open to interpretation. Arnoux and Prost occupied the front row, but they were both swiftly overwhelmed by Riccardo Patrese and Nelson Piquet, driving identical Brabham-BMW cars. When Patrese's engine blew, Piquet accelerated clear of Arnoux at a second a lap until his engine expired on lap twenty-four of fifty-four. Arnoux was then left with a ten-second lead over Prost, whose car was marginally damaged, costing him some downforce.

It was not an undue problem to Prost – as he understood that Arnoux had agreed to allow him through before the end of the race because he held a superior place in the world championship. Arnoux would later swear blind that he had made no such arrangement. Blithely, he ignored the instructions from the Renault pit wall to allow Prost past. According to Renault's Jean Sage, he gave

Arnoux a signal no less than five times to let Prost catch and overtake him. Arnoux drove relentlessly on, however. He was so far ahead he barely caught a glimpse of Prost in his mirrors. He took the chequered flag to great approval from the crowd – but then the time bomb that had been ticking at Renault exploded. Prost and Arnoux may both have been Frenchmen, but they had little else in common. Perhaps the fact that they were of the same nationality was even divisive. One country has room for only one monarch on the track. It is the same across the spectrum of sport. Jimmy Connors had an immense problem with John McEnroe, not just because he showed the same distinct lack of respect for authority and the same willingness to turn tennis into a street fight, but for one fundamental reason: in Connors' mind McEnroe was a rival for the same corporate dollar in the United States, and a threat to his prosperity and success. These men despised one another until they arrived at a place called middle age.

Arnoux, almost thirty-four, from the Grenoble region of France, was an unsophisticated man by his own admission. He had not won a race for more than two years and, by now, had an intense dislike of Prost. Arnoux did not lack popularity in France, however.

Prost's skills in the political arena of a deeply political sport ensured that he had the support of Renault's management. Arnoux's belligerence in disobeying team orders, and later refuting that he had offered to acquiesce to Prost, was like a suicide note. Yet it was Prost who left Le Castellet with his image blackened. He was accused of acting like a spoiled child who had not been allowed to have his own way.

Prost insists to this day that he was a victim of circumstance, not the author of the plot. On that summer's afternoon in Paris in 2008 he explained what had happened from his perspective.

'It's true René and I were never close,' he said. 'But we had only this one real problem, at the French Grand Prix. I was really angry with the Renault management for what happened. On the race morning, René and myself were in the motorhome with the team's sporting director Gérard Larousse and some others. We had a strategy to fight BMW [Brabham]. René was asked to use a little more turbo boost. Normally, BMW were a little quicker than we were, but they were more fragile. The conversation then turned to the drivers. It was suggested to René that if we reached a point where we are first and second, he should let me through because I was in a better position in the championship. I had nothing to say, you know. René said, 'Yes.'

'Everything worked very well. We were first and second. The team put out the pit board to tell him to move over. I was just behind at the time. I think the board read: "P1 Alain".' This is motor racing shorthand that is impossible to misunderstand. The management wanted Prost to be in first position the next time the Renault cars came past the pits. Prost continued: 'Arnoux did not let me pass. I was a little furious because I thought he had an advantage in having more turbo boost. This was a real help on a long circuit like Castellet. To be honest, at one stage I was not racing him as I knew what had been said. But with two laps left, I thought: "Shit, he is not going to let me past." Then I accelerated, but, of course, it was too late.'

Prost is still angered by the memory of the day. 'It was my worst race,' he said. There would be worse, many, many worse, in the years ahead, but this was a wound that cut deep. 'I was competing against the BMWs, not Arnoux,' he said, describing his rationale at the wheel that day. 'If I had known, I would have raced against Arnoux from the beginning. Maybe I would have still lost, but at least I would have raced against him. That was not correct at all.' Prost's

disappointment centred on the behaviour of the Renault management, not Arnoux himself. 'When the management was asked what
happened, they did not tell the truth. They left me alone – I was
called a bad loser. I had very bad publicity. Arnoux didn't say much
either; but that was also bad for me. This race was the first big
problem I had, you know.

'What happened was not correct at all. That was when I realised
when you fight against the top management of a big factory, they
are more aware of their own agenda and look after themselves.
You cannot be confident. It changed the real essence of the racing
spirit and the environment.' Renault president Bernard Hanon
tried to placate Prost in a private meeting, but the damage had
been done. Prost explained: 'You are proud to be part of a big
manufacturer, a small part of France, but the rules are different.
It's not your rules. But, then, I always considered I was an employee.'

To their rivals, the Renault team remained an enigma. A former
team employee, who does not wish to be identified, told me:
'Renault came to Formula One with a turbo engine, and because
it was unreliable at first, it was called the "yellow tea pot". We
also had Michelin tyres first, and a cook that everyone was laughing
at. Typical French, they said. Everyone else had sandwiches and
tea, but they started to come and look at what we did. You know
what happened, everyone else got a cook. It is true that Alain and
René never got on from the beginning. They were different types
of men. René did not have a great technical mind, like Jean-
Pierre Jabouille or Alain, but he was willing to learn. He was just
happy to be a Renault driver. Alain is a complicated man in his
mind. He can be very difficult to understand – but he was always
political. After the French Grand Prix in 1982, the team was
completely divided. The atmosphere was terrible. But I have to
say Arnoux was really quite happy with what happened.

No regrets . . . !' Yet Arnoux also understood he was now living on borrowed time with the Renault management. He was to find solace in the arms of Ferrari who signed him for the 1983 season.

Formula One found only further tragedy. In this joyless summer, when the lives of Villeneuve and Paletti had already been claimed on the racetrack, Didier Pironi's career as a grand prix driver came to an end in heavy rain in practice for the German Grand Prix just two weeks after the French farce at Le Castellet. Through no fault of his own, Prost was central to the accident. This incident was to have a profound effect on him.

Pironi had taken early to the track during untimed practice on the Saturday morning of the grand prix weekend at Hockenheim. The rain was remorseless, but there is a need for drivers to seek a wet-weather balance on their cars in case the grand prix should be raced in such conditions. Prost tells what happened that morning: 'Pironi was the first on the track. It was very wet. Didier was very hot, the car was good. He had strong possibilities to be world champion. He was with a new girl-friend. He was really strong, at the top of his business. Yet no one – certainly not me – understood why he was driving like he was from the beginning. After fifteen minutes or so, I went out. Derek Daly [Williams] overtook me coming down the straight towards the stadium section, not that fast as I think he had only been out for two or three laps. Behind Daly, Pironi saw him move over.' The Ferrari driver calculated Daly had switched sides on the track to present him with room. Of course, he had done no such thing. Suddenly, too suddenly, even for a man with lightning reflexes, Pironi's Ferrari was on a collision course with Prost.

'Didier did not see me, because there was a lot of rain,' said Prost. Afterwards, people estimated Pironi was travelling at

165mph when his left front wheel struck Prost's right rear. 'Pironi's car went up like this, like a plane taking off,' said Prost, directing a palm towards the ceiling of his drawing room. Prost's helmet was grazed as the Ferrari flew over him, pitched on its right side. 'Didier's car came down on its gearbox; then bounced and landed for a second time on its front end. That is what caused the car to break in the middle.'

Without brakes, Prost's Renault kept going into the stadium, a horseshoe-like arena of concrete stands that had been built for Hitler's rallies. 'I hurried back, and Didier was still in the car. A track marshal was already at the scene and not long afterwards Professor Sid Watkins [chief medic] arrived . . . Didier was conscious and really suffering. There was plenty of blood around his head. But it was his legs that were in a bad way, and as I looked I knew there was nothing I could do.' Prost heard voices discussing amputating Pironi's legs. He cannot be certain who was talking, but he remembers how he responded. 'No, NO, NO,' he shouted. But through the confusion Professor Watkins remained calm and Pironi was extricated from his car and taken to hospital. Prost felt emotionally bankrupt as he returned to his team's motorhome. Renault's Gérard Larousse came to see him. 'When is this going to stop?' asked Prost. 'What can I do?' Prost's mind was spinning like a turntable. 'We had all kinds of problems: polit-ical, on the sporting side and human accidents. I was asking many questions, mostly of myself. Everybody thinks I don't like driving in the wet – but it was almost my preference before this.'

Prost engaged in a deeply philosophical discussion with Larousse. Basically, he wondered aloud if it was worth contin-uing to race. Prost actually suggested to Larousse: 'Maybe I should stop.' Instead he vowed to himself that, from this moment onwards, he would drive racing cars on his terms. 'Gerard had said that if I don't go back in the car, it would be difficult,' said Prost. 'But he did not push me. I decided to go out again. But I also decided I should make it in my own way – can you understand that? I realised this day that I had to be more careful – because before I never really realised the dangers. I never realised you could have these kind of things.

'*From this point, I changed the way I drove. I remember 1982 as a defining moment.*'

Prost, who ended the miserable 1982 Formula One season with two victories and fourth place in the world championship, never did ask Pironi how he had been affected by the death of Villeneuve. 'I went many, many times to visit Didier in hospital in Paris,' he said. 'But we never talked about Gilles, because this was difficult. He never let me leave without showing me his leg. Every time, I felt sick.' Six months after the accident, on a chilly morning in February 1983, Pironi invited me to visit him at his home in Paris. He looked clear-eyed, smiling, boyishly handsome . . . everyone's idea of a grand prix driver. It was only when your eyes strayed towards the floor that you could see his heavily bandaged right leg, a reminder of how his career had been ended. He was waiting for his fifteenth or sixteenth operation – he couldn't remember the exact number of times he'd had surgery. This time he awaited a bone graft on his right leg. His left leg was held together by thirty-nine screws. Since leaving hospital the previous November, he had been required to return twice a week for inspections and dressings. He walked with crutches, and the pain was visible in his eyes. Yet he was consumed by a need to race again.

At thirty, he was financially self-sufficient. So, why did he want to risk all again behind the wheel of a racing car? 'The only explanation I can offer is that motor racing is my passion and

I'm ready to lose my life for that,' he replied. 'I would prefer to have two or three years fulfilling that passion than a hundred years of doing nothing.' Jackie Stewart had likened his accident at Hockenheim to an air crash, an analogy that Pironi's own recollections served to strengthen.

With remarkable clarity Pironi told me what had happened: 'It was raining, but I had to test a new tyre in case we were faced with a wet race. The car was good and I was the quickest on the circuit. I was happy with the tyre and on my fourth lap I was slowing down. I was following Derek Daly. He moved over to overtake Alain Prost, but I couldn't see Prost's Renault through the rain. Too late, I saw two big tyres and black rear wing. It was not a big crash. I touched his rear right tyre and my Ferrari took off. My car was flying very high. I could see the tops of the trees . . . it is like a film passing slowly through my mind. When I saw the tree tops, I thought, "This time, it will be very bad." I was sure I was finished because I was perhaps eight metres high and the speed of the car was always fast. I didn't feel any pain. I was upset at damaging the car and disappointed that I would have to use my spare. I couldn't imagine I was broken.'

And then, perhaps most chilling of all, he said: 'I realised something might be wrong when I saw the bones. At first, I thought they belonged to an animal I had killed. Then I saw they belonged to me. I was losing a lot of blood and after twenty-five minutes trapped in the car I heard the doctors say they were going to cut off my leg to get me out. I said, "No, no, I don't want that." I'm not saying that influenced the doctors, but they maybe felt I could wait another five minutes to be freed.' His injuries were severe: two breaks across the right shin, almost severing his foot from the leg; left leg broken at the thigh and shin; left arm and nose broken; cuts and bruises around his head.

Pironi busied himself at this time completing a new insurance policy for the Grand Prix Drivers' Association, of which he was still president, and with the affairs of his building and boat importing companies. But mostly he longed for the day when he could accept Enzo Ferrari's invitation to drive a Ferrari again. 'I would like to be world champion, and then stop racing again.'

Three years later, Pironi was dead. He never could drive a Formula One car again, but the Frenchman had found some compensation from the thrill of racing powerboats. When he crashed at sea in the summer of '86, he did not have the same good fortune as he'd had at Hockenheim. Prost sighed: 'Didier became fascinated by powerboat racing. He raced boats, like cars I would say. On the day he died, he was leading his race, but because there was a helicopter overhead making a film, he drove his boat over a wave and that caused the boat to crash. He didn't have to do that.'

England 1982: Keith Sutton, the young photographer from near Manchester, received a telephone call early in the year. On the line was Ayrton Senna, who told Sutton: 'I'm back.' After spending the winter in Brazil, contemplating a future in his father's business enterprises, he had elected to devote himself to becoming not just a racing driver, but the best racing driver the world had ever seen. He returned without his wife.

Senna would later reason, in that cold-eyed, calculating manner of his: 'If I was going to make it to Formula One, I had to give it all my time and attention. I couldn't do that if I was married, so we parted. I consider it to have been a very precious experience. We didn't have children, so no one else was hurt. It was simply that she wasn't made for me, nor I for her.'

He had accepted an offer to drive for Dennis Rushen, boss

of a successful Formula Ford 2000 team, in the British and European championships. Rushen had asked Senna to bring with him a cut-price £10,000 towards the budget. Senna had encouraged a Brazilian bank, Banerj, and another company, Pool, a Brazilian jeans manufacturer, to sponsor him. Sutton requested a meeting with Senna as he wished to place a proposal before him. They arranged to meet when Senna had a test day at Oulton Park.

Sutton still chuckles at his precocious early conversations with Senna. He said: 'I asked Ayrton at Oulton Park, "What are your ambitions?" Imagine!' Senna responded by claiming he wanted to become a successful Formula One driver. Sutton suggested: 'I might be able to help you. I've done a few grand prix races and I've seen how it works. I've noticed they send out these press releases. Why don't we do a press release for you after each race and send it out to all the media, to all the magazines I work for around the world? We could send some pictures as well – it would be a good way to get publicity rolling.' Senna agreed. Sutton had one further point to make. 'Obviously, I want to be paid,' he said.

With Senna acknowledging the need to put this relationship on a professional footing, Sutton went to work. 'I'd doubled my income,' he said. 'I used to scribble out the press releases by hand, and gave them to a lady I knew in Cheadle who used to correct the grammar and punctuation and then type it out. I had headed notepaper designed with a few of my mates in Manchester. We decided to use Ayrton's helmet in one corner and then took the colours across the page. At the bottom of the release, we advised people who wanted further information to contact me and printed my home address.'

By the end of the season, Senna had won twenty-one of his twenty-seven races and won both the British and European championships. The European championship was claimed over a weekend in Denmark that Sutton still remembers with affection. 'Ayrton said he wanted me to come to Denmark at his expense,' said Sutton. He called Bob Warren whose company, Travel Places, which moves Formula One personnel around the world with great efficiency, was persuaded by Sutton to send an invoice for two return plane tickets to Senna at his address in Norfolk. 'On the flight we had a heart-to-heart about the breakdown of his marriage,' said Sutton. 'He had been upset – but by this time he had a new girlfriend. At the same time, he said that he would be a Formula One driver within a couple of years and, when he did, he wanted me to come with him as his personal photographer. I said, "Yeah, yeah, yeah" and we left it at that.'

Senna's closest rival throughout the year was an Englishman, Calvin Fish. Perhaps Fish became the first driver to fully comprehend the nature of Senna's obsession. Fish told Christopher Hilton, the author of a stream of books on Senna, 'In 1982 when you were challenging him – and when I say challenging I mean wheel-to-wheel, overtaking him or leading him – it was as if he shouldn't be put in that position. He personally felt he was head and shoulders above everyone else and simply shouldn't be in that situation. He felt as if he was in a different league to everyone else. When it came to "I may get beaten today" he didn't know how to handle it. He'd either put you off the track or maybe crash trying to overtake you. It was very strange. Whenever it got to that point, it was panic and he'd go completely to the nth degree to get back in front.'

In Denmark, Sutton and Senna shared a room to keep the costs down. After Senna won the championship, the two of them went to a nightclub. 'Calvin was also there,' said Sutton. 'There was this one girl they both took a shine to. It was quite funny to watch them battling it out for her attentions . . . Anyway, we had a fantastic night out. It was the first time I'd seen Ayrton drunk – it didn't take much though. He was wheeling mopeds about the town. He also ended the evening with a Danish girl – another one – and he asked me to leave the room!'

In this year when Prost had seen so much grief, and learned more about the political landscape that is Formula One, Senna had taken another huge stride forward. Prost had proved he could win grand prix races, a fundamental progression in any driver's career; history is littered with the names of fast men who never won a Formula One race. He had moved himself to the front of the grid, literally and metaphorically.

For the moment Senna may have inhabited a parallel motor racing universe – and in football terms, he was playing for a non-league side while Prost was in the Premier League – but in his own way he had made it plain to all that he was a man who would not denied. Thousands of miles from home, he was in the heartland of European motorsport. He was gaining experience, he was absorbing information from reading, watching and exercising his curious mind. To him, this was like serving an apprenticeship. And he was quietly getting himself noticed.

5

FIGHTING WITH SENNA – AN ENGLISHMAN'S TALE

Late morning at the Circuit de Catalunya, on the northern reaches of Barcelona in the spring of 2008.

Martin Brundle arrived, as arranged, at the Red Bull Energy Centre in the paddock. He is a man with a heavy schedule, always, but as the Formula One cars would not be on the track for another ninety minutes Brundle placed his regular order with one of the girls at the counter that dominates the entrance. 'A cup of builder's tea, please,' he said.

The Red Bull headquarters has three floors, including a sun terrace on the top of the structure. It is said the Energy Centre takes twenty-five people two days to erect and nine trucks are required to transport it across Europe from race to race. On the first floor, there are three bars and a group of chefs preparing a constant supply of nouvelle cuisine dishes at a counter. This is food for the inner gourmand in us all. There is a terraced deck on this level and this is where Red Bull's squadron of young models can be found at times when they are not parading in the paddock. The girls are different at each race. The ground floor has a long counter where coffee and tea are dispensed, and there are a number of tables and chairs to the right and left. On the right side is where the team's workforce is catered for.

This is where we waited for our drinks to be made. They say this facility cost €12 million and it dwarfs the other motorhomes in the paddock in the way that the Empire State Building once again dominates the Manhattan skyline. Austrian team owner Dietrich Mateschitz – Mr Red Bull – has spared no expense.

Brundle led me beyond where the team dines to a room that needed a key to gain access. This was David Coulthard's private sanctuary at a grand prix, and as DC's manager Brundle had an entitlement to enter. Brundle has become such an accomplished broadcaster – his name was first on the team sheet as those responsible for the BBC reclaiming the contract from ITV to broadcast Formula One in a £200 million, five-year deal conducted a recruitment drive in late 2008 – that it is easy to forget he was a distinctly competitive racing driver. His fast wit, deep knowledge and an informative commentary on all things Formula One have won him a succession of broadcasting awards. Brundle's grid walk in the minutes before a grand prix swiftly became *live* television *par excellence*. From world champions to reigning monarchs, if you are on the grid, you are fair game to Brundle. But while he grants us access to a driver's mindset before a race – is Hamilton as calm as he appears? Is Raikkonen as rudely disinterested as he pretends? – his best work is reserved for his analysis and insight during the course of a grand prix. His secret is to tell us what the pictures we are watching *don't* reveal to the untutored eye.

He never won a grand prix – second at Monza and Monaco

were the closest he came – but Brundle drove in 158 Formula One races over a dozen years from 1984 to 1996 without ever getting his hands on a truly competitive car. He was the 1988 World Sportscar Champion and he won the Le Mans 24-Hour race in 1990. Brundle had announced his talent at an early age. As a teenager, he drove for Audi as team-mate to Stirling Moss in a touring car championship, but he had always yearned to race single-seaters – and this was where Brundle, a young man from King's Lynn in Norfolk, was first to encounter a young Brazilian named Ayrton Senna. His career would run parallel to that of Senna's, but ultimately, he would not be able to compete on the same plane as the Brazilian.

In 1983 that was not the case, nor the indication that it would be. In Coulthard's private domain at Red Bull, Brundle rolled back a quarter of a century in his mind. 'I was a year ahead of Senna as I'd already done a season in Formula Three in 1982,' he explained. 'I first saw him when he was dominating in Formula Ford, so I knew about him. What I found slightly weird was that when Senna was coming to Formula Three it was automatically assumed he would win the championship. I was a bit miffed.'

According to Keith Sutton, McLaren had made an offer to pay for the Brazilian's season in Formula Three. Senna declined – because Sutton suspected the contract he was being offered from McLaren would have required him to commit himself to the team for a number of years. There was nothing unusual in this type of arrangement being offered to a young driver of promise. Years afterwards, Lewis Hamilton would tie himself to just such a contract with McLaren as the burden of funding his progression through motorsport was beyond the means of his family. But Senna, with his sponsors from Brazil, and family support, could afford to retain his independence. He reached an agreement with West Surrey Racing, an F3 team based on a small industrial estate near Sunbury-on-Thames. Team principal Dick Bennetts had built an enviable reputation in the category and had already provided cars for Stefan Johansson and Jonathan Palmer to win the F3 championship in 1980 and 1981 respectively. Bennetts prepared a Ralt-Toyota for Senna. Brundle had a similar Ralt-Toyota, run by Eddie Jordan, a gregarious Irishman who would command his own story in the following years. 'I moved to EJ's team, relatively new at the time, as I had lost sponsorship from BP which prevented me from staying with David Price's team,' explained Brundle. Jordan, struggling to raise finance himself, had invited several drivers to test for him the previous summer. 'Senna was one of the few [for whom] I did this for nothing,' said Jordan, a man not renowned in the paddock as a philanthropist, it must be noted. 'Senna was something very special, but I knew inside that he would not drive for me. To be honest, I just didn't have the pedigree he was looking for. I was thrilled what he did in my car, but I felt he lacked something as a person then.'

Instead, Jordan dedicated himself to assisting Brundle to beat him. Brundle sipped his tea, and still sounded perplexed as to how Senna's reputation had grown at such an alarming speed. 'I couldn't understand that he was perceived to be a clear favourite to take the F3 championship,' he said. 'I am not saying I was offended, but it caught my attention. It was a kind of warning, wasn't it? I'd read a bit about him. Didn't he go home and give up his racing career? Anyhow, he turned up in Formula Three and won the first nine races!' Brundle released a slow smile, as he added, 'Which kind of confirmed he might be quite good.' By now Keith Sutton was sending his press releases to myriad

Formula One team bosses: Ron Dennis at McLaren, Bernie Ecclestone at Brabham, Peter Warr at Lotus, where an Englishman called Nigel Mansell was manfully looking to make an impression. 'But Ayrton really only wanted to know that I was sending them to Ferrari,' said Sutton.

From time to time Brundle and Senna exchanged small talk on the podium as the English driver was consistently second. 'He kind of broke me in half with his immaculate start to the season,' admitted Brundle. Yet if Senna thought the Englishman was history, he was to discover otherwise. Brundle again: 'Several things happened that year that I saw with him as a fellow grand prix driver later on. There was a race at Silverstone and Senna was so far ahead in the British F3 championship that he opted to compete on that afternoon in the European championship, as it was a combined race open to drivers from both championships. I was trying to score some points in the British championship to try and catch him up. About halfway through the final part of qualifying, I was easily the fastest of those in the British championship. But I was only twelfth, or maybe tenth on the grid, on the British championship tyres, which were harder and slower than the European ones, which were softer and faster. I didn't see much point in being the fastest British runner and yet so far back down the grid. I made a spontaneous decision to change tyres. So, near the end of second qualifying I said to EJ, "Let's go European." Bosh, I stuck my car on pole. That was the first time I had beaten Senna; and for the first time, he looked flustered. In the race, I pulled away at the front. And Senna just couldn't live with my pace – to the point where he crashed big time at the Woodcote Chicane.'

Brundle had claimed a psychological edge. One week later, the duel resumed at Cadwell Park, just four miles from Louth on the east of the Lincolnshire Wolds. 'We were trading pole position all through qualifying,' said Brundle. 'Until Senna dropped his car at the spot called The Mountain and hit a marshal's post. I went to look at his car – and it was a mess because they were primarily made of aluminium and pop rivets. How on earth he got out of that without a broken leg I'll never understand. As it was, Senna was out of the race. I won and I was starting to haul some points back.' Two weeks later, the battle between them intensified to another level at Snetterton, in Norfolk. Senna's attempt to recover from fourth on the grid meant he had to first hunt down Brundle, then find a way past him. The first part of the mission was accomplished by mid-distance of the race. From that point, Senna understood that only by taking an extreme risk could he hope to overhaul Brundle. For his part, the Englishman was in no mood to acquiesce.

With some inevitability, the two drivers collided as Senna tried a manoeuvre that Brundle covered. Senna spun into a barrier. Each man would tell you the other was to blame. Afterwards, Senna somewhat optimistically demanded a tribunal and spectators who witnessed the incident were asked to describe what they had seen. Well, as Brundle was something of a local hero in this part of the world Senna's search for justice was made in front of a prejudiced jury. 'I didn't get fined, or get my licence endorsed,' said Brundle, who chuckled at the memory. 'Ayrton was quite an emotionally driven man, wasn't he? He thought he was racing in Britain against the local favourite, so he thought the Establishment was against him.' Of course, Senna's sense of injustice would manifest itself later on a global stage rather than the repertory theatre that was the British F3 championship. But as he would prove, again and again during his career, Senna had an enviable talent for placing the past behind him; filed, but not necessarily forgotten. Besides, before the next round of the championship he had another appointment. He had a rendezvous at Donington to drive a Formula One car for the first time at the invitation of Frank Williams.

In his office at Grove in Oxfordshire, Sir Frank Williams has hung three portraits, two of them of racing drivers. The odd one out is Margaret Thatcher, a Prime Minister whom Williams, a fierce patriot, always viewed with great affection. One of the drivers is Piers Courage, who competed in just twenty-eight grands prix. Courage was a member of the brewing dynasty, an Old Etonian, who shared Williams' passion for racing cars. They befriended one another as young men and for a while shared a flat in Harrow. In the sixties, Courage toured Europe competing in various categories. Often, he slept in his car transporter. Courage's determination and, it's said, his debonair charm, propelled him towards the elite end of motorsport more than the riches of his family background. In 1969, Williams first entered Formula One with a private Brabham BT26 with Courage behind the wheel. Together, they scored memorable second places in Monaco, behind Graham Hill in a Lotus, and, at the US Grand Prix at Watkins Glen, behind Jochen Rindt's Lotus. In 1970, Courage rejected an offer to drive for Ferrari to stick with Williams, who had negotiated a deal with Italian company De Tomaso to supply him free chassis. Sadly, Courage was to become a victim in an age when all too often racing drivers perished in pursuit of their dreams. On lap twenty-three of the Dutch Grand Prix at Zandvoort, a plume of pitch-black smoke appeared on the far side of the circuit and Courage failed to come past the pits. On a fast part of the circuit, his car had left the track and hit a grass-covered sandbank. The car rolled and exploded into flames – Courage was just twenty-eight when he died. 'I remember clearly that when he died a nation grieved,' said Williams. Another twenty-four years would pass before a second driver was killed driving for him. The third portrait is of that man: Ayrton Senna.

Each day, when he is not at a grand prix, Williams comes to his office to retain a personal grip on what is happening within his team and within the complexities of the sport. He has been confined to a wheelchair since 1986, because his own unquenchable thirst for speed caught him out in a rental car as he rushed to make a flight from Marseilles after leaving a test session by his team at the Circuit Paul Ricard at Le Castellet. His car careered off the road and Williams sustained terrible injuries that left him a quadriplegic. He has never blamed anyone but himself for his disabilities – and he has most definitely never lost his lust for motor racing or the special men who drive fast cars with the most zeal. A man most lustrously typified in Williams' mind by Senna.

Williams had watched – and noted – the prodigious impact the Brazilian had made in each category he had competed in. Clearly impressed, Williams invited Senna for an audition in one of his cars even though he did not have a vacancy. In this business particularly, the smart men try to be one step ahead of the game. In time to come, if Senna became successful and in demand, Williams might have gained an edge because drivers do tend to remember those who offered them assistance when they were on the lower rungs of the ladder.

In 1983, Williams had arranged for Senna to drive a Formula One car for the first time, but he had arrived late to meet him at Donington through mildly embarrassing circumstances for an owner of a race team. 'My car broke down on the M1 about two junctions before the Donington exit – its marque shall remain nameless,' said Williams when we met at his team's HQ in the summer of 2008. 'I was rescued within the hour, but arrived a bit late; not a good start. Happily, the young man didn't see fit to give me a bollocking.' Senna had invited Brazilian broadcasters TV Globo to be in attendance, along with Sutton. Ever diligent, he wanted filmed evidence of his test to be shown at home in Brazil. Sutton has a photograph of Senna bare-chested, with his overalls tied around his waist, describing the characteristics of the car to Williams, listening intently with a clip board and pen at hand. Even then, Senna had an aura.

Williams watched as Senna drove, from memory, around thirty-five to forty laps of Donington. 'He was driving very much under control and well within himself,' he said. 'At the time Jonathan Palmer was our test driver and Ayrton posted lap times faster than Jonathan. We didn't decide when he stopped – Ayrton did. I think we wrapped up around lunchtime.' This was peculiar in itself, as most drivers, given a test in a Formula One car for the first time, tend to spend every available moment of daylight on the racetrack. Not Senna. He had learned all he needed, thanked the team and left.

Williams had no driver vacancy for 1984 as Keke Rosberg and Frenchman Jacques Laffite were under contract, but he retained contact with Senna, because he liked what he had seen and because he found in the Brazilian a young man who shared his own deep-rooted passion for motor racing. Williams remembered: 'Ayrton was living quite local, near Reading I think, so on a few occasions we had dinner. Ayrton had this five-speed Alfa Romeo 1300, a little four-door hatchback. He drove the thing down the middle of the road at 25mph in fifth gear while he was talking. I remember the judder-judder of the engine. I don't know if it was a put-up job to have me on the edge of my seat, but more likely he was just so absorbed with what he was saying that he forgot to change gear.

'I did say to him: "Do you always drive like a wanker?"'

'Ayrton said to me, "What do you mean?"'

'Well, when my wife was learning she wouldn't have driven a car like you.'

After his Williams test drive, Senna returned to defeat Brundle in the next F3 race at Silverstone. But the Englishman turned the tables at Donington. And then came fireworks at Oulton Park, a circuit in Cheshire that features rapidly changing gradients and blind crests. Brundle had now won four of the previous five rounds and Senna could no longer take the championship for granted. After all, Brundle cherished his own dream of graduating to Formula One. The fight between the Englishman and the enigmatic Brazilian had become sufficiently newsworthy for the sports editor of the *Mail on Sunday* to agree to my request to cover the round at Oulton Park. When I shook hands with Senna, he winced. I had not appreciated that forty-eight hours earlier his car had catapulted into a trackside on this circuit after the rear suspension of his Ralt-Toyota failed at 110mph during a special test session. The wreckage of the car was piled in pieces behind him, a sheet placed over the twisted metal as though it were a corpse. He was particularly anxious that photographs of his damaged car did not get published in Brazil. 'Of course, my family still worry and I wouldn't like them to see the pictures,' he explained.

Senna escaped more lightly. A bruised right hand seemed an acceptable price to pay for the high-speed shunt. 'He was a lucky man,' said Dick Bennetts, a softly spoken New Zealander, who had to organise a replacement car to be hired for £2,000, a substantial sum of money. The car would be returned in less than pristine condition after the race following another bust-up with Brundle. On the twenty-ninth lap of the thirty-five-lap fifteenth round of the Marlboro F3 championship Senna parked his borrowed car on top of Brundle's Ralt-Toyota. The Brazilian had made a desperate bid to overtake Brundle – the race leader – on the inside only to collide and ride up into the air, eliminating both cars. Back in the pits, a disgruntled Brundle told me: 'It should have been my race, instead all I've got to show is tyre marks from Senna's car down my helmet.'

Twenty-five years later, Brundle reviewed that accident through the lens of history. 'In that race I beat Ayrton off the line – I could always start better than him,' he said. 'But towards the end of the race, he pulled a move on me where there wasn't any room. They had to lift his car off my shoulder before I could get out of my car. Senna was prepared to have a crash with you to establish precedent and authority. Quite clearly, this was an indication of one of the traits we would see from him later in Formula One. I think at the time I was slightly bemused by this. I did think he was over the top. We ended up twice, possibly three times, being asked to explain ourselves to the stewards. Senna got very upset. His licence was endorsed and he was given the blame. As he would reveal in later years in Formula One, Senna thought the entire Establishment was against him. Certainly, he felt this was the case in Formula 3; it wasn't of course, but he brought an approach that no one had really seen before.' Brundle, it must be emphasised, was not averse to taking care of himself in the clinches. At twenty-four, he was heading in one direction only: Formula One.

His admiration for Senna as a driver was informed from that

season in Formula Three, when he learned sooner than most what a gift the Brazilian possessed. 'Sure, there was a sense that here was a man whose philosophy was unique in my experience,' he said. 'Senna let you believe he would rather have an accident than yield to you. But the car control that I saw from him, especially in the rain, was just extraordinary. He had a sixth sense where the grip was. One example stands out a mile. Early on at Silverstone I beat him off the line in appalling conditions. So I am heading down to Stowe [a fast right-hand corner at the end of the Hangar Straight] and it's soaking wet. I brake for the corner really nicely on the inside – only for Ayrton to go flying past me on the outside.

'I'm thinking inside the car, "Bye, see you . . . wouldn't want to be you!" At which point, after I have tippy-toed through the apex, he emerges in front of me, having done a wall of death on the rubbishy bits of old tyres where he knew there was more grip. Shortly after this, the race was red-flagged because of a big shunt involving someone else. We're back in the pits and I'm thinking I'm going to try that. On the formation lap for the restart I go steaming down the outside at Stowe, hit a puddle and just keep the car out of the barriers. Remember that all I am doing is going to the grid for the restart. Right, I tell myself, I won't be doing that in the race. Ayrton beat me off the line and we finished first and second. Talking to him on the podium, I said to him, "Your line wasn't so special at Stowe in the second part of the race, was it?" Senna replied, "I didn't try it. There was too much water to do that again." How did he know that? When a circuit is covered in water, you don't know how deep the lying water is. Anyway, he somehow knew not to try it again. That story is all you need to know to sum up the extraordinary ability of Ayrton Senna.'

★   ★   ★

Marlboro McLaren had committed themselves to testing promising young drivers from the Formula Three championship in one of their Formula One cars: Senna and Brundle were the stand-out candidates. They also included German Stefan Bellof, a driver of immense potential in F2. McLaren's John Watson had been enlisted to drive at Silverstone to establish a lap time as a benchmark on that chilly day in a British summer. 'We all blew away Wattie's lap time in about five laps, though he didn't need to impress us,' said Brundle. Out on the circuit, a man who had nothing to do with McLaren stood at the side of the track. Herbie Blash, from the Brabham Formula One team, had come specifically to watch Senna. He was not disappointed by what he saw even though Senna's first run in the car came to an abrupt end when the car blew an engine.

'We all did roughly the same time, but it was pleasing for me as Senna had already driven an F1 car before,' said Brundle. His father had accompanied him to Silverstone, and the two men walked around like children who had been given the keys to Santa's grotto. In the meantime, Senna negotiated a second run by pleading with Ron Dennis that his first period in the car had been compromised by an engine failure for which he was not culpable. 'Senna then went about three-quarters of a second faster than us,' recalled Brundle. 'We didn't get a second run. I don't know how Senna managed it, but he already had worldliness at that stage that Bellof and I didn't have. We were very excited to be driving a McLaren – a car with around 550 horsepower compared to the 160bhp of an F3 – but Ayrton's brain was ticking over. He never missed a trick.'

Not long afterwards, Sutton came home one day to be greeted with a message from his mother. 'She said she had taken a call for me from someone called Bernie Ecclestone – had I heard of him?' he said. 'I said that I had, and when I called him back he asked me how he could contact Ayrton. Of course, I gave him his address and telephone number.'

Bernie Ecclestone has been the most influential man in Formula One for more than three decades. He is the president and chief executive of Formula One Management (FOM), which, in simplest terms, makes him the paymaster of grand prix racing. At the last estimate, his private fortune totalled in excess of £2 billion. His vision brought Formula One from a small-time entertainment for petrol heads to a global audience of billions, as he understood the power of television. He took the financial risk in the earliest days of expansion, which is why he received – and still does receive – most capital gains from the commercial rights of Formula One. He is the Cecil B. DeMille of the pit lane. Like the Hollywood filmmaker, all Ecclestone touched made brilliant returns at the box office. He has not entirely escaped scandal, however. His £1 million donation to New Labour before Tony Blair entered No. 10 Downing Street coincided with Formula One fearing that a ban on tobacco advertising would have a profound impact on teams' budgets. Ecclestone's donation was returned – but only after F1 had been exempted from a tobacco-advertising ban. Privately, Ecclestone considers the episode as one of the few actions of his life that he has any regrets about.

To Ecclestone each day is a challenge to broker the next deal, even as he edges nearer his eightieth birthday. Heart bypass surgery in 1999 has not slowed him for a moment. 'I'd rather have heart surgery than go to the dentist,' said Ecclestone in a tone that implies he isn't joking. No sport has ever had such an autocrat in charge, or one with as much charisma. I have known him – and yet not known him at all – for almost thirty years. No phone call to his office has ever gone unreturned. To my knowledge, he has never told me a lie. If he dislikes a question, he swats it away. He agreed to see me for lunch for this book.

I arrived five minutes early at his office, identified only by its number and located opposite Hyde Park in a smart terrace in Knightsbridge.

I was shown into a waiting room behind the receptionist's desk that had an oval table and enough chairs to comfortably accommodate a board meeting of eight directors. On a sideboard was a bronze of two hands clasped together and another of a tray piled high with $100 bills. Those two pieces symbolised, not by accident, Ecclestone's business philosophy. His handshake is his bond – and, well, the money tray needs no explanation, does it? Another artwork, if it can be called that, is a framed 3D-caricature limited edition depicting a modern executive. He is sitting with his feet on his desk, a phone clasped to his ear and the sports pages open in front of him. The *Wall Street Journal* lies untouched at his feet, and his golf clubs are in a bag not far from an in-tray that is overflowing. On the wall is a certificate from BSU: Bull Snot University. It shows him to be a Bachelor of Bull Holada Bullada. Ecclestone's waspish sense of irony is at play as this is precisely the type of modern executive he loathes with a passion.

Once he had put his head around the door, we walked through a labyrinth of desirable streets and mews to a pub where he has a table permanently reserved. A glass of mineral water arrived at the table before he had time to sit down. Ecclestone lunched healthily on chicken –'No cabbage, thanks' – warmed peaches and an espresso. He took one phone call – someone was bidding on behalf of him and a partner at the Newmarket Sales. It would

be indiscreet to reveal at what point he ejected from the auction
– but let's say that he braked late.

Ecclestone remembered well when Senna first came to his
attention, at a time when another Brazilian, Nelson Piquet, was
in the process of winning his second world championship for
his Brabham team that had its headquarters on a small, non-
descript trading estate in Chessington, Surrey. Brabham took
Senna to test for them at Circuit Paul Ricard. The team's
engineers and management had deliberately set the car up in a
fashion that would make it difficult to drive at the optimum
speed. They wanted to know if Senna would notice. 'After two
laps, Senna came in and told us what we already knew,' said
Ecclestone, who ran Brabham for fifteen years from 1972. The
Brazilian had passed his first examination – the second hurdle
was to drive the car fast and that came as second nature to him.
But there was one obstacle that proved insurmountable.

'Ayrton would have driven for us except for Nelson,' said
Ecclestone. 'Nelson didn't want him for the same reason as we
did – Senna was good. We had all the excuses from Nelson's
sponsors telling us that it wouldn't be good commercial sense
to have two Brazilians in the team. We were on good terms
with Nelson and knew how good he was. We thought we knew
how good Senna was – but why get in an argument with Nelson
if there was a chance, no matter how small, that Ayrton wasn't
as good?' British driver Derek Warwick, who had raced against
Piquet in Formula Three, a rivalry as hard and uncompromising
as the one between Brundle and Senna, had already told me:
'Piquet was a master at destabilising people. He tried to get
inside my head – but he never did. But he would succeed with
Alain Prost. Bernie had a lot of time for Piquet; they were more
than boss and driver, they were mates.'

Senna would remember the lessons learned and one day he would use the power at his control to his own ends. Of course, limiting another driver's options would be elevated to an art form a decade or so later by Michael Schumacher. He was a man who preferred his team-mates at Ferrari to be his formally contracted outriders.

Incredibly Brundle went to the last round of the 1983 F3 championship at Thruxton one point ahead after being twenty-two behind at one stage. 'Eddie Jordan was brilliant, he just motivated me,' explained Brundle. 'On the start line, Senna would be alongside me and EJ would just look at me and say, "You've got the beating of this guy." EJ just told you all the things you wanted to hear.' Jordan had his own motivation for beating Senna. Having been given a free test drive by Jordan in 1982, Senna hardly spoke to him during this tumultuous fight with Brundle. The Irishman took a dim view of this. Brundle understood, though, that the odds overwhelmingly favoured Senna at the climax of a spellbinding season. 'I'd just won a round of the European championship at Donington, but, basically, I had detonated my engine,' he recalled. 'It was knackered. We had no money whatsoever in the pot. Halfway through the year I'd won the F3 support race at the Austrian Grand Prix – a race that included Gerhard Berger on home ground – but on the way home the team suffered a terrible tragedy. Our truck went over a cliff and my mechanic, Rob, was killed. Our three cars and truck ended at the bottom of a ravine. We had to rebuild the team. Senna, in contrast, had taken his engine in the boot of his car to be rebuilt at Novamotor in Italy.'

Apparently, Bennetts from West Surrey Racing had discovered

by scrutinising Brundle's car in a couple of races earlier that Eddie Jordan was running an engine different from the one he had. Novamotor's engineers agreed to rebuild WSR's power-plant, and Senna deputed himself to make the journey. Ron Tauranac, who built the Ralt chassis, had some new parts for the 1984 season, which he made available. Brundle said: 'I got his new push rod suspension and Senna was given new side pods with five per cent more downforce. At Thruxton, the side pods were just the ticket.'

Senna took pole, and after the Brazilian made a perfect start Brundle found himself chasing an American called Davy Jones. What the Englishman could not know was that Senna had taped up the oil radiator outlet to heat up the engine more speedily. Senna's benefit was that the temperature was at an optimal level within a lap or so rather than the usual six or seven. All he had to do now was to remove the tape before the water temperature rose too high. This proved none too easy. Ultimately, he had to unfasten his seat belts in order to reach the tape. This was a man whose mind never slept. Victory fell to the Brazilian with Brundle lagging home in third place behind Jones. 'I saw Senna have a wobbly moment when he took the tape off,' said Brundle. 'But if I am honest, he was a worthy champion. Afterwards, he was very magnanimous. I remember him saying I was the best British driver since Jim Clark. His parents had travelled from Brazil to be at the race – and I think their son and me had done each other an awful lot of good.

'We did chat a bit through the year, but there was an intensity about Senna that didn't allow you too close. I was busy trying to sell Toyotas to make a living from the family business, and I was married. We were both trying to find our way. He was a long way from home and, for the first time, I was beginning to realise that I could be a professional racing driver. Until that point I had been a hobby driver, but I could see that it was all coming together. We both leap-frogged into Formula One after our epic year. But let's be honest, Ayrton was destined to be in F1 anyway. In some ways, I was hanging on to his shirt tails. He was so highly rated that I looked good against him.'

Brundle's test with the Tyrrell F1 team at Silverstone convinced team owner Ken Tyrrell to offer him a contract for 1984. 'As I'd already driven a McLaren I flew in the Tyrrell and Ken was very excited about that,' he said. On the same bright, cold day Senna drove the Toleman Hart that Warwick had driven at that summer's British Grand Prix. Team designer Rory Byrne – who would later create world championship-winning cars for Benetton and Ferrari – urged Toleman to sign him on the spot. But Senna had no need to rush.

6

HOW PROST PROFITED
FROM THE SACK

In 1983, Alain Prost's mind was focused on winning the world championship yet he was not entirely oblivious to what was happening in Formula Three. 'Sure, when you come from karts and F3 yourself, you always look to see who is coming next,' he said. 'At the time, if you asked people from the outside they were talking as good about Martin Brundle as Ayrton Senna. If you asked who would be the top guy of the next generation, they were maybe a little bit more for Martin than Ayrton. But those who knew Ayrton from karts knew that he had an attitude, perhaps a little strange in someone so young, but he was already focused and obsessed. They liked that about him.'

Murray Walker, the voice of motorsport in Britain until his retirement, had also taken a keen interest in the drama being played out beyond the arena of Formula One. 'I spotted Ayrton Senna – and you'd need to be blind not to have spotted him – when he first came to Britain to drive in Formula Ford in 1981.

And the reason I spotted him, with brilliant acumen, was that he won virtually every race he drove in. I am besotted with motorsport, it's my life's passion.' He commentated on anything that moved, he said. 'I was always at something, partly because I was interested, but partly because I was bright enough to realise it could be of benefit to me in the future. I always applied myself to finding out and getting to know the drivers in lesser categories. I remember at the end of 1981 at Brands Hatch Senna asked me: "How do I get a video of this race?" I told him I'd send him one if he won. Well, surprisingly, he didn't win, but I sent him one anyway.'

Walker traipsed the country, from Thruxton in the south-west to Oulton Park in the north-west, chronicling for BBC Television viewers the showdown between Senna and Brundle while still broadcasting from Formula One races around the world. 'I felt sorry for Martin, subsequently, because Senna, like Prost, was not only a bloody good driver, but he was an outstanding politician. From the beginning I could see Senna had this obsession to win at all costs. I don't think his ruthless streak was something that he developed when he got to Formula One. I think it was there all the time. There's a very fine line between ambition and being determined to win and being the *Boy's Own Paper's* villain.'

Prost never presented Walker with any such conundrum. By 1983, the Frenchman had become a formidable force within Renault and within the world championship. 'Alain was a master tactician,' said Walker. 'He thought it all out and drove as fast as he needed to drive.' Wasn't that precisely what Prost pledged he would do following Pironi's accident with him that had such dreadful consequences for the Ferrari driver? 'Alain had such a quiet personality, he didn't shout,' said Walker.

'In interviews, I always had to say, "Will you speak up, Alain."
He never spoke in more than a whisper.'

Eddie Cheever, an American with Italian heritage, now partnered Prost, as replacement for Arnoux after he had joined
Ferrari. Cheever was an amiable man, and as an American of
Italian extract he sat comfortably within Renault's plan to exploit
those markets. But he was no match for Prost on the track.
Often, he was a second a lap slower. Of course, Cheever, like
any racing driver, looked elsewhere to understand this deficiency
in speed. He would complain that Prost was getting preferen-
tial treatment, and that his car was somehow inferior. At Renault,
they dismissed Cheever's claim. The management would point
out that Cheever experienced more mechanical breakdowns
because he was harder on a gearbox, or an engine, than Prost.

Although Prost put his Renault on the front row for the
opening round of the 1983 world championship in Brazil, he
finished seventh. Nelson Piquet, amid a mood of optimism
among the drivers, won the race. The regulations had banned
aerodynamic skirts, reducing cornering speeds and increasing
braking distances. John Watson suggested: 'The driver's role is
more important than it has been for the past four years.' Derek
Warwick, driving for a second season for Toleman, where he
had fought to retain his sharp sense of humour after a torrid
baptism in an uncompetitive car, also felt encouraged at the
prospect of competing on a more level playing field. 'It will be
easier to judge drivers this year,' he claimed. 'Last year, it was
too often a case of looking for who had the most grip and the
biggest heart.'

At the next race, in Long Beach, California, Australian Alan
Jones came out of retirement to drive for the impoverished
Arrows team seventeen months after he had quit Williams and

the sport. At almost fourteen stone, Jones's return cast an ominously large shadow in more ways than one. Among those with reason to treat the thirty-six-year-old former world champion's re-emergence warily was Watson, who did not have a conventional contract with McLaren. His manager at the time, Nick Brittan, admitted: 'The complication in John's contract arises purely from financial consideration, but, in my opinion, he is no more vulnerable than any one of half a dozen drivers. Jones is the most desirable commodity not signed up and I am sure there will be a lot of drivers examining the fine print of their contracts.'

This is mentioned for a pertinent reason: Watson would prove to be more vulnerable than Brittan acknowledged, but from a source other than Jones. Watson, in fact, qualified twenty-second on the grid at Long Beach with team-mate Lauda one place ahead. Astonishingly, Wattie won the grand prix on this street circuit with hardly anywhere to pass and Lauda finished second. I saw the race and still don't believe the result! Watson drove magnificently and the breaks for once went his way. Prost was eleventh – but his season was to fire up once the championship took anchor in Europe. In April, he won the French Grand Prix for a second time in his career; at Imola he was second in the San Marino Grand Prix, then third at Monaco, before winning his second race of the year, at Spa-Francorchamps in Belgium where he had started from pole. He now led the world championship with twenty-eight points, four ahead of Piquet. Prost was far from secure, however. 'I told the team we had to be careful because we could see Brabham becoming better.' Prost's profile had been significantly raised in France. Although he insisted that he had never been fully embraced by the French public when we met in Paris in summer 2008, and there is no reason to question the sincerity of that judgement, Prost felt at this moment that he was under unreasonable scrutiny. He wrote in his autobiography, *Mâitre de Mon Destin*: 'My position at Renault, the firm's diligent PR efforts on my behalf, and the fact that I was winning races had combined to make me the focus of French motor racing. I had become – albeit reluctantly – a star. Being a star has certain media advantages, but it also has all sorts of drawback. At home in Saint Chamond, I was being inundated with all kinds of requests, not to mention anonymous telephone calls and even threats. The situation was making life increasingly difficult for Anne-Marie and my son Nicolas. I hit on the idea of moving abroad. Accordingly, I made the necessary overtures to the Swiss authorities and, in May, I moved house, cutting ties with France.' Prost won again at the British Grand Prix, when he said in the glow of victory: 'I think I can become the first Frenchman to win the world championship.' Another win at the next race, in Austria, reinforced that sentiment. Then at the Dutch Grand Prix we witnessed something rare in Formula One: an error of judgement from Prost.

On the forty-second lap of a grand prix lasting seventy-two laps, Prost attempted to pass Piquet on the inside on the approach to Tarzan hairpin, situated at the end of the pit straight. It was a common overtaking spot, and one of the few places that Prost could hope to squeeze past Piquet, whose BMW engine had an advantage in power. But as Prost hit the brakes, his rear wheels locked and he collided with Piquet. The Brazilian's car ploughed into a tyre wall – and Prost's Renault travelled not much further before he left the track for good. Prost accepted that he had been the culprit. 'My fault,' he admitted. 'But I don't understand why it happened. He gave me enough room and I was not braking extra hard.'

While the Dutch Grand Prix had ended in disappointment for Prost, the McLaren team had taken a significant leap into the future at Zandvoort, a future that would involve Prost. The international airport at Amsterdam had been closing when a private aircraft made its final approach at midnight on Thursday 25 August, the day before practice for the grand prix began. On board the Lauda Air flight were Ron Dennis and John Barnard, the senior management team of McLaren International, and some mechanics. At approximately the same time, the team's new car with a TAG turbo-charged Porsche engine was nearing the completion of its journey from Dover to Zeebrugge. The ferry crossing was the final stage of a journey that had started two years earlier when the Porsche Formula One turbo had been conceived in the mind's eye of the McLaren management. It had proved to be an impossible race against the clock to have two new cars at Zandvoort, so Lauda, clearly the team leader, had been assigned to drive McLaren's first turbo-powered car. Lauda, in turn, was happy to supply one of his own aircraft – at a cost of £1,300 – to ensure the team could make a belated arrival after round-the-clock work at their factory in Woking. His generosity ensured an extra day's preparation for the team.

Dennis and Barnard had long since appreciated that without turbo power you were not at the races. The Renault-Elf team set the trend amid much smirking in 1977, when their car was far from reliable, and since then Ferrari, BMW, Alfa Romeo and the Toleman Hart engines had put the staple engine of old, the Ford Cosworth, in the shade. McLaren had made their decision to acquire a turbo two years earlier, in 1981. Dennis said, 'While some of the engines around has short-term gains, we felt they had in-built compromises. We wanted a purpose-built engine for F1 and went to Porsche. They were keen, but not keen enough to make the investment.' Dennis approached Mansour Ojjeh, whose family company, Techniques d'Avante Garde (TAG), had entered Formula One as co-sponsors of Williams. After delicate negotiations, Dennis and Ojjeh created an alliance that exists to this day; and the McLaren-TAG Porsche, a 1499cc engine developing around 600 horsepower, was unveiled in Holland. Barnard had apparently wanted to hold the engine back until 1984, when he would have finished a car specifically tailored to run the turbo power. Lauda objected to this strategy because he thought time was of the essence. He took his view to the money men at Marlboro – as Alan Henry, one of the oldest, best informed and most sober voices in Formula One journalism, reported. 'Never one to be thwarted Niki went straight to the top dogs at the Philip Morris organisation and told them what was happening,' wrote Henry. 'Niki said, "They came down hard on McLaren and told them if they wanted their money, they'd better get on and start using the turbo engine. Ron fully understood, because I told him what I was going to do. But Barnard was furious. They hated me for that!"' This was The Rat at work in his own inimitable fashion. On Saturday morning at Zandvoort, Lauda's car was clocked at 182mph, the fastest on the circuit, but in timed practice the turbo broke and he qualified in nineteenth position on the grid. 'We pushed too hard,' admitted Dennis. But McLaren understood what exciting possibilities lay ahead.

In Holland, a win by Arnoux propelled him into second place in the championship on forty-three points, putting him eight behind Prost. With three races remaining, at Monza, Brands Hatch (for the European Grand Prix) and Kyalami, Piquet had fallen fourteen points behind Prost. It appeared the Brazilian needed to produce three flawless races. Or hope for a meltdown within

Renault – a distinct possibility considering how the atmosphere had deteriorated. Prost feared a repeat of 1982. 'Typically, in a big team like this we had some strange decisions starting to be made,' he said. 'In 1982, I had eight races where I was leading and stopping for the same reason. It was caused by a small part controlling the electronics. It cost hardly anything – but it was a brand out of the Renault group and they did not want to change it for another more reliable one. As a driver, losing a chance in the championship because of that was frustrating. Keke Rosberg only won one race and he was world champion. I won two, but stopped eight times. I always remember the Austrian Grand Prix that year. I was leading by half a lap and I was thinking, "Please, don't happen this time." Then close to the end . . . pooop! That was really rough. Now again in 1983 there were problems beginning to happen. We could not use more power as we had problems with the turbos we used. At the same time, we were convinced Brabham were using bad fuel . . . rocket fuel. We had this real situation, but it looks like I was complaining all the time.'

There was another issue, central to the unrest within Renault and a deeply sensitive matter. Sometime in the summer, Prost allegedly became involved with someone close to the team. In France, the law of privacy has historically been used to bludgeon those who break it, so Prost's alleged indiscretion never became public. Except to those who knew . . . and therein lie difficulties of a kind that had nothing to do with the reliability of engines or anything else mechanical. A serious line had been breached, according to Prost's critics within Renault. His discomfort worsened on arrival in Italy.

He had been warned to expect a hostile reception, because a few weeks earlier at a test at Monza there were reports that bottles had been thrown at his car. Arnoux's presence in a Ferrari

made Prost a natural enemy for the *tifosi*. And before he journeyed to Monza for the grand prix, Prost received a threat that
he was a target for kidnapping. Renault treated these calls so
seriously that three security guards from the unit that protected
French President François Mitterand were detailed to accompany
Prost to Italy. In the event, the only mishap Prost experienced
occurred when the engine of his car blew. Piquet took victory
with Arnoux second; the title race had been blown wide open.

The Formula One circus moved from Italy back to Britain.
Brands Hatch is close to London, but the big city lights were
strictly off limits. Rosberg, the reigning champion, seemed an
appropriate man to gauge the mood of those battling to succeed
him. 'Piquet has the right attitude, trying his best and behaving
normally,' he said on the eve of the John Player Grand Prix of
Europe. 'Arnoux is behaving almost normally, too. But Prost . . .
he looks as though he is about to crack. He is unshaven and
has had bodyguards around him in Italy – crazy.' Prost had only
qualified on the fourth row, slower than his team-mate Eddie
Cheever. Nigel Mansell, who would have to wait for another
two years before he claimed his maiden Formula One victory,
at Brands Hatch, also thought the momentum had swung in
Piquet's favour. 'You need a car that handles well at Brands Hatch
and the Brabham does that,' said Mansell. 'Any one of the three
can still do it, but Nelson has lived with the pressure.' Piquet, on
the second row, confirmed he had felt a twinge of nervousness.
'But,' he grinned, 'if I'm a little scared Prost and Arnoux must
be in serious trouble.' Prost and Arnoux were duelling in the
classic Gallic manner for the honour of being the first Frenchman
to win the title. Arnoux, who had taken two wins and two second
places in the last four races, suggested: 'I am very happy. I have
my chance. I will play it.' Somewhat disingenuously, Prost argued,

'It will be a nice fight.' In the event, Piquet's nerves proved capable of taking the strain. Yet again, the Brazilian emerged triumphant as he took the flag ahead of Prost while Arnoux laboured to finish ninth. Prost had just a two-point advantage to carry with him to the final race in South Africa.

It was time, both men decided, to disappear. Piquet opted for some solitude at an Irish health farm. Prost escaped to his newly acquired home in Switzerland. After fourteen races, spread across three continents, the destiny of the championship depended on which man could deliver one last effort and on which team could provide the faster and most reliable car. In the years ahead, Prost would become a veteran of such occasions, but now he was a novice. Piquet had walked this way before, a couple of seasons earlier in Las Vegas. The Brazilian also had fewer media trailing him. In contrast, Prost had what appeared to be an army reporting his every move, because a greater contingent of French journalists than usual assembled at Kyalami. At last, there was an appetite in France to anoint the first French motor racing champion. But there was another factor in play: Prost carried the burden of having to vindicate, in the eyes of the Republic, the millions and millions of francs that Renault had invested in winning a championship. That amounted to more than hand baggage.

Prost, perhaps alone, sensed that Renault and France would have to continue to wait. He'd had serious misgivings about Renault's performance for some time, having not won since the Austrian Grand Prix three races back. His pessimism did not prove misplaced. From the start, Piquet dominated the South African Grand Prix. His team had gambled on giving the Brazilian a light fuel load in the belief that he could open up a substantial lead. Piquet ensured the strategy worked. He completed the first lap two seconds ahead . . . and then widened the gap between himself and his rivals. Prost's worst fears were fulfilled when, not quite halfway in the seventy-seven lap race, he drove into the Renault pit, unbuckled his seat belt and became a spectator. His turbo had ceased working. All his work had been in vain.

Almost unnoticed in the heat of the championship battle, Lauda's McLaren-TAG Porsche ran for a while in second place in the race. He was eventually forced into retirement when the electronics failed but the omens for the new season had been noted. Lauda, Dennis and Barnard said nothing for public consumption afterwards, but they knew in their heart of hearts that they had a package that was going to be hard to contain.

With Prost out, Piquet cruised home in third place to be acclaimed world champion for the second time in three years. 'I feel much better than when I won the first time, it seems more important,' he said.

At Renault, calls were being hastily made to newspapers across France to cancel advertisements that had been booked in the expectation that Prost would be world champion in one of their cars. 'Newspapers and magazines were just waiting to push the button to print,' admitted Prost. He had been deaf to this notion that the championship had been a foregone conclusion. 'Everyone else was ready to be world champion,' he said. 'But we had broken an engine many times, even in the last race. The Brabham was much quicker – and then there was the fuel they were using. Everyone knew what was happening, and Elf talked about protesting to Brabham because of this. But Renault did not want to protest; even though we could believe that with this protest we could have been world champions in just a few days' time.'

Yet the truth was there was no appetite inside Renault to protest, firstly, because this would not reflect positively on their corporate image; and, secondly, because there were those within Renault who did not want to stand up for Prost. 'I felt after the race that the ambience was very difficult,' said Prost. As disconsolate mechanics wearily packed away their cars for one final time, readying them for the long journey home as air freight, Prost made his way to the helipad at the circuit. As he waited for a helicopter shuttle to Jan Smuts Airport in Johannesburg, he chanced upon John Watson and a man called Paddy McNally, who worked with John Hogan at Philip Morris. 'Is it true Renault have sold their champagne to BMW?' ribbed McNally. The Frenchman manufactured a thin smile, then replied: 'Maybe I drive for an English team next season.' Looking at Watson, he added, 'Perhaps I take your place!' It was perceived to be no more than innocent banter between old team-mates, who had enjoyed a good relationship. At Johannesburg airport, the two drivers went their separate ways, Prost to Paris and Watson to London. Yet inside a matter of days, each man was to discover his world had been turned upside down.

In Paris, Prost had an appointment to keep with Renault's top brass at a season-end debrief that had been in the diary ahead of the debacle in South Africa. In London, Nick Brittan waited to strike a new deal for his man Watson. At that time, Lauda had squeezed Marlboro into paying him $4 million for 1983, and another four million for 1984. Brittan's negotiating position had been strengthened, he felt, by the fact that Watson had finished ahead of Lauda in the championship. He planned to seek a serious hike in Watson's salary.

At home in France, Prost placed one critical telephone call ahead of the meeting with Renault's senior management. He telephoned John Hogan, Marlboro's man in Switzerland. 'I wanted to know from John that, if something happened between me and Renault, could there be any possibilities for me with another team. John said, more or less, that there could be some possibility.

That was all.' Even though he had made this precautionary call, Prost had not anticipated what would happen when he walked into Renault's offices. He had supposed there would be an inquest into the failure of the team. He imagined a feisty meeting, with senior figures trying to get to the bottom of the mistakes that had stalked the team. Instead the management had concluded its own inquest. They had decided there was one culprit responsible for Renault's demise: Prost.

'At the meeting, it was suggested it was better for me to stop driving for Renault,' explained Prost. It was a very French solution; a very public execution involving one man's reputation being placed on the guillotine. At a stroke, Renault had absolved themselves of any blame. 'I did not know that this would happen even if I felt something a bit strange,' admitted Prost. 'I still had a Renault contract, but I did not fight at all.' He walked out of the meeting a disillusioned man.

Understandably, he informed Hogan of his fate, yet even as he made the call to Switzerland Prost insists he had no guarantee of finding another seat. 'When I left that meeting with Renault, I had no security that I could make a deal with McLaren,' he said. 'Maybe, I would have to stop driving for one year. I just did not know.' What transpired reshaped the career of Alain Prost – because the day he was shown the door at Renault turned out to be one of the best days of his life.

Hogan reports what unfolded. After calling Ron Dennis to tell him that Prost was available, he summoned the Frenchman to his office in Lausanne. 'Essentially, after he arrived we held Alain a prisoner,' said Hogan. 'I told him, in so many words, "You're not fucking leaving until you sign a contract."' There was a small matter to clear up. Had not Prost reneged on the last McLaren contract he had signed? In Hogan's office, Prost addressed his own history. 'Alain said to me, "I will not do the same again."' Besides, the contract Prost had torn up belonged to McLaren of another age. Under Dennis, McLaren had become a progressive team with a belief and a desire to return to the winner's circle.

Hogan admits now, a quarter of century after the event, that Ferrari also wanted Prost. 'I had my secretary tell Marco Piccinini from Ferrari that I was out of the office,' said Hogan. 'That was a bit naughty, I suppose.' Prost's manager, Julian Jakobi from Mark McCormack's world-renowned International Management Group (IMG), flew to Switzerland to conclude negotiations with Hogan. As an unemployed driver, Prost's bargaining position was not as strong as it would have been otherwise, of course. 'We signed a heads of agreement contract and Paddy [McNally] flew with him to London the next day to complete the deal with lawyers,' explained Hogan. Next, Nick Brittan received a call to be told that Watson would not be re-signed by McLaren. 'John Watson was a perfect gentleman,' remembered Hogan. 'I think he had seen it coming.'

Clearly, Niki Lauda had not. 'Niki crapped himself when he heard,' chuckled Hogan. It was nothing personal; purely business. Lauda knew that Prost would represent a much younger and faster rival than Watson, and therefore become a far greater threat to his ambition to win the world title again. 'I was getting ready to go out for Sunday lunch in Lausanne when The Rat called.' Hogan broke into a passable imitation of Lauda as he remembered the core of their conversation. '"Listen, you signed this arsehole Prost, I want to talk to you." So, Niki decided to fly from Austria to Geneva and I told him to meet me at a specific roundabout. He joined me for Sunday lunch with my family. Niki was upset, "Listen, this arsehole Prost . . ." I stopped him to remind him of one indisputable fact. "You've got a signed contract, what are you going to do?" He knew the car was red hot with the TAG Porsche turbo engine. The conversation was at an end, really. He was not going to walk away from a car that gave him genuine possibilities of winning races.'

Prost first heard of Lauda's excursion to meet Hogan when I relayed it to him in Paris. 'I didn't know that, you know there is always a story behind a story,' he said, in his phlegmatic manner. 'I had a No. 2 contract, Niki was No. 1. He had a lot of preferences. He could test the car first. He had the new development and he could decide if I tested or not. I tested after Niki and I could confirm what he had said as Niki was very good testing a car and analysing its performance. I could see I had no problem. Anyway, I was not in a strong position to negotiate. The only thing I discussed with John [Hogan] – and I suppose he talked with Ron – was that even if you don't want to pay me a big fee you give me some good prize money. At the end, they came with a good contract even if the fee [salary] was quite low.'

At the time it was speculated that Renault had been obliged to pay up the remainder of Prost's contract, which meant Marlboro had a fraction of his salary to meet. Only Prost and Hogan know the truth – but Watson made a salient point. 'Marlboro boasted they had got Prost at a price they couldn't refuse,' said the Ulsterman when we spoke in the days after the Frenchman had replaced him. 'Prost, though, doesn't come as cheap as Mars bars.' Watson's tone carried no rancour. He never drove in another grand prix, however.

To Hogan, signing Prost ahead of Watson had been a matter of business, nothing else. 'It was not a contest, unfortunately,' he said. 'With Ron's hard work and detailed planning, this was the culmination of bringing McLaren back from the dead.'

7

STORMY MONACO

British driver Derek Warwick was hired to replace Prost at Renault. After two seasons driving a Toleman Hart turbo, claiming two fourth places, a fifth and a sixth place in 1983 for an under-financed team, Warwick had declared his talent. At twenty-nine, Warwick – not Nigel Mansell – was deemed much more likely to be Britain's next world champion.

Having narrowly missed out on the world championship with Prost, Warwick sensed he had made a career-defining move, as well as assuring himself of becoming a millionaire. 'I was the hottest British driver,' said Warwick, stating an undeniable truth without a hint of arrogance in his voice. 'I'd just come off a string of results where I was the only driver to finish in the points in the last four races with a pretty difficult car and engine. I had good credibility. Alain's only words of wisdom to me when I signed the contract were to suggest, "If I can give you one piece of advice, Derek, don't learn French!" He thought this would stop me getting caught up in the political problems that he thought would eventually lead to the downfall of Renault.' Warwick took him at his word. 'After the first technical debrief I threw a bit of wobbly,' he smiled. 'It had been in French and English, half-and-half. The second debrief was all in English!' With Cheever also departed, Renault had a second new driver, Patrick Tambay, an urbane Frenchman with six years in Formula One, the last two of them spent driving for Ferrari. Warwick recalled: 'Patrick used to laugh, and say, "We have a team of two-hundred-odd people, all French, and now we have to speak English because of one Englishman."'

Warwick was affectionately known within the British media as 'Del Boy' after the TV character. Warwick's family had a company in Alresford, Hampshire, Warwick Trailers, and he had grown up wheeling and dealing, if in a more sophisticated manner that 'Del Boy' Trotter did in his fictional exploits around Peckham. 'I was kind of fortunate that I came up the hard way as I had a good upbringing with my father – very much a working back-ground,' said Warwick. 'I came through stock cars and I got a bit lucky as I found a couple of sponsors which allowed me to do well in Formula Three and come up through the ranks. It was quite an extraordinary way into Formula One – not like nowadays when these young guys are coming in with full budgets. We always had to buy one tyre at a time, not a complete set!'

Warwick's contract with Renault encouraged him to seek a new home in Jersey. Achieving permanent residence on the island is no mean feat, and requires an application to the Chief Advisor to the States of Jersey. One day much later, Warwick told a few of us how that had gone. 'I remember I had to be interviewed to prove that I was suitable, financially, to live in Jersey,' said Warwick. 'Quite proudly, I told them of my business assets, of the value of my home in Hampshire and how much I was being paid by Renault. When I'd finished – and I thought I was doing all right in life – I was asked: "Is there anything else, Mr Warwick?" I wasn't doing perhaps as well as I'd imagined!' Warwick never managed to take himself too seriously, unlike some of his contemporaries.

'You know that little circle that you thought was the most important thing in the world called Formula One? Well, when you were in that circle you thought no matter how many billions were outside it they were looking at you,' said Warwick. 'Honestly, that's what keeps those people inside the circle alive. I think Bernie thinks there is nothing else out there. But when you get outside that circle, you see it's not even a circle; it's a dot. I'd been on Jersey for a couple of years and I was at a friend's house for dinner, and remember I'd been on the back pages of national newspapers quite a lot in that time, when a woman looked at me across the table in a drunken stew, and said: "You look a bit big for horses." She thought I was a jockey. Not everyone is into Formula One.'

On the day we met in the spring of 2008, he had just arrived at Southampton Airport from Jersey, where he still lives and, furthermore, owns a successful car dealership, Derek Warwick Honda. He wore a dark suit, with a British Racing Drivers' Club pin in his lapel, and an open-necked shirt. He is a man with a naturally sunny disposition, but this visit had a sombre agenda. Warwick had flown to the mainland to attend the funeral of David Leslie, fifty-four, a friend who had successfully raced touring cars after driving in other branches of motorsport all his life. Leslie had died in a plane crash that claimed five lives. Warwick had mourned the death of other racing drivers: Villeneuve, Elio de Angelis and Michele Alboreto and he was saddened again to have to deal with the loss of another fine man.

Perhaps few men had a greater appreciation of his sport's merciless capacity to change the lives of a family in an instant than Derek Warwick did. In 1991, his younger brother Paul was killed when the suspension of his car broke when he led an F3000 race at Oulton Park. Paul Warwick was just twenty-two. 'I still have bad days,' said Warwick. 'I feel cheated. I feel angry with Paul even though it wasn't his fault. He was my hero and he died on me. I could see him being sensational in a racing car. He was much better than I was. He was better looking, faster and more professional because he picked up on what I did and improved it. When I heard Paul was dead, it was like a massive part of my heart had been wrenched from my body.' Warwick shared those dark, harrowing memories the last time we had met when he had returned to a Formula One car in the Grand Prix Masters Series that began in South Africa late in 2005, and where I had gone to write the story for the *Mail on Sunday*. He was fifty-one years old, and his family had misgivings about him driving a 180mph Formula One car again in the company of Mansell and his old Renault team-mate, Tambay, as well as other men with greying hair and broadening waistlines like René Arnoux and Eddie Cheever. Each one of them was a survivor. As the German driver Hans Stuck suggested wryly, 'At the time we were doing F1, sex was safe and motor racing was dangerous.'

Warwick had not taken much persuasion to drive a Formula One car again. 'I needed to know if I still had the commitment to corner at 160mph as I did as a younger man,' he explained. Warwick had driven in 147 Formula One races and some will tell you he was the best driver never to have won a grand prix. The death of his brother – his best friend and his protégé – still haunts him. 'At times of my life, I bring Paul into what I am doing but, mostly, I put him in a little compartment in my mind that has a massive lock and key,' he said. 'I won't let him out. Sometimes, I can't remember him; that's how far I had to put him away to survive.' The floral tributes at Paul Warwick's funeral spread over 500 yards. One came from Ayrton Senna.

Warwick knew that he would have to confront his loss again at David Leslie's funeral, when so many drivers of his generation, and other personnel from motorsport, would congregate to pay their respects. But as we took coffee at Southampton, he rewound his life to the time he succeeded Prost at Renault. 'You felt enormous responsibility because you were filling big shoes,' he said. 'Alain was never going to be a journeyman. But when I arrived at Renault there was an excitement I had not felt before. I think they'd had their fill of Prost. I suspect a Frenchman and a French team was never really going to work unless they pulled the magic rabbit out of the hat and won the world championship. On the other hand, I suppose Alain felt aggrieved not to have won the championship because they should have done. He was out-psyched – not the team – by Piquet.

'Piquet destabilised every driver out there. I raced with Nelson in 1978 and he won the BP F3 championship, and I won the Vandervell F3 title; he won thirteen races, I won twelve. He tried to unsettle me – but he never did.' Warwick's case was made by Piquet himself when he gave *F1 Racing* an insight into his *modus operandi* in June 2008. This is Piquet on Nigel Mansell:

'I first met Nigel Mansell when we were racing in British Formula 3. While I was at the front winning races, he was a wanker driver – always at the back. After that we were in Formula 1. I raced for Bernie Ecclestone at Brabham for seven years and never had a contract. Then Frank Williams called me and asked if I wanted to join Williams as team-mate to Nigel. I said to

Frank, "I will come and drive for you on one condition. I want to be No. 1. I want to be undisputed the best driver. I know how to develop a car, I know how to win the championship and I want to help to do that again." His reply was: "No problem."

'So we had a 19-line contract – everything was sorted. Then, before the start of the 1986 season, Frank had his accident. I arrived at the first race and had no T-car [spare], nothing. But I could not talk to Frank as his problems were 100,000 times bigger than mine were. So I kept my mouth shut and did my job. Then I started to fight with Nigel. It was an English team with an English driver and I was a two-times champion. He was nothing. Like Hamilton and Alonso at McLaren last year – it was the same. Nigel was a nice guy. I tried to start a fight with him because I wanted to divide the team. So I said his wife was ugly. The problem is people in England don't fight with their hands like they do in Brazil. I tried everything I could to get him to hit me. I called his wife [Rosanne] everything under the sun. But I had nothing against him, he's not a bad guy really.'

Behind this insidious streak of his nature, Piquet could just as easily launch a charm offensive with a perma-twinkle in his eye for women of all nationalities. 'Nelson had an ability to get the press behind him,' said Warwick. 'He was a joker and he'd be in the knickers of any woman with a slight sign of a heartbeat! He was an all-time good old boy for journalists and mechanics. He fitted the mould. Alain was perceived differently – perhaps he was not so popular because of the hatred Formula One had for Renault for bringing in turbo engines.'

The search for Warwick's replacement at Toleman Hart for 1984 had been narrowed down to one candidate: Ayrton Senna. His options had become slim, too. 'At the time, Toleman was probably the only door open to Ayrton,' said Bernie Ecclestone. Yet Senna still negotiated with Alex Hawkridge, the team principal of Toleman, as though he had bountiful choices. By now, photographer Keith Sutton had already experienced this side of Senna, this need to cut a deal on his terms, something that was an essential element of the man and a prevailing feature of his life as a Formula One driver.

Again, Senna asked Sutton to become his personal photographer for 1984. Again, Sutton declined. But with Senna at home in Brazil over the winter, Sutton had shown his own entrepreneurial flair. 'I'd made a good relationship with the head of Arai helmets in Europe, and I talked to him about offering Ayrton a contract with the company,' he explained. 'He came back with a proposal that would have given Ayrton a $100,000 deal – and I was on ten per cent which would have meant a huge amount of money for me. I put the offer through to Ayrton, who by this time had a Brazilian manager. I was told they'd think about it. Actually, it seems they approached other manufacturers, presumably to see if they could get an improved deal. Then, I got the word from Brazil to tell Arai they didn't want to accept. But this message had been sent without Ayrton getting a better offer – and they never did. The next call I took from Brazil asked me to go back and clinch the deal with Arai. Well, the boss of the European operation in Holland was no longer interested as he knew what had been going on. He sent Ayrton a telex that read: "Dear Mr Senna, I'm sorry but we don't have a helmet big enough for your head."'

Perhaps the man who wrote that has felt, to this day, something in common with the guy who turned down The Beatles. But hindsight is always 20-20, right? Sutton's services were still wanted by Senna, no matter the stinging rebuke. 'Ayrton talked of setting up a company and putting me on a salary, and paying all my expenses to travel and stay at all the grand prix races,' he recalled. 'It would have given me a chance to get into F1 at no cost to myself. But the only problem was that he wanted me just to photograph him. I'd moved into a three-bedroom terrace in Towcester, close to Silverstone, and planned to set up a little agency called Sutton Photographic with my brother, Mark. Ayrton's offer was just too limiting, so I declined. He was very upset – he wasn't used to people saying "No" to him. I thanked him and I told him the reasons why I couldn't do it. After a while, he came round and said that he still wanted me to be at his first race in Formula One that just happened to be in Brazil. He paid for my flights – and put me up in a hotel on Copacabana Beach in Rio de Janeiro. That was a thank you, he said, for my three years' work with him. I carried on photographing him, as it was my job. But the intimacy was over as far as he was concerned. He always asked about my family – he was a real family man. That side of him never changed.'

In Alex Hawkridge's office in Brentwood, Essex, Senna had sufficient self-confidence to call all the shots. The Brazilian's position had been unequivocal: either Hawkridge agreed to insert a buyout clause in his contract, or he would walk out of the door. Money was not an issue, Hawkridge would confirm later. But Senna wanted to be able to leave the team at a time of his choosing. In short, if Senna had an approach and he wanted to leave, he simply had to tell Toleman before he put pen to paper and pay them an agreed amount of money. While Senna hammered out his terms of employment with Hawkridge in his office, there was an open telephone line to the Brazilian's lawyers in São Paulo. The meeting lasted until the early hours of the morning as Senna insisted on a wording of the contract that was precise to his needs. This was a man unlike most racing drivers, in a range of ways.

With the deal customised to his satisfaction, Senna had officially become a Formula One driver. He flew to Rio de Janeiro for his debut in his home country, if not his home city where the Brazilian Grand Prix is held these days. Senna's family swamped the paddock as he waited to drive in the race he had rehearsed for since he was four years old. He qualified on the eighth row of the grid – but his race was short lived as his car lost turbo boost pressure after a mere seven laps had been completed.

This Brazilian Grand Prix was won by – Prost. After his bitter eviction from Renault, this was a cathartic moment for the Frenchman and a cause for elation within the McLaren-TAG Porsche partnership.

Senna's own disappointment was exacerbated on his return to England. He had worn sponsorship patches on his overalls, as allowed by the team, but he had failed to inform them that he would be wearing them, as he was obliged to do under his contract. A small point, perhaps. Yet Hawkridge felt a necessity to remind Senna of the terms of his contract – the contract in which the small print had been debated word by word. According to witnesses Hawkridge reduced Senna to tears. This would happen again in much more serious circumstances in his bitter disputes with Prost, but Hawkridge had been the first to expose the fragility of his Latin temperament under emotional duress.

To compound matters for Senna, Martin Brundle, his old nemesis from F3, had crossed the line in Brazil in fifth place. 'Senna was quite bitter about that, because I'd started better than him, and because he had found the Toleman was quite a difficult car,' said Brundle. 'He was chippy, and tried to devalue my result. I was quite surprised. It wasn't his style, but I think a bit of frustration was creeping in.' Brundle came second at a later race, in Detroit, but the Tyrrell team was later excluded from the 1984 world championship for an infringement of regulations. Yet that was no stigma on Brundle – even though he felt he had been less than properly prepared to make his entrance into Formula One. Nor, for that matter, had Senna. 'We were both unfit,' said Brundle. 'I've got a wonderful black and white picture at home in my gym of the two of us on the podium at Donington, after we had raced nose-to-tail in an epic F3 battle. We both look shattered. We just didn't know the levels of fitness we needed for Formula One. When Ayrton first raced in F1 he had major difficulties. He could barely turn the steering wheel, at times. That was when he realised he had to do something about it. We both did.'

In his second race, in South Africa, Senna finished sixth to claim the first of the 610 points he would eventually score in the world championship during his career. In that race, Prost came second behind his team-mate, Lauda. Clearly, a pattern had already developed: over the course of the winter the McLaren-TAG Porsche had become the team to beat. While Alboreto brought Ferrari a win in Belgium, the San Marino Grand Prix fell to Prost. Shortly afterwards, Prost met Senna for the first time. He has never forgotten the meeting.

Before the following round of the world championship, a contingent of grand prix drivers agreed to participate in a celebrity race to open the new Nürburgring circuit. 'I was coming from Geneva to Frankfurt on a scheduled flight, and Ayrton was due around this time,' said Prost. 'Mercedes had arranged a car for me and Gerd Kremer asked if I would bring Ayrton to the track. On the way down, we chatted and he was very pleasant.

Then we got to the track, practised the cars and I was on pole, with Ayrton second. As racing drivers, we were really taking the fight for pole position seriously, but, after this, it is a race that is supposed to be fun, no.'

Each of the drivers involved was to be at the wheel of a Mercedes 190E, a car just being launched on to the market by the German manufacturer. To Senna, this was a showcase event; the celebrities could treat it as a jaunt, but not him. 'After practice, Ayrton didn't talk to me any more. It was very funny at the time,' said Prost. Yet, what happened next startled Prost. 'In the race, Senna jumped the start completely . . . then pushed me off the track and someone hit me at the back,' he said. 'If someone was ready to jump the start in this kind of ambience, I thought he must have a strange mentality. I could never have done that. I realised how Ayrton was *really* like at this race. A great start, no?' A template had been made that would last for the next decade of racing.

After Lauda took victory at the next grand prix, at Dijon in France, the next stop on the calendar was Monaco. There is no other race circuit comparable in the world. For all but a handful of days each year, the streets of the Principality are congested with the symbols of the extremely rich: Ferraris, Bentleys, Mercedes–Benz, Porsches and Rolls–Royces meander through Casino Square, or around the harbour, at twenty miles an hour. Women in fur walk poodles, or dogs small enough to sit on their laps in the cocktail bar of the Hôtel de Paris, or at the dining table. The boutiques are not so vulgar as to place price tags on items in their window displays. Apartment buildings all have one or more concierges in braided uniform. All would-be owners are means-tested: only the super-wealthy are invited to take residency. Traffic policemen wear white gloves, and use a whistle to keep an orderly flow of cars moving at snail's pace. Crime is non-existent – except perhaps during the week of the Monaco Grand Prix when hotels increase their normal room rate by, minimally, a multiple of three and insist on guests paying for at least five nights regardless of how long they actually stay. Restaurants and bars are equally as dexterous at altering their tariff to match the mood of the moment.

Against the purpose-built monolithic grand prix tracks of modern times, in Malaysia, Bahrain, Istanbul and, waiting in line, Abu Dhabi, the Monaco Grand Prix is an anachronism. It is next to impossible to overtake on streets that are narrow and lined with Armco barriers. If it was proposed today as a location to race cars at 180mph, those making the presentation would be led away by men in white coats and administered mind-altering drugs. Similarly, if it were mooted that it should be removed from the calendar, on grounds of safety, there would be uproar, not least from the drivers. This race is sacrosanct. The roll-call of winners at Monaco includes legends of the sport: Fangio, Moss, Brabham, Graham Hill, Lauda and Schumacher, but for ten years the streets of Monaco were the exclusive domain of Prost and Senna.

This first confrontation in Formula One between them in the summer of '84 could not have been predicted. Prost was in a car setting the pace in the world championship while Senna was in a car without history, albeit one now racing on more competitive tyres from Michelin after Toleman jettisoned Pirelli. Prost had qualified on pole with Nigel Mansell alongside in a Lotus-Renault. Senna was on the seventh row. But the intervention of atrocious weather suddenly levelled the playing field. In driving rain, Senna brought his Toleman Hart alive.

At the start, Prost took the lead, but Mansell barged past on the tenth lap. For the first time in his career, the moustachioed British driver was leading a grand prix. Mansell held this position for a mere five laps, though, before he crashed. The margins for error in Monaco are measured in centimetres. By then, Senna had stolen a path through the menacing confetti of flying water to claim fourth place. The Brazilian's fearless progression continued unabated until he cut down Lauda to take second place. He was almost thirty-five seconds behind Prost – but in clear air he began to make swift inroads into the Frenchman's lead. Prost's mind, do not forget, had still not erased the memory of Pironi driving into him on a dreadfully wet day at Hockenheim two years earlier; nor would it ever. Prost felt the race had to be stopped – and let his feelings be known as he crossed the start-finish line by gesticulating that the grand prix should be halted. Senna carried no such baggage – and he continued to claw Prost back to him.

But on the thirty-first of the 77-lap grand prix, Clerk of the Course Jacky Ickx intervened. He adjudged it to be too dangerous to continue racing and, with Senna practically breathing down his neck, victory was awarded to Prost. However, due to the limited distance covered by the drivers only half points were awarded. Consequently, Prost received 4½ points for winning and not nine, as he would have done for a conventional victory. But on this afternoon those venting their spleen were Senna and Toleman. They felt they had been denied victory because, had the cars been allowed to continue to race for a handful more laps, they believed that Prost would have been swamped and passed. Senna contained his anger in public, but later he told Hawkridge, 'Well, what do you expect? This is the Establishment we're taking on.'

Writer Christopher Hilton tracked down Ickx to hear his

verdict. 'It was a controversial decision,' Ickx told Hilton. 'Some people thought it was right, some people didn't. For a long time, Senna thought it was a mistake because he thought he could win the race. I understand his disappointment. He had the race in hand, he was sure to win it and suddenly it disappeared – so he was upset for a number of years.' But Ickx, who achieved twenty-five podium finishes in Formula One, and won the Le Mans 24-Hour race a preposterous six times, remained adamant that conditions had deteriorated to a point where he could not place the drivers at further risk. 'On the screens [in race control] you see everything, people going off here, spinning there, having a major problem in another place and there is a moment where overall you have to judge if the race is safe or not. I decided in the circumstances that this was enough. Formula One is terribly difficult to drive in wet conditions. Monaco is not so fast, but it is impossibly narrow. The job of a professional driver is already dangerous. You don't have to push it beyond that. Prost and I spoke several times afterwards. He said to stop the race was a benediction.'

Maybe it was then, but at his home in Paris twenty-four years later Prost had another viewpoint drawn from the passage of time. He lost the 1984 world championship, as we shall see, by half a point. 'Because of this half-point, Monaco was not a win, it was a bad memory,' he argued. 'If you think, one lap, or two more laps, we would have had full points and, even if Senna had overtaken me, I would have had at least six points for second place. But no one knows what would have happened if we had kept racing. When the race was stopped, it was raining more and more. Nigel had crashed, Niki had crashed. I slowed down a little, but I had more and more trouble with the brakes. I always thought the race would be stopped. Stories circulated, though, that because Jacky Ickx was a Porsche driver he decided to stop the race. What a pity to hear that. If you look backwards, Ayrton, even at that time, because of his attitude to racing, had power with the media. He was new, it's normal that he gets attention. I have no problem with that, but the polemic with Jacky, when the track was becoming more and more wet, was not acceptable.'

The first seeds of dissent between Prost and Senna, sown in that celebrity race at the Nürburgring, had taken root in the rain on the affluent streets of Monaco. The season continued to be dominated by Lauda and Prost, however. Lauda rarely matched Prost in qualifying – the younger Frenchman was prepared to accept more risks – a balance that would later be reversed against him. Yet in race trim the wily Austrian managed to be extremely competitive. Lauda won the British Grand Prix at Brands Hatch – where Senna was third – only for Prost to respond with a victory at the German round of the championship at Hockenheim. At home in Austria, Lauda drove to one of the most extraordinary wins of his colourful career. With Prost already eliminated by an accident caused by an oil spillage from the blown engine of Elio de Angelis, Lauda heard an enormous bang as he held fourth gear at full throttle. 'I thought that was the end of that, and I began to slow, looking for somewhere to park,' said Lauda. 'Then I began to fish around to see if there were any other gears working. I got third, then I found fifth . . . so I thought, "Let's go on and see how far we get."' Lauda navigated the last ten laps to take the chequered flag first. Those points would prove to be invaluable to his attempt to win a third world championship, fully seven years after his second title.

Senna found fresh headlines for an altogether different reason. In midsummer in Dallas, on a new circuit where the surface had to be continuously repaired with quick-drying cement, the Brazilian had ignored instructions from Toleman team manager Peter Gethin not to go out on the track to practise. Senna insisted that no one could judge better than he if it was appropriate to drive or not. Gethin still pulled rank and voiced his displeasure with the Brazilian – and perhaps at that moment the Toleman team accepted an inevitable truth. Senna would not be with them beyond this first season.

Indeed, Senna had been assiduously courted for months by Lotus team principal Peter Warr. He had wanted to sign him for 1984, but the team's sponsors, John Player, insisted on keeping Mansell for their British market. Warr had not abandoned hope, however, and Senna had calculated that Lotus represented an advancement of his career. At the Dutch Grand Prix at Zandvoort at the end of August, Hawkridge had a huge shock when he was shown a press release on Lotus headed paper that Senna had signed for them. Hawkridge had been negotiating with potential sponsors and this news had wrecked his credibility because he had been unaware of what Senna planned. Was the Brazilian not honour-bound by a contract to tell Toleman *before* he signed for another team? Senna explained that events had accelerated beyond his control. No matter what had actually passed, Lotus had invited journalists to lunch at their motorhome to announce the arrival of Senna to the team for 1985. Mansell was to be the driver displaced.

Later, Senna said: 'The whole thing at Zandvoort was disgusting. I was very annoyed with Peter Warr – no release, no news was supposed to go out at all. Before anything could be said, it was my desire and duty as a professional to inform Toleman that I was one hundred per cent leaving plus where I was going. It was a bad start in my relationship with Warr, but this is Formula One and I have learnt from it.' Senna may have sounded contrite – but his mission had been accomplished. He had a drive for the next season that he reasoned, rightly, would be a rung higher up the Formula One ladder. So what if the lines of communication had become blurred. Isn't truth the first casualty in any battle?

Yet Hawkridge knew of one sanction that would harm Senna. So, at the next race, the Italian Grand Prix at Monza, he banned the Brazilian from driving. Instead, Swede Stefan Johansson drove and he finished a splendid fourth in a race won by Lauda. Senna returned for the next round, the Grand Prix of Europe at the Nürburgring, but crashed on the first lap. Prost won – which meant that for the Frenchman the championship hung on the final race of the year for a second consecutive season. Lauda went to Portugal on sixty-six points with Prost on 62½. Prost could win the Portuguese and still not be world champion if Lauda finished second in Estoril. 'Before the race Jean-Marie Balstre [president of FISA] had us in his office,' recalled John Hogan. 'Balestre said, "Let me show you the plan for when Alain wins the world championship." There was a parade planned to go along the Champs-Elysées – I was rather stunned. I said to Balestre, "Hang on, he hasn't won the bloody race yet."'

The omens for Prost looked good, though, when he qualified on the front row where Piquet held pole. Lauda had to start in a distant eleventh place on the grid because his engine had been down on power during qualifying. On race morning Lauda was fastest man on the circuit in warm up – in those days the drivers had a thirty-minute session to tweak their cars some hours ahead of a grand prix – but his engine had developed a water leak. A new one had to be installed before the grand prix, hardly an ideal scenario for the Austrian. For Prost, there was nothing to do but wait and think, think and wait. Certainly, his nails had been chewed to the quick.

While the two men had fought hard against one another all year long, there was no perceivable tension between them. Hogan said, 'Niki and Alain got along really well, it was one of the great partnerships. From what I've read, Moss–Fangio was obviously a great partnership [at Mercedes and Maserati], but I can't think of too many more. There were a lot of pretend partnerships – but Lauda–Prost was in the Moss–Fangio league.'

From the start of the race, the dice rolled kindly for Prost. On the first lap, Piquet spun. Initially, Prost lost ground to Rosberg (Williams Honda) and Mansell, who was driving his final race for Lotus, of course, to accommodate Senna. But by the ninth lap Prost had threaded his McLaren into the lead with Lauda nowhere to be seen. Certainly not in his mirrors. But Lauda had been on the move, impressively, decisively, demonstrably on the move, and eighteen laps from the end of the Portuguese Grand Prix the McLaren pit crew showed Prost the sign he dreaded most: 'Lauda P2'. Lauda had done all that he needed. While Prost drove home to his seventh grand prix victory of the season, it was not enough. Lauda's second position meant that the Austrian was world champion by half a point. On the podium, Prost cut a disconsolate figure. Out of respect, Lauda kept his own celebrations to a minimum. It is now a matter of Formula One legend that Lauda actually told Prost, 'Don't worry, next year you're going to be world champion.' That was the act of a man who has met and shaken hands with those twin impostors Kipling told us about: triumph and disaster.

Later Lauda would say, 'Ron Dennis congratulated me and said how pleased he is. I don't believe him for a minute.' He had cause to be sceptical. In mid-season Dennis had opened contractual negotiations with Lauda for 1985 by offering him $2 million – half of his current salary. In 1981, when Dennis had wanted Lauda to come out of retirement, he knew the Austrian held the bargaining power. Lauda drove a typically hard deal, then told Dennis, 'You'll be paying just one dollar for my driving ability, all the rest is for my personality.' At the time Dennis bit the bullet – but now he had Prost. Some say that McLaren had printed posters acclaiming Prost as 1984 world champion and taken them to Portugal. Lauda understood precisely how the Frenchman had won favour inside McLaren and, in a non-wilful manner, explained: 'Prost had an unerring instinct for consolidating and developing his position in the team.' After the initial approach from Dennis, a derisory offer in Lauda's opinion, the Austrian held tentative talks with Renault over a contract for 1985. Those negotiations for a variety of reasons never properly took flight. But with the championship, Lauda had a new currency to trade. In the end, Marlboro massaged Dennis into improving McLaren's offer to $3.8 million, according to the Austrian's account.

That night in Portugal, Mansour Ojjeh hired a restaurant for a lavish party, in celebration of McLaren's triumph in the constructors' championship and The Rat's third world title. Later, the celebrations shifted to Paris. Hogan again: 'Lauda won the championship, but Prost had to go to Paris anyway. I was sat with Niki in the back of a car with Alain up on a podium. The French had turned it round and made out as if Alain had won. Niki smiled, and said to me: "I feel sorry for that little fucker, he won seven races and I won the title by half a point."' Hogan, who views Prost with great affection, as a racing driver and a man, could not prevent himself from laughing at the memory. 'Very Niki!' he said.

Lauda may have viewed the arrival of Prost into the McLaren

team as unwelcome news, as Hogan recalled, but the two men actually worked in tandem without any rancour or jealousy. From the beginning, Lauda had the respect of Prost; and Prost soon won the admiration of Lauda with his clear, concise work as well as his speed. The old sorcerer and the apprentice combined to decimate McLaren's rivals as they delivered the constructors' championship. But what Prost understood was that Lauda was playing the end game. He realised that the endless hours of devotion he had given the team outside of the race car had endeared him to his engineers and mechanics. He was the future – Lauda the past. Undoubtedly, that was the way that Ron Dennis read the situation.

8

CHAMPION DU MONDE

Jo Ramirez never had his name in lights in Formula One. He was strictly back-of-the-house – but no less appreciated down the pit lane for that. Ramirez joined McLaren just before Christmas 1983 and remained with the team for the next eighteen years. He loves motor racing, and he lived for the men involved. Alain Prost and Ayrton Senna were near the top of the list of those who called him a friend.

This is Prost on Ramirez: 'Jo was one of the greatest enthusiasts of the sport that I have ever come across, and he devoted himself totally to McLaren. His sense of humour, enthusiasm and electricity were a great motivation for the whole team. He arranged everything for the drivers, making our lives easier, many times above and beyond the bounds of duty.'

Ramirez was born in a suburb of Mexico City, but he would not be offended to be described as an Anglophile after years of being domiciled in England. To him the McLaren was an extension of his family. 'From the beginning I was team coordinator and my job never really changed – but the teams were so small then,' he said. 'Ron was team manager, he was the team principal, he was the owner, he was the boss, he was everything. But he was involved in things above just the running of the team, so I used to do all the functions that Ron couldn't do because he didn't have the time. He did the big deals and got the money. It meant for the first time that if I wanted something, it was possible. Ron would just tell me, "Don't worry, if you need it, just get it." It was such a change – before I'd had to worry about every single penny.'

Ramirez invited me to his home in the hills above Fuengerola on the day after the 2008 Spanish Grand Prix in Barcelona. He had been unable to attend the race as builders, due to unseasonably wet weather, had fallen behind in the construction of the swimming pool he was having landscaped into the front of his property. In this region, on the road to Mijas, and a twenty-minute drive from Malaga Airport, it appears that every home is built on a hillside and that included his traditional Spanish-style villa with imposing views of the valley running down to the sea in the far distance. He had planned to live here in retirement with his wife, Bea, but he was denied that dream as, sadly, Bea died before the villa was completed. He has tried to console himself by immersing himself in local life, but Bea's death has left a vacuum in his life. Yet he remains a man to whom laughter is a gift and he wears his sixty-six years lightly. His only daughter, Vanessa, still lives in England.

He had prepared a salad for lunch, and mixed a dressing to his own recipe. A chilled bottle of Spanish white wine proved to be a perfect accompaniment for his memories. In his study, a super licence that had been issued to Ayrton Senna, and given to Ramirez as a memento, hung on a wall. He has an enviable collection of drivers' crash helmets: over time Senna presented him with three, and Prost two. In his impossibly neat garage – and this would meet the approval of his old boss Dennis, a man meticulous about cleanliness and order – he has memorabilia from a lifetime in motorsport. In pride of place is the Harley-Davidson that drivers Mika Hakkinen and David Coulthard bought for him when he retired from McLaren. He rides most weeks with a group of friends. Ramirez never misses a grand prix on television and he writes a column for a Mexican publication. His heart has never left the pit lane.

When Ramirez first saw Prost, he had been working for Shadow, a team long since vanished but one that gave an opportunity to many drivers, among them Alan Jones who made his earliest discoveries about Formula One with them before piecing together a championship season for Williams. 'We had a problem with the clutch bearing and I asked the McLaren guys to borrow a lathe,' explained Ramirez. 'Alain was having his first test session with the team at Circuit Paul Ricard in Le Castellet and he came into the garage to change his overalls. He was eager to meet anybody from Formula One and I found he was a really nice young man. Just afterwards, John Watson also came into the garage to change. Of course, I already knew John as he had been around some time. We had a little chat and I asked him about Prost. He said, "No matter what you do, the fucking Frog is quicker." John was not an aggressive man, but it was clear that it was already very difficult for him with Alain's speed and natural ability.'

Ramirez moved from Shadow to ATS, and then to Theodore, teams that existed in the late seventies and the beginning of the eighties without threatening to become anything other than a footnote in the history of Formula One. When Ramirez first clapped eyes on Senna, he was working for the Fittipaldi team, founded by Wilson Fittipaldi as Copersucar, but a team that only established any real credibility when his younger brother, Emerson, drove for them as a double Formula One world champion. 'We were testing at Silverstone and I was chatting with Emerson when a very young Ayrton Senna came in to say hello. They spoke in Portuguese – but I understood as I had learned Portuguese when I had spent three months in Brazil on the car.' Emerson Fittipaldi had attained legendary status in Brazil, winning his first world title for Lotus and his second with McLaren; in later life he would conquer North America as well by becoming CART champion and twice winning the Indianapolis 500. If Senna ever idolised a racing driver – and that's highly dubious – it would have been Fittipaldi.

With Senna still in the garage, Fittipaldi instructed Ramirez, 'Look at this guy, remember him because he is going to become one of the greatest ever in the sport.' At that moment, Senna was competing in Formula Ford, but Ramirez felt that Fittipaldi's opinion went beyond his support for a fellow Brazilian. 'I could see from Ayrton's eyes how determined he looked.' In the years that followed, Ramirez would witness at close quarters as Senna's determination manifested itself in Formula One in a manner not previously seen. 'I never saw anyone with such a frightening will to win,' said Ramirez. He was a man making a judgement from a cast list of the highest calibre during his years at McLaren: Lauda, Prost, Rosberg, Berger, Hakkinen and Coulthard.

Ramirez joined McLaren at practically the same time as Prost. As the team reduced the world championship to a duel between Lauda and Prost in '84, Ramirez had one of the best views in the house. 'Niki was established within the team, but he became in awe of Alain as he was always quick,' said Ramirez. 'Niki started to use different ways to battle Alain – he was such a strong character and he had so much experience. Niki was smart, as you might imagine, and he concentrated on setting up his car for the race and accepted he could not fight so much with Alain in qualifying. It was a good combination, the two men got on really well. I must admit that I thought it was wrong that Prost, who had won seven grand prix races, could lose the championship to Lauda, as he won only five. In 1985, Niki knew that he was going out of Formula One. He accepted that somebody young was going to come up and beat him and he would rather it was Prost than anybody else because he liked him.'

With his merciless humour, John Hogan, the man holding Marlboro's purse strings, felt that Lauda had lost his edge for the 1985 season from the first grand prix of the year in Brazil. 'I was standing with journalist Alan Henry in the pits at the end of qualifying and Niki came in and parked the car,' said Hogan. 'I asked Niki, "Did you enjoy that? You haven't got a bead of sweat." Lauda snapped back, "What do you mean?" Alan watched Niki leave and then smiled, "You've got him . . . The Rat's rattled!" That was fine. I mean, Niki had come back and won the world championship and that had been a big ask. It was absolutely tremendous – but the following year he went into taxi-driver mode.' In this business, prisoners are taken on sight; and seldom do they get shown the courtesy of the Geneva Convention. Prost won five races against Lauda's solitary win in Holland.

To Ramirez, Prost was an easy man to accommodate within the team. 'Alain had a manager, but he came once a year for contract signing otherwise we never saw him,' he said. 'Sometimes Alain would bring a friend to the races, but mostly he was on his own. We hardly ever saw his wife, Anne-Marie. Alain was such an easy driver to deal with, or to talk with. He was down to earth. I am not sure he ever realised how good he was. I remember when we were testing once at Monza, a guy who was running in Formula Three, or some small formula, asked if he could have a word with Prost. He wanted to know from Alain how to take the Parabolic Curve.' This is a third-gear, high-G-force landmark corner in Formula One that leads on to the pit straight and is critical to obtaining a good lap time. 'Alain took me to one side and said, "What can I tell him?" He really wanted to help the guy, but it was something that he didn't know how to explain. With the great drivers, what they do is always instinctive, isn't it?' It is.

Prost's first race of 1985 began the process of exorcising his deep disappointment at losing the previous season's world championship by half a point. He won the Brazilian Grand Prix from Michele Alboreto's Ferrari. Alboreto had laid down a marker; and he was to be Prost's most serious rival all year. The next race on the calendar will never be forgotten for a different reason, however. Because the next race in Portugal would be the first grand prix to be won by Senna.

As at Monaco in 1984, Senna's 22-carat talent shone in the rain that fell at the circuit inland from the Portuguese coastline. In just his second race for Lotus-Renault, the Brazilian put his car on pole position, the first illustration of his blistering pace in qualifying that became a hallmark of his career. Martin Brundle would have been inhuman if he had not felt a twinge of envy as he watched from his Tyrrell cockpit. He thought he'd had a shot at getting a drive with Lotus himself, as he explained. 'I can't remember in fine detail what happened – I've had quite a few knocks on the head since then! – but I'd have loved to have driven for Lotus then. As a Norfolk boy I lived just down the road, not that this mattered. I just couldn't get out of my Tyrrell contract. I was on a three-year deal, renewable each year on 30 November. I went on holiday to Barbados hoping that Ken Tyrrell couldn't find me by that date. But guess what? Some bloke from the hotel came down the beach looking for me with my new contract in his hand. Ken had also had a copy delivered to my accountant at home. Old Ken never really missed a trick when it mattered . . .' Those who filled Guildford Cathedral at a memorial service for Ken Tyrrell in November 2001 included Brundle and Sir Jackie Stewart, who won his three world titles with the man who began his Formula One team from an old timber yard in Surrey.

Brundle had been left behind by Senna, a pity, as who knows what he might have achieved in a competitive car against a man he had troubled as they reached for the stars. In Estoril, Senna ran away with the Portuguese Grand Prix. By the tenth lap he led his team-mate Elio de Angelis, driving in second place, by twelve seconds. No one could live with Senna's sustained speed in the inhospitable conditions. At the flag, Senna was 1 minute 02.978 seconds ahead of second-placed Alboreto. In Formula One terms that meant Alboreto had finished in another post-code – and he was the only driver Senna had not lapped. Lotus mechanics had flooded the pit wall to salute Senna, who took his hands from the wheel and punched both fists towards the sky. Team principal Peter Warr rushed to meet the Brazilian's return to *parc fermé*. As Senna braked to a standstill, Warr jumped around in front of his car in a frenzy that those familiar with Basil Fawlty, the TV alter ego of John Cleese, would surely recognise. Warr had dispensed with Mansell for Senna – and he felt instant vindication. Seventeen of the twenty-six cars that started the Portuguese failed to finish – and Senna confessed to his own moment of high drama. 'On one occasion I had all four wheels on the grass, totally out of control . . .' he said. 'But the car came back on to the circuit.' Not by accident, it can be assumed.

Senna had achieved more than his maiden victory; he had turned the Lotus team in his direction at the expense of De Angelis. Brundle had been out on to the circuit at Estoril as a spectator with a vested interest after he had retired his own car with gearbox problems. 'It was a very wet day – and Senna just thrashed them, didn't he? Rosberg crashed in the last corner and his car was stuck there for ages. There was no safety car back then. We'd drive around crashed cars and splashing water and just try to get to the end as best you could. After I was out, I went to see Senna from out on the circuit. I can still see him now splashing into the *parc fermé* area after the race. Peter Warr was there with his arms out, it became an iconic photograph. But more than anything what defined Senna was qualifying. In the turbo era, we'd bolt on a set of tyres that were good for four miles, creep out of the pits and then blast it with 1,250 horsepower. No one, though, wanted to be the one who screwed up Senna's pole position lap. He had that sort of hold on us. We'd all be coasting back to the pits, having shot our qualifiers and melted our engines, but all the time you'd be looking in your mirrors for the McLaren with the Day-Glo yellow helmet. You didn't want to be the one to get in his way. There was a special stigma about Senna's hot, banzai lap at the end of the session. My abiding memories of Senna are those qualifying laps.

'We all worked in a not dissimilar way. You envisage the lap and then go and try to deliver it. We can all go out and find a few tenths of a second – but when you need to find a second out of yourself that's a step very few drivers can take. You can go out on new tyres, make an extra special effort to brake two or three metres later everywhere and pull a big time out of the bag. But Senna would find a second – you can't do that.'

The Brazilian won pole at the next race, the San Marino Grand Prix, and he ran clear at the front until he ran out of fuel four laps from the end. The cars were restricted to 220 litres of fuel, and with thirsty turbos there was an onus on drivers to manage fuel consumption. Prost mastered this challenge, just as he understood how to preserve his tyres and his brakes during a grand prix. McLaren technical director John Barnard – at this point still a partner in the business with Dennis – thought Prost exceptional in this regard. 'His ability to separate the tyre feel and chassis date was unbelievable, to me anyway,' Barnard said. In France, they coined a name for Prost: *Le Professeur.*

While the Brazilian had headline-grabbing moments, this season was to be dominated by Prost, although Lauda's supporters will argue that the defending world champion had more than his share of misfortune. Lauda experienced a catalogue of technical difficulties with his car.

Prost was not cursed in this direction at all. He won at Monaco again, then came third in Canada, third in France and returned to winning ways once more at the British Grand Prix at Silverstone. Alboreto's victories in Canada and Germany kept him in contention, though. But what had become abundantly clear – perhaps from the first race when Hogan had a chip at him – was that Lauda had arrived at a crossroads. He had become increasingly aware that he needed to devote more and more time to his flourishing and expanding airline, Lauda Air. He had to decide between his business and continuing to drive a Formula One car around in circles. When he had declared his dissatisfaction with driving in Canada 1979, his team boss at Brabham,

Bernie Ecclestone, had not contemplated the contractual noose he held over the Austrian's head. 'I told Niki if he wanted to stop, he should stop right away,' said Ecclestone. Even then, Ecclestone was an unconventional player in this sport. He did things in his own style, a maverick who played the cards as they fell. 'During qualifying at one race, we had five sets of tyres for Niki and Nelson,' remembered Ecclestone. 'After they'd used two sets each, Niki was slower than Nelson and came in to get the third set of tyres put on his car. I told him the tyres were for Nelson. Niki complained, "But I am the No. 1 driver in this team." I told him, "Not today, you're not."'

Lauda had been a throwback from another era, and he had proved himself all over again in a younger man's world. The facial scars he still carries are a reminder of how close he had been to dying in a racing car – and in mid-season in the summer of 1985 he concluded it was the moment to rearrange the priorities of his life for a second time. At his home grand prix in Austria, he announced that he proposed to retire at the end of the season. Prost responded to the news of his team-mate's impending departure by winning the race. The world championship was in his sights.

But Lauda had one parting gesture in store, however. He beat Prost into second place in the Dutch Grand Prix by two-tenths of a second, in a nerve-tingling battle that would provide his twenty fifth – and final – victory of a remarkable career. By his own admission, after this last act of bravado Lauda went into survival mode. Who could blame him? At the sharp end, Prost now had the lead in the title race for the first time since the Brazilian Grand Prix. The Frenchman duly illustrated his great consistency by winning the Italian Grand Prix to nose, no pun intended, ever closer to the crown. He could not, would not, be denied; not again, not this time. Senna scored his second triumph of the season, in the Belgium Grand Prix that had to be rescheduled from spring to autumn to allow the track to be resurfaced. There was not a soul in the paddock, or the greater world outside, who doubted his talent now. Senna's intense attitude to his work had not gone unnoticed, either. Warwick suggested: 'Ayrton was special from the start. He was one of those guys that when you saw him in the paddock in the early days, the way he walked, the way he spoke, it was special. It was almost like he was put on this earth for different reasons. I can't explain it any better than that. He had that magical presence about him. You knew he was in the room without seeing him. I think he carried that mystique all the way through his career.'

But it was Prost who was destined to become world champion in the autumn of 1985, with Senna monitoring him for future reference. Prost was close to becoming the driver that Senna planned to become; or planned in his mind even then to one day usurp. In early October, Prost arrived at Brands Hatch with the maths uncomplicated. If he claimed two more points than Alboreto in the European Grand Prix in Kent the title would be his. In Britain, this actually became the sub-plot of the afternoon.

The race is remembered as Nigel Mansell's first grand prix victory at the seventy-second time of asking. Mansell demonstrated his courage, as well as his car craft, to seize control of the race from Senna. A crowd of 75,000 gave the Englishman a tumultuous reception as he took the chequered flag, and he admitted that he cried all the way round the circuit on his slowing down lap. Over the years, Mansell had broken his neck, he had broken his back and he said, 'lost a fortune before I had one to lose.' This was payback time – for him and his wife

Rosanne who had never lost faith in her husband's ability to succeed even when the odds looked unfavourably stacked against him. It would have needed a heart of stone not to have shared with the Mansells their jubilation; and, yes, relief. Even better days beckoned for Mansell, but this had been the moment when he announced that he had the credentials and the skill, as well as the 'bottle'. Only one man had a more profitable day – Prost.

The Frenchman had a miserable start to the grand prix. Off the grid, he had to take avoiding action to miss Rosberg who failed to get away ahead of him. Prost drove on to the grass and by the end of the first lap he was a distant fourteenth. Surely Prost had travelled too far, and had had enough near misses, to be made to endure yet further heartache? Inside his McLaren, he did not permit himself such morbid thoughts. Instead, Prost did what he had become renowned for: he drove with his mind alert to all possibilities. He kept cool and he made easy, easy progress. Then the afternoon became easier still when, on lap eighteen, he could see smoke billowing from Alboreto's Ferrari. The Italian would not be scoring any points. On lap thirty-eight, the halfway point, Prost pitted for new tyres and with a softer compound he felt his car far more responsive. He still had to get himself into the points, with his ultimate target to finish fifth to sweep the two points that he needed to be declared champion. On lap fifty-six, Stefan Johansson retired and Prost passed De Angelis. He was running in fourth place – he was driving to the Promised Land. As he drove hard and fast into Clearways, the corner that slings the car on to the pit straight at Brands hatch, for the seventy-fifth and last time, the chequered flag had never looked more beautiful. The mission that began as a child, when his father had introduced him to go-karts on holiday in the South of France, had been accomplished on an autumnal afternoon in the south of England. 'I didn't gesticulate wildly, but I do remember my eyes misted over my visor,' said Prost, recalling how he had reacted to the realisation that he had become world champion. That day he climbed past where Mansell stood on the traditional third step of the podium, because they had put in a fourth step to accommodate the presence of the world's new Formula One champion. According to Prost's memory, the celebration party lasted until the small hours of the next day. At thirty, he had become the first Frenchman to win the world championship – and to this day he remains the only Frenchman to have taken the title – but this had not been a priority to Prost.

'France has not a big consideration for the champion, like Brazil, Argentina or England has,' he said. 'The public in France likes me a lot, but we don't have this perception of keeping champions at a high level. It does not mean very much. It is difficult to be a French driver in an English team – because the relations between the French and English people are always a little tricky! But because I never had the French mentality, I always had a good relationship with English people and an English team. I always said I don't like some French attitudes; sometimes, I never felt one hundred per cent French, to be honest.'

The season had still to be wrapped up, in South Africa and Australia. Mansell won the next race at Kyalami – proof, if proof were needed, that in future he would be a championship contender. Prost came third; then he kept a promise to himself to have an audience with the Pope. On the way to the last grand prix of the season in Adelaide, Prost and his wife Anne-Marie detoured via the Vatican where an appointment had been made for them to meet Pope John Paul II. 'I have never concealed the fact that I am a believer,' said Prost. After his visit to the

Vatican, he reported, 'The Pope is the person who has made the most impression on me. On meeting him, I immediately appreciated his greatness.'

Senna was another profoundly religious man. We would become accustomed to him praising God – and Senna did this much more than Prost ever did in public. To some, this was an unnecessary and, perhaps even disturbing part of Senna's personality. At Adelaide, he had forced Mansell off the track on the first lap. Had this anything to do with the fact that Senna had claimed that during the first day's qualifying the Englishman had 'blocked' him on a quick lap? An eye for eye, perhaps? Mansell was unamused to have travelled so far to have raced less than a lap – but on this occasion he absolved Senna of blame. 'We had a bit of a scuffle, but Ayrton had no part in putting me out of the race,' he explained. On the grid he'd had a technical failure and that was the cause of his exit.

Later in the race, Senna had driven erratically as he battled with Alboreto and Rosberg until his engine gave up the ghost. Still, this had been a demonstrably good season for the Brazilian. Rightfully, Prost won acclaim for becoming world champion with such distinction, but Senna had battled his way to fourth in the drivers' championship. He was a man laying down a marker.

Senna was also proving to be different. He looked after his own interests and that was his entitlement – but did he not compromise his devout faith with some of the decisions he took? It is for others to judge, but, at times, we will see there is a *prima facie* case for him to answer. What is beyond dispute is that his second season in Formula One had been profitable: he had won twice, finished second twice, come third three times and, quite brilliantly, claimed pole position at seven of the sixteen races.

Senna's fierce, uncompromising style, so apparent from his earliest years in Britain, had not been diluted now that he was competing against the best drivers in the world. He was not a man to yield an inch – and that was now clear to all. His team-mate Elio de Angelis, who had set out as Lotus No. 1, finished behind him, and the Italian was shown the door after six seasons with the team. De Angelis signed for Brabham, but, tragically, he drove in just four more grand prix races before he was killed at a test at Le Castellet the following year.

Lotus boss Peter Warr had identified the driver he wanted to join the team: Derek Warwick. He had the required speed, he had experience of Renault engines like those run by Lotus, and he was just what the team's British sponsors, John Player, wanted: a British driver with personality and enthusiasm to market. Yet when this development was put to Senna, the Brazilian promptly stamped his feet and told the team's management this was unacceptable to him. At twenty-five, he held this amount of clout inside a team that had been in business since 1958 and had won seventy-five grands prix and created five world champions: Jim Clark, twice; Graham Hill; Jochen Rindt; Emerson Fittipaldi and Michael Andretti. Senna's veto kept Warwick out of the team.

'I think it was a compliment to me, but at the time I didn't see it that way,' said Warwick, on that morning we had coffee at Southampton Airport. 'Nor did you guys in the British press. It was seen as a selfish act that destroyed a promising British racing driver's career. No matter how you analyse it now – and I bear Senna no malice whatsoever – he destroyed my career as a top grand prix driver. Even now, my wife Rhonda won't hear of his name in the house. I never got myself back into the eyes of the people that mattered. What stands out in my mind was that through the whole episode Ayrton was selfish enough, focused enough, thick-skinned enough not to give a shit what you wrote, what I said, or what everybody else thought. All he knew was that Lotus couldn't build two equal cars – which was right. He wanted the spare car – which was also right. He also knew I was quick, and he didn't want me in the car. He also knew I was British and I'd get the team behind me no matter his own reputation.

'When Renault suddenly left Formula One at the end of 1985, my contract was torn up and I'd got nowhere to go after being vetoed at Lotus by Senna. Yet at Christmas, I got a card from Ayrton wishing me all the best for 1986! But for all that happened, I respected the man.' Brundle also understood. 'I think this type of behaviour is unquestionably a defining point of the great champions: they have all been utterly selfish bastards. Look at them: Lauda, Prost, Senna and Schumacher. All of them got their elbows out, galvanised the team around them, demanded all the best aspects of the resources, then, on top of that, they wanted to disadvantage their team-mate as well. And it's right, isn't it? Well, in a way it is and, perhaps if I had my chance again, I'd try and do the same. You tried to maximise your own opportunities, but that extra step of trying to minimise the chances of your team-mate, so that you had the whole team focused on you, just didn't cross your mind then. Schumacher took it to another level, didn't he? He was like a man with his own test driver.'

With that decision to deny Warwick a drive at Lotus, Senna had established himself as a driver with increasing muscle in the political arena. He would not allow sentiment to blur his mind. One day he would have what Prost presently owned – the world championship. If that meant being ruthless, so what?

9

STREET FIGHTING MAN

Alain Prost found himself a man much in demand after he had returned from Adelaide. He was feted at dinners, and required to make any number of personal appearances as the new world champion. Two dates stood out, however: one, an evening among family and friends in his home town of Saint Chamond, where a gymnasium complex had been named after him; the second, the formal occasion when French President François Mitterrand conferred on him the highest award the Republic has to offer, the *Légion d'Honneur*.

Prost had won twelve of the thirty-two grands prix that had been contested over the past two years and he had been on the podium on eight other occasions; with McLaren, the man had become a *tour de force*. All the time, Prost was working on the team, invisibly, but with great industry. He had nudged Lauda into the shadows at McLaren and forged a strong bond with Ron Dennis and Mansour Ojjeh. He spoke a language that technical director John Barnard appreciated and could act on. He had also absorbed some hard lessons – one in particular. Fame is not attained without a price. 'Time and accessibility, they have gone,' he said. 'I used to have driver heroes, a Stewart or a Lauda, I even had heroes among journalists when I started out. You become a hero of sorts yourself, and you wonder about those values. The spontaneity goes; you've been betrayed, attacked too often. You find it harder to believe: not in yourself, but in others. A public life isn't your own, but then I think all drivers are masochists. We seem to be masters of our own destinies, but we are not. I hate demagoguery of all kinds, the ritual praising of everyone in the team after a race, but it is true: we are hostages to others, to luck, to fate.'

Prost made another observation at this point in his life, at this tranquil moment in his career. 'Formula One is at least honest about itself. There is no trickery, no fraud, whatever people think. Sure, there are sharks. In F1, they swim out in the open.'

Murray Walker may have attracted a wider audience through his verbal *faux pas*, but this should never be confused with ignorance. Walker studied harder than most to acquire his facts around the paddock, and there was no one who wouldn't speak with him. He was sharply observant, too. 'Prost was hard-working, intelligent and he was bright enough to realise that one of the ways to beat your team-mate was to get the team on your side. By that I mean everybody from the research and development guys, the designers, the engineers and the mechanics. He had a sympathetic personality, drove absolutely brilliantly and he was – and I am sure he still is – an absolute master politician. The contrast between him and straightforward John Bull-like Nigel Mansell, in political terms, is black and white, night and day. Prost was brilliant on every front. Although he was to meet his Waterloo, wasn't he?'

Derek Warwick viewed Prost from another perspective, from being on the road as a rival. 'Alain was so quick with such little effort,' he argued. 'I think that's what amazed us. It was such a natural thing for him to drive fast.' As it was for Warwick, Senna, Piquet and Mansell and almost all the other drivers on the grid; but what Warwick meant was that Prost achieved his speed, his consistent smoothness, with an economy of effort. 'When Nigel got out of the car – and for me he is one of the greatest British racing drivers of all time – we used to take the mickey out of him because he would collapse in a big heap, drenched in sweat. But when I look back, that's how he drove a racing car. He used every ounce of energy, mentally and physically, and when he crossed the finishing line he was fried. Perhaps we didn't give him that credit at the time because of all the antics he'd got up to when he was acting. A grand prix was rarely straightforward for Nigel!

'But when I remember the way he set up a car, it was always a very nervous car that he drove from the back end; that's how he was quick, the car was always moving and it could always be pulled around by him. Prost used to prefer a little understeer, and he was a very traditional driver. He wasn't flamboyant which is why he looked so effortless. Alain taught me – and I suspect a lot of others including my brother Paul – what skills you needed to be a quick racing driver. You have to think of the team as a whole. You have to know its weaknesses, as well as its strengths, you had to know how to build that team around you. You also had to have a feel for the car you were driving. At testing sessions, Alain was never the quickest. He might put in a quick lap in the last fifteen minutes, but he didn't really care. All he was doing was testing for the race weekend. At a grand prix, he would do nothing spectacular on a Friday. Then Saturday, bang; Sunday, bang. And that was spectacular — that's why he was called the professor.'

Five and a half months separated the last race of 1985 from the first race of the new season, in Rio de Janeiro. Lotus had given their second seat to the Earl of Dumfries, known in racing circles as plain Johnny Dumfries. He had competed against Senna in F3 and he was considered no threat and would make no demands to embarrass the Lotus management. The team was now to be moulded in the image of Senna. While Renault had withdrawn from the sport as a constructor, they continued to supply engines to Lotus and Tyrrell. For this season, the cars were restricted to carrying a maximum of 195 litres of fuel, placing further responsibility on a driver to balance speed against fuel economy. In a test at Rio, several weeks before the Brazilian Grand Prix, Williams charged Nigel Mansell with running full race distance. He ran out of fuel two laps from the end. It was an ominous warning to all.

Mansell had another issue he wanted to address at this test in Brazil. He specifically sought out a discussion with Senna. In his autobiography he explained what had been on his mind: 'I had seen him [Senna] try some dangerous moves and was rather worried about him. He didn't seem to have too much respect for the other drivers and I thought it was worth talking to him before the new season. We had quite a long talk. I said that it was obvious that he and I were both going to be quick in the coming season and that we should both try to be professional as well. If one of us had the line into the corner, the other should let him go and try to pass at the next opportunity. There was no point in us having each other off. Ayrton agreed and we shook hands.'

And what happened next, you might ask? On the first lap of

the Brazilian Grand Prix, Mansell tried to pass Senna and mayhem ensued. 'I got alongside, my right front wheel level with his shoulder and began braking, but he suddenly came across and hit me,' recalled Mansell. 'I braked hard to avoid an accident, but his left rear wheel hit my right front and sent me off the road into the Armco, tearing off my left front wheel. We did not talk about it afterwards, but I learned an important lesson about racing him that day. His tactic was to intimidate and I refused to be intimidated.' Mansell proved faithful to his prediction.

But in the first instance, the Englishman had his hands full closer to home. His team-mate for this season was Nelson Piquet, who had joined Williams after seven years with Brabham. Keke Rosberg had been signed by McLaren from Williams to replace Niki Lauda. Prost and Rosberg appeared genuinely to get along. In contrast, Piquet set out to antagonise Mansell and their relationship ebbed and flowed like a storm tide.

Even with Lauda retired, this was a period in Formula One's history when the competition was intense, the calibre of driving high and the men involved were race hardened and not shy to start an argument. Four of them stood out above the others in '86: Prost, Senna, Mansell and Piquet.

Between them they won all but one grand prix – Gerhard Berger claimed the Mexican round of the championship for Benetton BMW. The first six races had unfolded like this: Piquet won in Brazil; Senna in Spain; Prost in San Marino and Monaco; and Mansell in Belgium and Canada. At Jerez in Spain, Senna and Mansell had produced a classic encounter. Near the end of the race, Mansell lost twenty seconds due to a pit stop for fresh rubber. He returned to the track behind Prost, who was trailing Senna. The Englishman found a way round Prost to go in pursuit of Senna. He had four laps to close a six-second deficit. Mansell's pit board acted like a red rag to an enraged bull: each time he saw that he had narrowed the gap he charged harder through the next lap. By the time Mansell exited the final hairpin he was almost magnetised to the Brazilian's gearbox. The Englishman's car screamed in anguish as he flicked through the gears, but he ran out of road and Senna's Lotus had taken the flag before Mansell finally passed him. Senna's winning margin had been 0.014 seconds – or ninety-three centimetres. 'Physically, I was at the end,' admitted Senna afterwards. 'But winning is the best medicine to regain strength. In the evening I drove the race again in my mind. I wanted to enjoy my victory once more that way.'

Mansell, clearly defined as No. 2 driver at Williams, had no orders to defer to Piquet on the racetrack. The team had enough to contend with having to learn how to deal without Frank Williams, paralysed in a road accident in March that year, to concern themselves with the increasingly tense rivalry between their drivers. Piquet had to hack it alone. Senna's second win of the season came in Detroit, where he was on pole. In all, he took eight pole positions this season, an incredible exhibition of his speed and commitment that Brundle alluded to earlier. Senna's intensity in a racing car – and there is a haunted look in the man's eyes before he leaves the pits on a qualifying run – is brilliantly encapsulated in his own words by Chris Hilton for his book, *Ayrton Senna: The Hard Edge of Genius*, which was published in 1990. Asked to discuss his mind's mechanism at the start of a grand prix, this is how Senna responded:

'I may look slow, but people don't know what a Grand Prix is. There are so many things you have to do, think about, and even learn in those few hours before the start. For me the only way to be stronger is to concentrate deeply. I try to remember everything, every small detail of my preparation. You must think of everything in this enormous turmoil at the start. It is wrong to recognise people, except your mechanics perhaps. I run the whole picture in my head. I inspect the surface of the track. That is important to determine your tactics in the race and your choice of tyres. I believe I am the only one who does that. I go through a sort of checklist like a pilot, except we have nothing on paper. After the warm-up lap I check everything once more. People always think the start of the race is something terrible, that your heart beats like mad, that your brain is about to explode; but it's a totally unreal moment, it is like a dream, like entering another world. Your spirit goes and the body sets itself free. When you accelerate there is only one thing that matters, not to fall behind, to take the lead. Really the most beautiful moment is when the light turns red. Everything in me is programmed then, everything is discharged, bang, bang, bang, the tension, the waiting for hours, minutes, it all disappears.'

It is a revealing insight into the man. If driving to Alain Prost was an art form, to Senna it was a form of spiritualism. '*Like entering another world . . .*' Those four words surely, act as a self-portrait of the man.

If Prost conserved tyres, brakes and fuel, Senna insisted that they should work to the limit, and sometimes beyond. If Prost wanted to win, Senna *had* to win as anything else was failure. He was defined by his victories. After Senna's win in Detroit – a Mickey Mouse track in Motown in a forlorn attempt to make Formula One connect with an American audience – Mansell claimed victories at the French Grand Prix and the British Grand Prix in successive weekends. Prost came second at Le Castellet and third at Brands Hatch, but that weekend was ruined for him by an accident to his close friend, Jacques Laffite. On an afternoon when he was driving in his one hundred and seventy-sixth grand prix – equalling the record of Graham Hill – Laffite's Ligier Renault crashed into a barrier at Paddock Hill Bend during a multicar shunt on the first lap. The race had to be red-flagged. 'Jacques was in a mess, with broken legs, ankles, heels and pelvis,' said Prost. 'I went with him as far as the ambulance. The pain was so terrible he blacked out. I was shattered.' Likewise Mansell sympathised with the plight of Laffite, a friend and one of the most popular drivers in the pit lane, but there was an upside for the Englishman from the Frenchman's accident that prevented him from driving an F1 car ever again. A restart meant that Mansell had a second chance because, in the original race, his Williams had ground to halt when his driveshaft failed. Second time around, Mansell defeated Piquet into second place in a race that sucked the breath from both men because of the frenetic pace at which they ran. Prost, in third place, had been lapped by both Williams.

Mansell was on a roll, having won four of the five previous races, and he headed the championship for the first time in his life. He had a four-point lead over Prost. Yet this was a championship with an abundance of life left in it. Piquet won three of the next four races, with Prost successful in the other one. Crucially, Mansell finished on the podium in three of them. No man could claim to have an upper hand. Three races remained: Mansell had 61 points, Piquet 56 and Prost 53.

Yet this suddenly became inconsequential to Prost. Just before the next race in Portugal his brother Daniel died of cancer. He was a young man, not yet forty. Prost accepted his responsibility to drive at Estoril, but he was in sombre mood with no real appetite for what he was doing. Of course, in the car he had to apply blinkers to ignore the distress of his family because it is vital to avoid emotional distraction when driving at almost 200mph. Outside the car, he surrounded himself with just a few of his closest confidants from the French media who never tried to exploit their relationship with him into hard copy.

In the race, Mansell led from start to finish, consolidating his hold on the championship. Prost claimed second which, given the emotional complexion of his weekend, represented six valuable points. He has never spoken publicly about his brother other than to say, 'Daniel's death taught me life is short and fragile. I am afraid of sickness and old age.' Prost's private life is – and always has been – just that: private. Senna adopted the same attitude. They were stripped bare, emotionally and physically, at a race weekend, but outside their workplace neither man hunted stardom in any of its forms. In particular, Senna was a man almost impossible for all but those closest to him to comprehend. As he once put it: 'The helmet hides feelings that cannot be understood.'

Prost's performance in Estoril somehow illustrated that sentiment. But the Portuguese Grand Prix did little to alter the state of the title race as Piquet finished third. Senna had run a strong second but his Lotus ran out of fuel on the last lap and he was classified fourth. His championship hopes, like his car, ran out of gas right there. The next day Prost attended his brother's funeral.

Perhaps he drew strength from adversity; perhaps not. But the season was about to tilt in his direction as fast, and as cruelly, as it would unravel for Mansell. In the penultimate grand prix of the year in Mexico, Mansell was left stranded at the start after he had qualified in third position. Did first gear fail him, or did he fail to engage first gear? Whatever, everyone else slipped past

Mansell until he squeezed his car into second gear and finally got off the line. Mansell fought back to finish fifth, but his lead in the championship had been reduced after Prost secured second place and Piquet took fourth. With one race left the championship table now looked like this, allowing for the drivers to count only their eleven best results as the regulations demanded: Mansell, 70 points; Prost 64 points; Piquet 63. To defend his title Prost had to win the Australian Grand Prix with Mansell finishing outside the top three.

I flew from London to Adelaide to cover the story – and the Australian Grand Prix provided us with a compelling and dramatic climax to the year. Prost was central to every scene in the defence of his title. 'Actually, I like this situation,' he said before the cars had taken to the streets of the capital of South Australia. 'It's like driving for your life, you have to win. For Nigel, it is more difficult, because he has choices he can make.' We had travelled south to the other side of the world with a summer wardrobe only to be confounded by the coldest mid-October weekend anyone in Adelaide could recall: it was as though the race director had borrowed from Hitchcock to play with the drivers' minds. My room at the inaptly named Sunny South Motel was like an icebox at night.

Prost, conveniently in the circumstances, understood that a cool mind would be needed to prevail. His McLaren would not match the raw power of the Williams of Mansell and Piquet, which meant that during qualifying his focus was on setting up his car for the race, not a quick lap. Rosberg, driving in his last grand prix before retirement, openly offered his assistance to Prost, a team-mate he admired as a driver and as a man. Rosberg was a man's man. He smoked, liked a drink and drove to the limit and, at times, beyond. In a race car, he was reckoned hard but fair. Outside the car, he was excellent company. Rosberg's misfortune at McLaren was that he never properly integrated with technical director John Barnard and rarely found the set-up of his car to his liking. In some drivers, that could be dismissed as a lame excuse for not delivering. Yet Rosberg's record in wringing the life from some spectacularly bad racing cars before he joined Williams meant that his evaluation carried the weight of a sworn affidavit. Rosberg's offer to help Prost, in whatever way he could, was indicative of the respect in which the Finn held the Frenchman. 'For me, it would be a joke for anyone else to be world champion,' said Rosberg.

Let us start this extraordinary grand prix at the end. Nigel and Rosanne Mansell spent the last fifteen minutes of the race inside a caravan parked at the rear of the Williams Honda pit. Chalked on the window of the makeshift team headquarters was the information that it was for sale afterwards, for 3,395 Australian dollars with a 10 per cent discount for cash. It seemed a ludicrously cheap, shabby and inappropriate funeral parlour in which to bury Mansell's lifetime ambition to win the Formula One world championship. But then the thirty-two-year-old Englishman had never walked easily on the glamorous side of the tracks in a sport too often embraced by beautiful people who measure heartache in terms of running short of vintage Dom Perignon midway through a dinner party.

Mansell had held the third place he needed to be champion with only forty-four miles remaining in the Australian Grand Prix. Forty-four bloody miles . . . of a star trek that had started sixteen years earlier. The left rear wheel of his Williams had unravelled at almost 200mph as he travelled down Dequetteville Terrace – called the Brabham Straight for the purposes of the grand prix. Sparks flew into the air like a random firework display. Rosanne, who had been watching from a monitor in the caravan, rushed into the Williams garage, hurdling toolboxes in her anxiety to glean information from someone within the team. 'What's happened to Nigel?' she asked, breathlessly. When she was told that a rear tyre had exploded, she looked exhaustedly at the screen in the garage. 'I don't believe it . . . yes, yes, I do,' she said. Rosanne had lived through all the hard times her husband had endured, the dreadful injuries he had sustained in a racing car, and she had willingly agreed to the sale of their home to keep him on the track. So, she had journeyed to Adelaide in hope, but definitely not in expectation of her husband going home as world champion.

As I watched the stoical Englishman walk away, arm-in-weary-arm with his wife, Prost was beginning to celebrate the successful defence of his world championship, an accomplishment last achieved by Jack Brabham in 1960. Prost could be found in Marlboro McLaren's HQ eating a bowl of strawberries. He felt nothing but sympathy for Mansell. He had twice been beaten to the championship within sight of the winning post and he was not about to gloat at the expense of the Englishman. 'I feel sorry for Nigel,' he said. 'He really deserved to win the championship.' No one, however, could suggest that Prost was anything, but the worthiest of champions. He had come to the streets of Adelaide knowing that he *had* to win. He did just that with a masterful drive, sprinkled with the slice of luck that deserted Mansell on the afternoon he needed it most.

Prost was not scheduled to make a tyre change, but a puncture altered his plans and he stopped for fresh rubber on lap thirty-two of the eighty-two-lap race. His pit stop became chaotic when the hydraulic jack refused to slide under the front of the car. This crisis was resolved when McLaren mechanics bodily lifted the car into the air – but the stop had lasted seventeen seconds. Prost emerged fourth, some twenty seconds behind Mansell and fifty seconds adrift from race leader, Rosberg, who was revelling in his grand finale. But as Rosberg tried to calculate how he could assist Prost, he suddenly heard a noise that he disliked from the rear of his McLaren. The Finn braked to a standstill on the sixty-third lap as he suspected his engine had been at the point of destruction; instead, when he examined his car he could see the noise had come from a delaminated rear tyre.

On the next lap Prost caught and passed Mansell to take second place, but the Englishman's third position still assured him of the championship. Then, calamitously Mansell's tyre, and his dream, exploded.

The Williams team could not ignore such overwhelming evidence that the tyres would not, after all, last the distance. They radioed Piquet, now leading the race and heading towards the championship, and advised him to pit for new tyres. He took the option on offer to him. Later, Piquet admitted: 'The final decision had to be mine and all the information suggested I had to stop. The car was vibrating. I knew I might be losing the championship – but I was alive.' Prost assumed the lead of the grand prix – and was never threatened by Piquet who had to settle for second place in the race. What Piquet did not know was that the McLaren team were praying Prost would have enough fuel to reach the chequered flag. Inside his McLaren, Prost feared he was running on vapour as his onboard computer informed him that he would not last the distance. He had run out of fuel at the German Grand Prix in the summer, a hard enough disappointment to swallow, but imagine this: imagine losing the world championship because the last of the 195 litres of fuel he was allowed to carry under the regulations had been consumed a minute too soon. 'Theoretically, he should have run out,' said Ron Dennis. 'The computer monitoring his fuel said he was down, but fortunately it must have been an error – one that worked in our favour.'

As soon as he had driven past the chequered flag, he parked his McLaren. He released his seat belts, climbed from the car and jumped in the air in a moment of pure ecstasy. A picture of this moment hangs in the study of his apartment in Paris, a rare souvenir on display from a lifetime of Kodak moments. A picture that could be legitimately captioned: 'Alain Prost – a street fighting man.'

The odds had been stacked heavily against him from the start. A week before the race, Prost and Mansell had met in an airline lounge at Singapore Airport and he had offered to help the Englishman combat the challenge of Piquet, if his own prospects looked bleak. They may not have been house guests of one another, but there was cordiality between them that lasted until they became team-mates some years later at Ferrari. They both played golf from a single-figure handicap and within hours of arriving in Adelaide they were on the tee in the Pro-Am of the South Australia Open. Mansell partnered Greg Norman, while Prost played alongside another Australian, David Graham. Prost knew that relations between Mansell and Piquet had worsened as the championship neared its climax. And, frankly, if Prost could not be champion he preferred the thought of Mansell being crowned as his successor.

In the event, Mansell's title hopes vanished in a catherine wheel of rubber. And John Hogan from Marlboro suspected that if any man could get the McLaren to the line on a fuel gauge registering empty, that man was Prost. 'Alain was never going to fail to win; in those circumstances he'd win on the smell of an oil rag!' chuckled Hogan. Jo Ramirez also realised how Prost's conservation of the rudimentary elements of his car had been vital to his triumph. 'I remember looking afterwards at the brakes on both our cars,' explained the team coordinator of McLaren. 'There was no way Keke could have done another ten laps before he ran out of brakes. Alain could probably have done another race on his! He was so gentle on the brakes, on the tyres, the gears, everything. He was so smooth. It was unbelievable, and hard to understand how he did it. We used to say to him, "Alain, if you are going to do a quick lap let us know; otherwise, we will miss it." He just didn't look quick – even Senna would remark later how smooth Prost was.' Ramirez had smuggled Prost's wife Anne-Marie to the podium ceremony. 'Alain was not supposed to have any chance of winning this championship,' said Ramirez. 'When Alain saw Anne-Marie at the podium – and he did not know that we could get her there – the two embraced and there were tears. It was lovely.' This was a snapshot of Prost rarely seen. He has been meticulous in keeping his family out of the spotlight and that is something that has been respected in France and Switzerland where he maintains his homes in utter privacy. Hogan offered a postscript to the season with a mischievous glint in his eye. 'I thought Keke was going to be like lightning in that car,' he said. 'I'd always had the highest admiration for him. He was one hundred per cent committed on every lap. But Barnard had a theory that Keke couldn't drive the car the way Alain liked it and John insisted on the cars being more or less the same. Keke got the hang of it in the last race . . . he went like shit off a shovel but it was too late.' Sometime that evening, Hogan said to Prost, 'You are going to beat Fangio's record of five world championships, aren't you? Alain said to me, in that nonchalant way of his, "Oh, yeah." But he was really looking for Fangio's record and he got to four by the end . . . but it wasn't to be.'

Rosberg was not the only departure from McLaren. Barnard left for Ferrari with a commission to establish a base from which to work for the Scuderia from near his home in Guildford. He had already sold his shareholding in McLaren International to Mansour Ojjeh in 1985 for the expedient reason of wanting a decent house and some capital. Dennis and Barnard's relationship had become increasingly tense – and Dennis felt aggrieved when his erstwhile partner allegedly held negotiations with BMW Motorsport in the summer of 1986. In the end, the scale of Ferrari's offer and their willingness to allow him to operate from England seduced Barnard and he left the team before the Italian Grand Prix. Dennis, in his inimitable manner of speech, told journalist Alan Henry: 'We had achieved everything together that we had set out to do and there was a variety of choices available to myself and John. The easy route for both of us, and certainly the easy route for me, would be to have no change. But when faced with all the things that affected that decision to either continue together or not, we split. Each's contribution was inaccurately perceived by the other, and I think there was more of an inaccuracy on his side as to what I was contributing in generating finances, and all that sort of thing.'

Regardless of the disruption, Prost prevailed for a second year, but Williams won the constructors' championship with some ease. Perhaps Rosberg best captured the excitement and emotion of a year's racing that had started in the searing heat of Brazil seven months earlier and ended on an unseasonably cold and overcast Australian afternoon. 'At the end, Williams have had a fantastic season,' he said. 'But Prost drove a great race. You can't take that away from the little Frog. He's great.'

Behind the scenes, the Honda management had been unimpressed that neither Williams driver had won the world championship. And, privately, Dennis accepted that the TAG turbo that McLaren had funded to win the last three world championships was nearing the end of its competitive life. Dennis knew that he needed to obtain manufacturer support as soon as he could. Join up the dots . . .

For Senna, the season ended when the Renault engine in his Lotus failed at around the halfway mark in the Australian Grand Prix. He had shown a strengthening capability to mix it with Prost – and Mansell and Piquet – but he was competing with an inferior car and engine. Things had to change – and fast.

10

BIRTH OF THE DREAM TEAM?

Ayrton Senna duly had Honda engines at his disposal for 1987 as Lotus had switched from Renault to the Japanese manufacturer. With the engines came Japanese driver Satoru Nakajima, whose son Kazuki currently drives for Williams. Lotus also had new sponsors, Camel, a brand of cigarette from tobacco giants R.J. Reynolds. To Senna, this was a pivotal season. He had to know if Lotus could provide a car commensurate with his own ambition. An Englishman called Tony Jardine ran the Camel account – the same man who had been McLaren team manager when Prost entered Formula One. After he had left McLaren, Jardine switched to the marketing and PR side of the business. He had worked with Lotus on the John Player account through a company called CSS and had already established a rapport with team principal Peter Warr. 'I became quite close to Peter,' he said. 'He could be a hard man and at the beginning he gave me a lot of kickings. However, I won his confidence – and I was involved with Peter making clandestine phone calls in the back of the motorhome to Toleman to try to get Senna to Lotus for 1985. To Senna, there was a bit of romance about Lotus because of Jim Clark. Also, the team had Gérard Ducarouge who was the man of the moment as a designer.

'I knew Ayrton from his F3 days as I shared a house in Egham, Surrey, with Dick Bennetts from West Surrey Racing, who ran his car, of course. In the house was also Davy Ryan [a McLaren man to the core then, and now] and Razor Grant who had been James Hunt's chief mechanic. That house was party central. We served jugs of gin and tonic and there were lots of Kiwis in flip-flops and shorts even when it was snowing. Senna knew who we were and what we did. He had his road map – he knew who could help him.'

How did Jardine think Senna compared with Prost? 'Senna was a totally different character. You noticed nervousness about Prost, but Senna already had an aura. He had this look – I wouldn't go as far as to say it was imperious – but he had total confidence. He knew where he was going whereas Prost wasn't like that. Prost had doubts when I knew him at the beginning, but once he was in the car he was okay. Another difference: Prost could never concentrate when you were talking, and his eyes darted all over the place. Senna absorbed it all – and unlike Prost he formed relationships with all the members of the team. He'd stay behind all hours. He'd go down and see the Goodyear guys in the tyre-fitting bay; he was a cute operator.'

Clearly, Prost developed these traits himself after he had left McLaren the first time around in the days when Jardine had been with the team – because that is a feature of his behaviour that everyone who has been in contact with him remarks upon. Jardine's own career path took another turn at the end of 1985. He left CSS to establish his own business. He had no contact with Lotus in 1986, but towards the end of that year he received a call from Warr. He remembered: 'Peter came on the telephone and said, "How are you getting on, Chap? We're missing you, what about if we can get you back on board?" Naturally, this was the chance of good business for me. He arranged for us to meet him in the museum at the Lotus factory at Hethel, in Norfolk. It was all very clandestine. In the gloom I could see a bloke in a mac. Peter introduced this man to me as W. Duncan Lee from R.J. Reynolds. Lee explained that their Camel brand was coming into F1 and that Peter thought I might be the right man to handle their account. I was invited to go and pitch for the business at the company's head office at Winston Salem, in North Carolina.'

The scale of the R.J. Reynolds headquarters was mammoth. The company dominated the landscape of the town. 'I had to walk right through the dining room where all the employees had lunch and there was a dais at one end where some of the board would eat,' recalled Jardine. He suspects that some of those same executives appeared just a few years later in the book *The Barbarians at the Gate*, an investigative work about the controversial leveraged buyout of RJR Nabisco. 'It was arranged for me to have a private lunch with W. Duncan Lee and Lester Pullen, the feared Englishman who was chairman and chief executive. Pullen had an accent from the English aristocracy, no doubt advantageous to him within an American company. He fired six questions at me that put me on the spot.'

The first related to Lotus founder Colin Chapman and American John De Lorean. Chapman's company designed a car for De Lorean, who was funded with subsidies from the British Government as he built a factory to manufacture them in troubled Belfast in the early eighties. The Government's

$18 million vanished into a black hole through a company registered in Panama and the story created headlines and controversy on both sides of the Atlantic. 'Lester Pullen wanted to know if I knew where the money was!' said Jardine.

'Next up, Pullen said: "I understand you have a close relationship with Peter Warr. If it comes down to some political decision between us and the team, who are you going to support?" You get the picture of the level of my interrogation? Anyway, I was squirming and doing the best I could to come up with some answers, and I suppose I must have survived. For question number six, Pullen looked at me hard and said: "If we give you this business, you have to ensure I have an apartment right over the start-finish line at Monaco. Do you think you can fix that?" I replied – in a way I hoped was convincing – "I am sure I can."'

Pullen turned to Lee and asked him: 'Duncan, have you hired this young man yet?'

'No, sir, I have not.'

'Make sure you do, then. Delightful to meet you, Tony.'

Jardine had not the faintest idea how he was going to make Pullen's wish come true, but that was a worry for another day. He had the account and that was what mattered. Besides, the Monaco Grand Prix was the fourth on the calendar at the end of May and there would be time to pull some strings with contacts in the interim months. Jardine had good connections and, doubtless, the Camel budget would withstand whatever money he had to spend to rent the apartment. The opening race in 1987 was once more in Rio de Janeiro.

No one at Lotus would openly admit as much, but the team was on trial. Senna had been with them for two years and he was beginning to have reservations about their capacity to provide him with a car good enough to allow him to win the world championship. He was in Formula One for no other reason than to be champion. If Lotus could not deliver, he would switch allegiance to a team that could. Formula One is a rumour factory at the slowest of times. With a man of such prodigious talent as Senna, the factory was on overtime. It was speculated that Ron Dennis had met with Senna before the season began. Some, like Jo Ramirez, felt that contact between the two men had happened even earlier. 'Ron signed Stefan Johansson for 1987 only after he had failed to get Ayrton from Lotus,' said Ramirez. 'Peter Warr put Ayrton's money up and up, apparently. Ron said something like, "We haven't got Senna, but now Lotus don't have enough money to do a good car so I don't think it's going to be a problem."

'Keke Rosberg at the time thought it was the best thing that could happen to Senna. Why? Keke reckoned that everyone had talked up Ayrton as the biggest star in the sky and that would be his downfall for one reason: Keke argued that if Senna was in the same car as Prost he would be a nobody. Prost would make a meal of him, said Rosberg. Keke in 1986 could not live with Prost, for whatever reason, and in the end he said that Alain was unbelievable. Keke was a good guy, very honest. He respected very much what Prost did.'

Senna was the last to arrive in Rio de Janeiro, a city renowned worldwide for its carnival, football and the beautiful women who boulevard on the beaches of Ipanema and Copacabana, brought alive to a wider audience by the lyrics of pop songs. Senna had preferred to remain at his home 250 miles away in São Paulo as late as possible as he knew that he would be the focus of attention twenty-four hours a day during the Brazilian Grand Prix. He took refuge in a secret apartment, a recluse in his own country. Senna had become an idol, an inspirational figure in a nation where millions exist below the poverty line. In time, Senna's popularity rating would be on a par with that of Pele; yet already adulation for him in Rio ran wild. Nelson Piquet might have been world champion twice in the previous six years, but it was Senna's picture that adorned house-high posters on the road from the city to the racetrack. His annual salary was not much less than the $5 million McLaren paid Prost. In Rio, such a sum might have been thought obscene as tens of thousands of people live in poverty in favelas, the slums on the fringes of the city with ramshackle homes that would be condemned if they stood on allotments in Britain, yet the Brazilian public did not protest Senna's wealth. Senna was a source of national pride – and if that sounds pretentious it cannot be helped. It was the truth – and a truth that never left him in life and one that followed him to the grave.

To the frenzied approval of the local crowd, Senna, briefly, led that Brazilian Grand Prix before his race was prematurely ended by engine failure. It was a less than ideal beginning to a pivotal season for Lotus who had come under enormous strain to try to hold on to their most prized asset: Senna. Prost encountered no such disappointment. He won his twenty-sixth grand prix – in his 106th Formula One race – by more than forty seconds from Piquet. Prost was now driving to a new destination, somewhere called sporting immortality. Victory had moved him to within one win of equalling Jackie Stewart's record of twenty-seven grand prix wins. At thirty-two, the Frenchman had, staggeringly, won twenty-one of the previous sixty-four races staged around the world. On that triumphant day in Rio, Dennis showed no reluctance in placing Prost in the pantheon of motor racing gods. 'Alain's the best,' he said. 'He has a lot of personal discipline and is a very quick, very clean, very committed driver. His motivational level is higher than ever. After this season, he will probably be the most successful champion in the history of motorsport.'

Mansell won the next race from Senna in San Marino when Piquet was prevented from racing on doctors' orders after he had crashed heavily during practice on Friday. Prost was forced into retirement after just fourteen laps by an electrical fault. But Mansell and Senna would claim bigger headlines a fortnight later at the Belgium Grand Prix at Spa-Francorchamps. It is not often that one Formula One driver has to be pulled off another in a garage in the pit lane. Mansell had won pole with Senna in third place on the grid. It is important to know their positions. When the race began, Mansell accelerated into an unimpeded lead, but the grand prix was red-flagged on the second lap after a crash involving Britain's Jonathan Palmer and Frenchman Philippe Streiff. At the restart, Senna muscled his way into the lead at the hairpin. Mansell trailed him halfway round the lap until, on the exit of Pouhon, he detected that Senna had suddenly slowed. Mansell thought he might be in trouble – but he also felt it was not 'beyond the realms of possibility that he was trying a dirty trick on me, dabbing the brakes to unsettle me'. Regardless of what Senna had or had not done, Mansell tried to seize the advantage. He moved left and drew alongside the Brazilian to pass. 'The next thing I knew I was being pushed off the circuit,' reported Mansell. The Lotus and the Williams left the track in unison. Senna's car went no further than the gravel trap, but Mansell in his guise as John Bull forced his car back into the race. Yet his Williams had sustained too much damage and became unmanageable to handle. He retired on lap seventeen.

In a blind rage, Mansell headed along the pit lane until he reached the Lotus garage. He saw his prey, Senna. Then he pounced . . . and grabbed the Brazilian by his overalls and pushed him against a wall. Mansell pulled the zip on the front of Senna's overalls beyond his chin towards his nose. 'Next time you do that, you're going to have to do a much better job,' snarled Mansell. Before the incident could escalate, three Lotus mechanics arrived to yank the Englishman away. News of Mansell's assault on Senna swiftly reached the media. The story was soon on the wires and running around the world.

Senna's version of events was short, and not without a hint of gallows humour. 'When a man holds you around the throat, I don't think he has come to apologise,' he said.

As he would do repeatedly throughout his career, Senna claimed to be the aggrieved party. 'I couldn't believe what he was trying to do – overtake on the outside at a place like that,' he said. It was a classic motor racing incident: Mansell and Senna, complaining in turn that they had been a victim of the other. The truth was probably somewhere in the middle. Mansell had chosen to take a stand against Senna's exuberant style of driving; Senna had elected not to be intimidated by Mansell. The road was not wide enough to accommodate them both. But it was the wild look in Mansell's eye as he entered the Lotus garage that, perhaps, indicated where most blame could be laid. It takes peculiar circumstances for one racing driver to actually want to start a fist fight with another.

Later that week, Mansell's syndicated column appeared in an Australian newspaper with these words printed under his name: 'I don't think I've ever felt so angry in my life. When I climbed out of the car, I had only one thought on my mind – and that was to get Senna. He was lucky some bystanders kept us apart after we'd had a bit of a scuffle. There could have been a mess

on the garage floor.' After publication of his column, Mansell
was asked to comment on the contents by some of us in the
English press. From his home on the Isle of Man, he denied the
sentiments attributed to him. 'I said no such thing,' claimed
Mansell. My own story in the *Daily Express* – for whom I was
working at the time – appeared under the headline: 'Mansell
denies a Senna vendetta'.

Mansell insisted in our interview that the matter had been
closed in the Lotus garage. 'What happened is history, and
forgotten,' he vowed. 'I'm going to the Monte Carlo Grand Prix
[the next race] to enjoy myself and hopefully break my duck
there. There will certainly be no question of a vendetta. We are
both professional people, and what outsiders may not understand is how a lot of adrenaline can pump through a grand prix
driver – and that sort of thing can happen in the heat of the
moment.' Almost a decade later Mansell addressed the incident
in a reflective mood in his autobiography, which was published
after Senna's death. 'I was painted as the bad boy, although the
reports did not mention that the accident had been forced upon
me,' he wrote. 'To this day I don't condone my actions and I
am not trying to justify them. I would certainly never do anything
like that again, but in those days Senna would do anything to
win, and he needed to learn there was one man out there on
the track who would not be intimidated by him. He knew that
when we were side by side, I wouldn't give an inch and he
wouldn't scare me off. The problem was that he and I were both
incredibly competitive creatures, cast out of the same mould, if
you like. To both of us winning was everything, but the difference was that I have always played by a sportsman's rule, Ayrton
wanted to win at any price. At least we both appreciated how
quick and talented we were as drivers. I think that Ayrton only

had that with one or two opponents throughout his whole career – probably just Alain Prost and myself.' Mansell could be right.

After the fracas at Spa – a race won by Prost to place him at the head of the championship – Mansell and Senna occupied the front row on the grid at Monaco. Would there be another coming together, another collision of wills between two men who had never knowingly surrendered an inch on a racetrack, we wondered? Certainly, Prost considered the atmosphere menacing, as he told me at the time. 'It's bad when you have drivers locked against one another like this,' he said. 'It is bad for Formula One and bad for the sport. I don't want to talk about Nigel or Ayrton because that is their problem. But the way it is at the moment is unhealthy. Even for me, I am not comfortable having them around me on the track.' Prost was at a loss to comprehend what Mansell had done at Spa. 'I like Nigel and he is a good friend, but I don't understand what he did in Belgium. It is something Nigel has to control if he is going to be world champion one day. The Williams he drives is fantastic, better than my Marlboro McLaren.'

Mansell, however, relieved the tension with a clean departure from the line and began to drive impressively over the horizon. In twenty laps he built a ten-second lead. But Mansell's luck was out – on the thirtieth lap he lost all turbo boost pressure and his day was over. Senna capitalised on the Englishman's demise to clinch his first triumph on the streets of Monte Carlo, where Prost had reigned supreme in the previous three years. Only British driver Graham Hill had ever won Monaco three times in a row before Prost. Hill epitomised the sixties, rakish in appearance with a matinee idol's moustache and a fondness for partying. Prost's style, two decades later, was far more conservative, but no less brilliant on the eye for that. The Frenchman's élan and smoothness suited the streets of Monte Carlo as he produced consistent lap times, one after the other, year after year. Everyone will tell you that the Monaco Grand Prix is one where a driver's ability can compensate for the shortcomings of his car. It is also the grand prix that is the best known in the world and, as such, coveted by generation after generation of drivers. Senna's victory had just improved his CV dramatically.

Tony Jardine was unsure whether to laugh or cry when he met the Brazilian afterwards. Let him recount how he had appeased the will of Lester Pullen, but still faced a PR catastrophe due to the intransigence of Senna. 'I did finally get the apartment Pullen wanted, on the start–finish line, but it had taken two months to set up and required, shall we say, some persistence to persuade those who had originally rented the place to let me have it!' Isn't money a wonderful language in any negotiation? 'Once we had the R.J. Reynolds party into the apartment, I was told that one of the board members had a Brazilian wife and she was potty about Senna,' said Jardine, almost ageing as the memories returned. 'The last request from Pullen was that if Senna won I had to get him to the apartment after the press conference was over so that the board could meet him. Well, Ayrton won in the active-suspension Lotus Honda in distinctive yellow livery, the Camel colours. The place went berserk, and after he had done with the press I said to Ayrton that he must come with me to the apartment to meet the people from Camel.

'Senna replied, abruptly: "I don't go to any apartment."

'Me, "Ayrton, please."

'Senna, "Fuck off, no."

'And then Senna left . . . aaaaaargh! I was thinking of every excuse under the sun. As Senna was running away in the wrong direction, I caught him up and told him the story I had concocted to get us both off the hook. "Ayrton, I'll have to tell them you're ill." He didn't care what I told them, he was gone. By the time I got through the streets, jammed with people, and cleared security to reach the twelfth-floor apartment I was in a lather. Immediately, I was asked: "Where's Ayrton?" What was I to do? I just told them a bare-faced lie, "Ayrton asked me to pass on a message . . ."

'Senna, oh man. He never happily or willingly did PR. I always had to put a gun to his head. He'd argue in response: "I do it for you on the track, that's the best PR of all." I tried to reason with him that off-track was part of his job, too. Even so, I used to go to the house he shared with Mauricio Gugelmin [a Brazilian driver who made it into Formula One] in Esher. We got on really well – except he didn't do PR! Him and Mansell were difficult men. We really did earn our money. In Nigel's Lotus days, he divided the team. It was him against Elio. Nigel was starting to show promise, but then threw away the race at Monaco in 1984 in a Ducarouge-designed Lotus that was a fabulous car. He got past everyone and took the lead. But I remember Peter Warr watching and saying aloud, "He's going to crash, I tell you he's going to fucking crash. Wait for it." Sure enough, Mansell crashed. He told me afterwards that the car had lost grip on a white line in the road.' Mansell would also tell you that Warr was no friend of his inside the team and agitated against him until he had replaced him with Senna.

The 1987 season became a duel for the title between Piquet and Mansell. Memorably, Mansell won a classic confrontation between them in front of 100,000 people at the British Grand Prix at Silverstone. At the end, thousands poured on to the circuit to produce the kind of wild celebrations usually witnessed in Italy when a Ferrari wins: that afternoon the term *Mansellmania* passed into the lexicon of motorsport. It was a mob scene without malice. Mansell had sold Piquet a 200mph 'dummy' on the Hangar Straight on the sixty-third of the sixty-five-lap race. 'I was surprised Nigel caught Nelson,' said Frank Williams. 'I always worry they might take one another off – but they are both winners. Any risks they take are calculated.' That night Mansell could be found at his rented caravan at the BRDC campsite barely 100 yards from the pit lane. He was slumped content-edly, if exhausted, in a candy-striped garden chair. He looked like a bank clerk on his annual holiday to the south coast. 'Anyone going to put the kettle on for a cuppa?' he asked. Mansell had retrieved a twenty-eight-second deficit to overhaul Piquet. His good friend golfer Greg Norman said, 'That was like scoring nine birdies on the back nine!' Mansell's win was invested with more satisfaction than ever as the man he had defeated so dramatically was his team-mate. 'Nelson was cold and callous when he said he has won two championships and I have lost one,' said Mansell. 'He has these ways of stirring the competi-tion – but he cannot hurt me out of the car.'

To suggest Mansell and Piquet disliked one another is rather like declaring that Chicago's law enforcement officers were less than enamoured with Al Capone. Mansell and Piquet were men from different worlds: the Englishman from a Midlands family full of middle-class virtues, the Brazilian from a wealthy South American background. But before this season was over, Piquet would be declaring his allegiance to a new team. At the centre of this switch was one man: Senna.

During the German Grand Prix in the summer, Senna had informed Peter Warr from Lotus that he was in negotiation with Ron Dennis. A few days after the race, Senna's solicitors wrote to Lotus and confirmed he would not be with them in 1988. Clearly, reading between the lines Warr knew that Senna had reached a deal with McLaren. In response, Warr acted decisively. Before the next race in Hungary, he flew to meet Piquet to make him an offer for 1988. The Brazilian accepted – and Williams lost not only a world champion but the prized support of their Japanese partners.

Senna had been made aware that Honda would follow him from Lotus to McLaren; and Piquet had arranged for Honda to leave Williams for Lotus. Williams had been badly snookered.

Senna, too, had been left in the dark. The first he learned of Piquet's signature on a Lotus contract was when he turned up to drive the car in Hungary. He was unamused – and rebuked Lotus for being 'unprofessional'. But on what grounds was not entirely clear. Had he not already handed in his notice? Perhaps Senna thought he was due the courtesy of hearing ahead of a press release what Lotus intended. But this was wishful thinking in the extreme; in Formula One there is rarely anything as straightforward as a transparent deal. Senna had used Lotus to get himself in reach of the top rung of the ladder – and Lotus had benefited from a driver who took their car to loftier heights than it would have done in other hands.

With Senna's signature, had Dennis secured Formula One's Dream Team? One man who thought so was Alain Prost.

11

THE DAY SENNA TOSSED
AWAY $1,500,000

Prost wanted to secure an understanding on that afternoon we met in Paris in June 2008. He had a point to make, one central to the heart of this story. 'It is important to tell you that I was very close to Ron Dennis and Mansour Ojjeh,' he said. 'We were even talking about me having shares in the team, we were having these kinds of discussions. You know, that was my team. Every time Ron had a meeting with a prospective sponsor, I was coming with him. We had a meeting with Honda people to try to have the engines for 1987. We spent two or three days in Tokyo. It did not happen for legal reasons, I think. Williams had a contract and that meant McLaren had to wait. We also talked together about drivers when we knew that Keke Rosberg was to retire. At that time, the team was looking at Nelson. But I was pushing for Ayrton . . .'

Jo Ramirez confirmed that Piquet visited the team's head-quarters, which had been relocated to the Woking Business Park, in the Surrey commuter belt, and built to the highest standards. Behind the smoked-glass windows, McLaren had expanded to having 130 employees on the payroll. The reception area would not have shamed an international hotel, and Dennis had included a thirty-seat theatre for sponsorship presentations, slide shows or media conferences. At most, McLaren planned to build seven cars from this factory that had only two customers for 1987: Prost and Stefan Johansson. To Dennis, the only way to plan success was to lavish attention on the smallest detail; it is the way he has always worked and the way he still does. McLaren do not have sponsors, he argued. McLaren sold corporate image to commercial investors – 'We don't like the word sponsors because it's not a charitable act,' he insisted. No matter the semantics, his record withstood the minutest scrutiny.

So, Dennis was comfortable that Piquet would be impressed with what he found at McLaren. Ramirez recalled how Dennis was unimpressed with Piquet, though. 'Piquet came to the factory late one evening and he was shown around by Ron,' said Ramirez. 'Ron told him loosely what was being planned for the future. But, it seems, all Piquet was interested in was how much Ron was going to pay him. That completely pissed off Ron. From then on, we knew Piquet was out.'

Prost's support for Senna caused Dennis to question his motives. 'I told Ron that I thought Ayrton was a driver for the future, and that I thought he would be best for the team,' he said. 'I was close with Nelson, but I thought it better for the team to have the younger driver.' The Frenchman had no agenda: he just wanted McLaren to be competitive. Also, he had no history of bad blood with any of his previous team-mates with the exception of his fallout with René Arnoux after the French Grand Prix in 1982. Prost had cohabited at McLaren with Watson,

Lauda and Rosberg without a problem. Besides, after all this time within the team Prost felt ultra secure in all his professional relationships. He had worked hard to gain the respect of everyone at McLaren, from the canteen staff to the boardroom. How could Senna possibly destabilise him? In Prost's mind, it made sense to have a man who, clearly, had made himself into a serious contender for the championship, inside the same team. In Prost's mind, he would have the beating of any man in the same car.

It must be stressed that Dennis had monitored Senna from his earliest days racing in Britain: again, an example of his attention to detail. Dennis, it may be recalled, had given the Brazilian a test drive at the end of 1983, but he had no vacancy in his team. In the summer of '87 the landscape had changed, of course. Johansson – one of the sport's really good guys and fast, but not quite fast enough – had been signed as a stopgap in the wake of Rosberg's retirement. Dennis had shown the world that he could manage Lauda, a wily champion with a strong mind, and Prost, a faster, younger man with a ceaseless appetite to learn and a fine grasp of what was needed to make him respected with McLaren. Winning motor races and dedication to technical detail soon gained him all the friends he needed. If that was interpreted to be the work of an astute politician, what did he care?

Similarly, Dennis had no misgivings. Prost was an honourable man, and Senna mixed aggression with intelligence in a manner that had not been seen before. He alerted the world to his success at a press conference called before the Italian Grand Prix at Monza, in September, when McLaren announced that Senna would join Prost in their driver line-up for 1988. In front of the media, Prost was a model of bonhomie and appeared genuinely delighted that the Brazilian had signed. 'I am sure you would like to know about the new partnership with Ayrton,' he said. 'I think in the past we have shown we could have two equal No. 1 drivers. I know that Ayrton is very professional and I will help him integrate into the team. We have to work together but, of course, I will do my best to beat him on the track.'

After four seasons in Formula One, and a thorough apprenticeship, Senna had at last found himself at a team that he knew could make him world champion. McLaren had won the title for three of those four years that he had been competing, with Lauda and twice with Prost; and, although Williams had been too good in 1987, Senna knew that they would lose Honda's engine to McLaren for 1988. Senna also understood that after a year working with Honda at Lotus, he had at least one critical edge over Prost. He had already won the trust of the Japanese engineers, and, most importantly, he had earned their respect as a driver of limitless courage. At that press conference in Monza, Senna happily sang from the same hymn sheet as Prost. 'From a personal point of view I am very happy to work with Alain,' he said. 'Two top drivers working together can only make a team stronger.'

Of course, this was not the view he had held when he exercised his veto to deny Derek Warwick a drive with Lotus; but Senna would argue with some conviction that McLaren, unlike Lotus, had proven resources to support two cars, and two ambitious drivers. With time, we discovered just how hard Dennis had found it to negotiate with Senna. Perhaps no driver, before or since the Brazilian, ever demanded as much detail in a contract as Senna. Some of those involved in the protracted process might joke that the Magna Carta could have been penned with fewer debates. At the end of his career, reliable sources inform me that

Senna's contract ran to almost 140 pages. What we know for a fact is that in 1987 the sum being disputed, in the final throes of hard bargaining between Dennis and Senna, was $500,000. Or at least, that's how it appeared on the surface.

In rapid time, Dennis had restored the fortunes of McLaren. More critically, the team had been fashioned, enlarged and refined in the image of the man who had – and still has – a fastidious eye for detail. Lauda, then Prost, had brought to life Dennis's desire to rule the world, not for the reward of money alone, but for the satisfaction of being acknowledged as masters of the Formula One universe. From the moment he walked through the front door of McLaren, Dennis said, 'As a team, we exist to win.' The capture of Senna was integral to maintaining that pledge. However, if he thought Lauda had been a hard man to negotiate with, Senna raised the stakes to an unfamiliar and unsettling degree.

At his wit's end as the negotiations stalled, Dennis suggested that one way to resolve his differences with Senna was with the spin of the coin. Senna had not the foggiest idea as to what Dennis was talking about. Dennis explained the principle of a coin toss, but, given the nature of the two men involved, he felt compelled to draw diagrams and write out rules. Dennis explained: 'Ayrton was an incredibly tough negotiator. In the end we came to a complete stalemate over the last half million dollars. So I suggested we flick a coin. He didn't even understand what that meant. I explained that this was the simplest way to break the deadlock. I then had to draw pictures of a head and tail to be absolutely sure that there was no doubt as to the interpretation. So, we literally wrote on a piece of paper the rules of this simple thing, as Ayrton still did not have a complete command of the English language. I won the toss – something for which he never, ever forgave me and I paid a million times for that.' The sting in this tale (or was it in the head?) of the coin toss only became apparent to Senna after the contract had been finalised and endorsed. 'It was about ten days later when it suddenly dawned on Ayrton that, in fact, it wasn't half a million dollars he'd lost, but one and a half million dollars,' said Dennis. The contract covered three years, you see. Senna conceded that he had tired of the bargaining, and this utterly alien concept of spinning for the difference in the terms being offered, and those being demanded by him, was as good a way as any of overcoming the tedium. 'It's true, when I was negotiating to join Marlboro McLaren we got to a difficult moment right at the end trying to arrive at a figure,' he said. 'If I had held out I could have got what I was asking for. I could have pushed a lot harder, but I was getting fed up with the negotiations. I spun a coin, I called wrongly . . .'

Senna had called heads and in the time it took for the coin to land tail-side up the Brazilian was $1.5 million lighter in the pocket. Even at the rate Formula One dispenses with money, can any man have ever lost so much in so short a time span? Yet to Senna this was of secondary importance – the negotiation with Dennis had been reduced to a tug-of-egos. Truly, the money at stake was almost an irrelevance; to men like Dennis and Senna it was just a measuring instrument to inform them which one had the upper hand. As Senna said, 'A lot of people claim winning is the only important thing, but few really mean it.' To Senna, this was an opportunity to win that he felt was worth a little pain in the wallet. In later contractual negotiations with McLaren, however, Senna fought as hard for time out of the car as he did for money. Obviously, his primary position was to have lots of both!

Ramirez had an interesting take from his home in Spain in

2008. 'Alain was happy about Ayrton coming,' he confirmed. 'Had we had Senna and said that Prost was coming, he would not have accepted that. Yet Prost welcomed him with open arms and an open mind.' These sentiments must be weighed against history, against the passing of time and, crucially, against the fact that Ramirez was a good friend of Senna until the day he died.

John Hogan already had Senna on the books at Marlboro before the contract with McLaren had been drawn up. 'I'd been made aware of Senna when a friend had championed him to me,' he said. 'I did a personal contract with him when he was driving for Toleman; he'd been a Marlboro driver from day one. As for Alain, he was very much of the view that you have to beat the best somehow, so he had no problem that Ayrton was in the same team. Ayrton did not hold that view. He stopped anyone that was any good from getting in the other car. He whinged like fuck.'

As the 1987 season unfolded, it became clear that Prost could not bridge the gap to the Williams of Piquet and Mansell. Yet on a late summer's afternoon in Portugal, Prost still contrived to drive into Formula One history. On 20 September, he won his twenty-eighth grand prix to break the record he had held jointly with three-time world champion Jackie Stewart. The world title Prost had held for the past two years may have been destined for other hands, but Stewart appreciated more than anyone what the little Frenchman with the crooked nose had accomplished in Portugal. 'If I were racing today, I'd like to think I would model my approach on his,' said Stewart, speaking to us from the paddock at Estoril.

'Alain is so committed to the job that everyone takes his ability and talent for granted. What puts him above the rest is attitude. He is patient and mentally able to deal with whatever situation confronts him. All the great drivers have started off with latent talent. That is their God-given gift. What separates them from the rest is their ability to think clearly, positively and without emotion. And that's not easy for a Frenchman. But Prost is single-minded and dedicated – he is my ideal grand prix driver.'

They had played 'La Marseillaise' as Prost stood on the top step of the podium and he had good naturedly whipped off Gerhard Berger's cap in deference to the French national anthem. Berger had surrendered victory to Prost by spinning his Ferrari less than three laps from home. He spun because he was pursued not just by Prost's speeding McLaren, but by his reputation. The amiable Austrian admitted as much when he said disconsolately, 'I knew I had to have a three-second lead for the last two laps to keep Alain behind. I had to take a risk and it was not possible to control my car.' Prost offered sympathy. 'It was marginal for me, too,' he said. 'Marginal on fuel, tyres, brakes and, yes, on the driver because it was such a physical race.'

They had played a scratched copy of 'God Save the Queen' and Dennis, alongside his driver, beamed in delight that his team from Woking had played such a prominent part in assisting Prost's journey into the pages of history. Prost just smiled, and continued to smile. 'I am going to enjoy my win tonight . . . I am going to enjoy it all week,' he promised. Stewart, a man of dignity and integrity, a man with an enduring passion for motorsport that consumes him to this day, placed in context what Prost had accomplished. 'I was so proud when I passed Juan Fangio's mark, then Jim Clark's,' said Stewart. 'I know how great Fangio was. And I revered Jim Clark – he was everything a racing driver and a man should be. So I put a great value on that record of wins. I've had it for nearly fourteen years. It is long enough and it is so good that a man like Alain is taking it.' While Prost was showered with praise, Senna disappeared almost unnoticed after finishing sixth, but his performance merited credit as he had recovered from twenty-second place after needing an unscheduled pit stop.

Senna's own outside interest in the 1987 world championship came to an end two races later in Mexico, in controversy. In qualifying on Saturday, Senna's Lotus rode a bump in the Peltrada Corner that leads on to the start-finish line. His car became airborne and he smacked into the tyre wall at high speed. Clearly, he was a shaken man as he climbed from his car and slumped on to his haunches. Senna would be required to start the grand prix from the fourth row. In the race, he ran second for a spell behind Mansell, but he was relegated to third by Piquet. Then, nine laps from the end, he locked his brakes as he tried to change down through the gearbox without a working clutch. His Lotus spun to a standstill. Nigel Roebuck reported for readers of *Autosport* what took place next: 'Senna beseeched marshals to come and give him a shove. This they failed to do to his satisfaction and, after stepping from the Lotus, he proceeded to slug one of them. Or was it two?' The stewards later fined Senna $15,000 for his unbecoming behaviour. For a man with such a clean mind on the racetrack, he was capable of making some irrational decisions.

Relationships within Williams were hardly convivial either. In victory in Mexico, Mansell condemned the driving antics of Piquet, who finished immediately behind him. 'I didn't enjoy the second part of the race because my team-mate tried to have me off, which I didn't feel was very professional,' said Mansell. 'I have never had a problem with Nelson, but he has always had a problem with me.' Mansell had reduced Piquet's lead in the championship to twelve points with two races remaining. But Mansell sensed – as Prost would sense later in his relationship with Senna – that Honda had a preference for his team-mate to be world champion. He voiced those concerns before he left Mexico, too. 'All hell is going to break loose in the team,' predicted Mansell. 'Frank Williams may have to step in and Honda will start applying pressure. Of course, they won't want me to win in Japan.'

As it transpired, Mansell had a huge accident in qualifying in Suzuka and did not race again that season. Piquet had the final laugh. Mansell had won six races – twice as many as Piquet or anyone else – and earned pole position eight times, yet it was the Brazilian who was crowned champion for a third occasion. And as he left Williams Piquet effectively walked out of the door with Honda's engines packaged to follow.

Senna did likewise at Lotus. In three years with the Norfolk-based team, Senna won six grands prix, delivering two of them, in Monaco and Detroit, in this his last season. He was third in the world championship – behind Piquet and Mansell in the devilishly fast and reliable Williams-Honda Turbo. Significantly, Senna had finished ahead of Prost for the first time. The Frenchman had won three races, in Brazil, Belgium and Portugal, but he had accumulated eleven points fewer than Senna. That must have pained the Frenchman, but not because he had finished behind Senna. What hurt him was that the McLaren had been outshone by the Williams team. Still, at least Prost could feel optimistic about the future with the imminent arrival of Honda's engines. That was a warm thought to carry into winter.

Senna had devised a plan of his own for that winter, one that he shared with Prost's first team-mate John Watson when they undertook a week's conditioning training at Willy Dungl's health centre in Austria. 'McLaren sent their drivers to Willy Dungl since Niki Lauda's days,' said Watson. 'It's where drivers get a fitness check, and receive a training and dietary programme. I happened to be there at the same time as Ayrton on a week's training programme. We were bicycling through the hills in Austria, when Senna asked me: "What is McLaren like? You were a team-mate of Prost – what do you think about him?" I said to him, "Alain's a tremendous driver and very clever with the team. The team are truly focused on Prost. Any driver who has been in the team with him would seem to be No. 2. I would suggest that you come into the team and feel your way and get to understand how Alain works, how his favour in the team is established."'

Watson recalled with barely disguised awe the manner in which Senna responded – and had Prost heard what the Brazilian had to say he would have received an early warning of the rough road that lay ahead of him. Senna told Watson: 'No, I don't think so. I am going to go and make myself physically and mentally stronger than anyone else in Formula One. I am going to make Prost come to me not me go to him. I am going to go in there and I am going to blitz him.' Here was a man on a mission; and that mission had just been spelled out in unequivocal terms.

12

MISSING IN ACTION

As the cars drove uphill on the throttle, passing in a blur apartment buildings unlikely to have been devalued in the global economic downturn, Josef Leberer watched the leaders cresting the blind brow into Casino Square. He had eyes for only one driver: Senna.

We followed the action together on a TV screen in BMW's motorhome planted in the paddock alongside the harbour at Monaco. Leberer was smiling and grimacing in unison as the race neared its conclusion. After two decades within the sport, his nerves on race day are still as taut as piano wire.

Only this time the man central to his attention was Bruno Senna, not Ayrton. Leberer's role these days is to ensure BMW's gifted Polish driver Robert Kubica, a natural rival to Britain's world champion Lewis Hamilton, is in the best physical and mental condition he can be. This was a job he once performed for Ayrton Senna. But Leberer's place in Senna's life went far beyond his contracted function of masseur, fitness trainer, nutritionist and cook. Over the years, Leberer became Senna's closest confidant in the paddock, perhaps in life. And one mournful day, mindful of his special place in Senna's affections, the Brazilian's family would specifically request Leberer to share Ayrton's final flight. 'It was the longest flight of my life, and the most intense experience of my life,' said Leberer.

Little surprise, then, that he should be interested in the fortune of Senna's nephew, Bruno, as he raced on the streets where his uncle will never be forgotten. Leberer provides Bruno with help whenever he can, as does Gerhard Berger, a man who struck a deep friendship with Ayrton during their time together at McLaren, a bond that lasted throughout his lifetime. 'I was with Bruno on the grid before the start of his GP2 race [a series which launched Hamilton and Kubica into Formula One],' explained Leberer as he watched Senna retain his nerve over the closing laps last spring. 'He has the same focus as Ayrton.' Berger is also conscious of the physical resemblance between the Sennas. 'I look at Bruno and he reminds me so much of Ayrton – he is a copy,' said the Austrian, an accomplished, brave driver, who for a time became team principal at Toro Rosso. Bruno had been a promising kart racer as a child – but any hope of him becoming a racing driver was placed on ice for ten years after the fateful events at Imola in 1994. 'He's a few years behind his rivals, because no one in the family wanted motorsport any more,' said Leberer. 'But he's learning so quick, he's like a sponge.' Ayrton's sister Viviane accepted her son had to be allowed to follow his own dream and she blessed his return to the circuit. Berger acted as a willing mentor.

Leberer said, 'I still remember Ayrton telling me that he had been karting with Bruno on the same track where he had grown up at home and he was very complimentary of his young nephew.

215

He told me, "You can see he's really good – he's going to be better than me.'"

Leberer remained focused on the television in the motorhome until Bruno Senna – whose father Flavio Lalli was killed in a motorcycle accident in 1996 – claimed an important and poignant victory in the presence of his mother. As Senna celebrated inside his car, and shortly afterwards mounted the podium, Leberer dabbed a tear from his eye. He was riding an emotional ghost train back through time. 'It's just so special to see Bruno win here, of all places,' he said. Senna revelled in the moment. 'I'm delighted to score my maiden victory in Monaco,' he said afterwards. 'Rest assured, I have every intention of adding to that tally in the future.' Bruno may be from a different generation, but those sentiments were of a kind his uncle would have recognised and approved.

Josef Leberer had started life under the wing of Willy Dungl, whose clinic in Austria was renowned as a haven for sportsmen – and, on occasion, politicians – to rest and rehabilitate from injury or surgery. Those who benefited from the treatment at Dungl's included Olympic skiing champion Franz Klammer, a host of footballers, and racing drivers like Lauda, Watson, Prost and Senna. In September 1987, Dungl asked Leberer to attend the Portuguese Grand Prix as a prelude to joining the McLaren programme for the following year. 'I never heard anything over the winter, then three weeks before the first grand prix of the new season in Brazil I received a telex from Jo Ramirez at McLaren to tell me I would start with the team in Rio,' he recalled. 'I had just two weeks to prepare myself. It was exciting – but it was also daunting.'

McLaren had left testing their new car, the MP4/4, quite late.

The design team had come under the command of the newly appointed McLaren technical director Gordon Murray, who had been behind Brabham's world championship winning cars in 1981 and 1983, with American Steve Nichols occupying a pivotal role. They busied themselves over the winter months to create a car they hoped would be the envy of their rivals. Their work was clearly not in vain.

Like they say in the business, the car worked right out of the box. More than that, it worked damned fast. At the final test in Imola, just eleven days prior to the Brazilian Grand Prix, both Prost and Senna posted times two seconds quicker than a Ferrari had lapped round the Italian track. Senna had been quickest of all, an ominous warning for Prost. But Prost was not dispirited; like Senna, he understood as he left Italy that McLaren and Honda had developed a car that would provide an opportunity to rule the world.

When the drivers reached Rio de Janeiro, Leberer had already arrived. He was exhilarated and anxious in equal measure. 'I told myself, "You are working with Prost and Senna, McLaren and Honda, and this is Rio de Janeiro – what else could you want?" But there was no one behind me, not Willy, no one, and I knew I had a big responsibility.' In fact, Leberer occupied a unique position in Formula One. 'It is a credit to Ron Dennis that he wanted to employ someone like me to take care of the drivers,' said Leberer. 'He was the first guy who really understood how important it was to look after them in this way. Ron was a man two steps ahead.'

Leberer's job description was complex. He planned the drivers' meals, often shopping himself, and he prepared and cooked food. He was a nutritionist, a masseur and a fitness trainer. 'I told Alain and Ayrton what to eat, not the other way around,' he explained.

'We didn't have the motorhomes we have now, nor all the chefs that the teams have today.' Leberer had a small cooker, little space in the McLaren motorhome and a lot of imagination. All his produce had to be fresh, so his menus would be determined country by country. Even the dressings he used were home made and wholewheat bread was shipped around the world from Dungl's clinic. His methodology had not been seen before. He brought with him to races organically grown cereals from Austria that had been vacuum packed to preserve their nutrients. He also had supplies of dried fruits. Breakfast for Prost and Senna was prepared the night before. 'I soaked the cereals and dried fruits overnight so they became easier to digest,' he explained. 'There was no sugar, but plenty of minerals that are proven to energise slowly into the body as fuel for when needed.' Senna swiftly grew fond of Leberer's breakfast cereal that he called 'Josef's Muesli'. Prost was not so keen on this concoction, and often took porridge instead. The drivers arrived at the circuit before 8 a.m. and, at the beginning, happily sat down with one another at meal times.'I thought that was important,' said Leberer. 'Time was short, so sometimes Ayrton and Alain ate while talking to their engineers. At the start, the atmosphere between them was good.'

Before first practice, Leberer served soup and salad. After qualifying, the drivers had a proper meal. 'At this time, we didn't do a lot of red meat,' he recalled. 'But it's changing now and at BMW we will have red meat once a week. Then, I served a lot of fish and brown rice or vegetable rice. They complained that the brown rice looked dirty, but they became used to it! Also I cooked all kinds of pasta and there were always fresh vegetables. Afterwards, I prepared fresh fruit salad.' Leberer devised an energising drink before they became fash-

ionable or commercial. He will not divulge his recipe – mocking
the inquiry with a little light-hearted contempt. 'Does Coca-
Cola tell you how they make their drink?' he asked. Leberer's
skill was to make Prost and Senna believe they were being
treated as equals. He is a serious man, but one without pretens-
ions; he is not tall, but he is strong. Both Senna and Prost
realised from the beginning that they could depend on his
discretion. He never betrayed a confidence. 'Please do not make
me sound important,' pleaded Leberer. 'I was just there to serve
Ayrton and Alain.'

Senna's demands included a night-time massage. 'Ayrton liked
a massage at the end of the day just before going to sleep,'
recalled Leberer. 'I'd go to his room, Ayrton would clean his
teeth, then lie on his bed. I could always tell when he was feeling
especially tense. I relaxed him with a massage and by using reflexology. It was possible to feel the tension flow out of his body.
Sometimes, he fell asleep as I massaged him. I'd turn out the
lights and leave. In those years, you must remember, it was much
harder on drivers. They had to change gear manually, operate a
clutch, and the cars were heavy to drive and they didn't have a
headrest or neck brace. I was working on Ayrton's back a lot,
and I was very precise in what I did. He liked that.'

Leberer, in fact, had to deal with an early crisis on his first
weekend with the team that had nothing to do with Senna's
back. On the first day of practice at Rio, Prost had an accident
with a substantial impact. 'Alain was white and complained of
a headache,' said Leberer. 'After we'd got him back to his hotel
room, he called me in my room and said, "Josef, my head is
bursting."' Leberer felt his own pulse quicken. '"Oh, my God",
I thought, "Dungl is not here and I must do something." Sure,
I was a little frightened. I knew that if I failed to do something

right this could be my first and last race.' Yet his instincts took over once he approached Prost's room. 'I did what I had trained for,' he said. Leberer used acupuncture, reflexology and other skills he had at hand, but will not divulge. 'Alain's head was the problem, so I tried to get energy down through his body. After I had treated him I left Alain to rest. I was drained by the time I got back to my own room. My last thought before I fell asleep was "Oh God, let it go well."

'An hour later my telephone rang. It was Prost, who asked, "Josef, what have you done?"' Leberer's heart flipped. What *had* he done, he wondered. Prost soon put his mind at rest. 'It's incredible, I feel fantastic,' said the Frenchman. 'In fact, so fantastic I am hungry.' The next day Prost had recovered sufficiently to seal third place on the grid for the Brazilian Grand Prix. His team-mate had done even better. To the jubilation of the Brazilian crowd, Senna had placed his McLaren on pole. On race day, the eyes of Brazil were on Senna; yet, disappointingly, his inaugural grand prix for his new team in a brand new car was hijacked by gremlins. His car jammed in first gear on the warm up lap. Once back on the re-formed grid, Senna tossed his arms in the air and the start was delayed. His car was pushed away and he hurried back to the pits to access the team's spare. He had to start from the pit lane, of course; but with the speed the car had shown in testing there was still much to be optimistic about. The day could be rescued, he must have thought, as he set out in pursuit of the other cars. But after thirty laps Senna was shown a black flag to disqualify him – because the Brazilian had breached regulations by changing cars when the race had only been delayed, not stopped and restarted. Prost drove to victory, his fifth win in Brazil in seven years, in that serene manner that was the hallmark of the man. As for Senna, this would have been the worst possible result, and in Brazil of all places. But it would have served only one purpose: to stiffen his resolve.

Vengeance was swift, however. At the next race at Imola, Senna again won pole and this time there was to be no technical glitch to thwart him, or stewards to intervene. Prost delivered the team a one-two — a result that was to become familiar in this year of enduring triumph on a monumental scale for McLaren. All their rivals finished a lap down. It was an astonishing show of strength from the team from Woking. Already, there was an overwhelming sense that there was little for the other teams to do other than to form an orderly queue behind McLaren.

To Senna, it was also a result of mammoth personal significance. He had triumphed over Prost in an identical car; he had beaten *the man* fair and square. 'From the beginning, Ayrton had only Alain in his sights,' said Ramirez. 'Whenever we talked to Ayrton, he asked: "What tyres is Alain using? Which springs?" If you told him Piquet was coming quicker, he wasn't interested. Alain was his goal.'

By the time we reached Monaco the story dominating the British popular newspapers was insulting remarks Nelson Piquet had made about Nigel and Rosanne Mansell in the Brazilian edition of *Playboy*. Piquet suggested 'Mansell was an uneducated fool with a stupid and ugly wife'. For the first time that year, Rosanne had accompanied her husband to a grand prix, and Piquet let it be known that he was willing to apologise in person to her in Monte Carlo. She refused point blank to meet the world champion. 'If Piquet approached me I would walk away,' said Rosanne, a woman of immense dignity and a pillar of support to her husband. She declined to comment further on Piquet's rudeness. Piquet had one interesting observation to offer us, however. 'Alain and Ayrton are going to be fighting all season, just like me and Nigel,' he said. The man may on occasion have lacked class – but on this one he saw the future more clearly than most.

On the circuit, woven around the harbour, and snaking through Casino Square, on streets more accustomed to the sedate passage of Bentleys, Mercedes and Ferraris, we witnessed a more edifying spectacle, a performance in qualifying from Senna that took the breath away. Of all places, it is imperative to start the Monaco Grand Prix from the front of the grid. It exists in this modern world of New Age circuits, in countries like Malaysia, Turkey, Bahrain and Abu Dhabi, as a playground representing unique commercial opportunities to combine business with pleasure. The racetrack, rising and falling between five-star hotels, boutiques, ludicrously priced apartments and a casino with a million untold stories of misery, is laughably narrow, bumpy and hemmed by Armco barriers and the Mediterranean. The drivers are required to make an estimated 3,000 gear changes during the course of the grand prix, and those wanting a favourable berth for their yacht when Formula One comes to the Principality need an income from a decent sized hedge fund and an acquaint-ance with the harbour master. They have been called the haves and the have-yachts. This is the only grand prix in the calendar that is staged over four days rather than three in order to accom-modate a day of devotion to parties and deal-making. In Monaco, even the hard times are good. Drivers consider the circuit a chal-lenge unlike any other. It demands of them absolute commit-ment, flawless judgement and unwavering concentration. The roll-call of multiple winners of the Monaco Grand Prix is impres-sive: Juan Manuel Fangio, Stirling Moss, Graham Hill, Jackie Stewart, Lauda. Prost and Senna lodged comfortably within the club formed ahead of their time.

In May 1988, Senna pieced together a sequence of laps around Monaco that caught the attention of all for their precision, consistency and sheer hostility. Time and again, he gnawed precious fractions of a second from his previous lap. Ultimately, he covered the 2.068-mile circuit in a staggering 1minute 23.998 seconds. Prost – second fastest – was 1.5 seconds slower, an eternity on a stopwatch. And the Frenchman was 1.2 seconds quicker than Berger, who qualified in third place for Ferrari.

Senna had made even hardened, cynical observers blink in astonishment. Marlboro's John Hogan has since watched that lap again on DVD and claimed: 'It is the most extraordinary piece of driving and focus and concentration you have seen in your life. He doesn't lift for anyone in his way. He just doesn't fucking lift his foot from the throttle. And they know he's not going to lift – they spot him in their mirror and instinctively get out of the way. It was said – and I don't know how true it is – that he used to hold his breath on a lap round Monaco. Certainly, he went into an almost hypnotic trance before he went out of the garage. You could see his eyes glaze over.'

How did Senna interpret what he had accomplished? 'Sometimes, I think I know some of the reasons why I do things the way I do in the car,' he said. 'And sometimes I don't think I know why. There are some moments that seem to be only the natural instinct that is in me. Whether I have been born with it or whether this feeling has grown in me more than other people, I don't know. But it is inside me and it takes over with a great amount of space and intensity.' This appraisal by Senna was captured on tape by distinguished Canadian author and journalist Gerald Donaldson a couple of years later, and published in his book *Grand Prix People*. Kindly, Donaldson invited me to repeat the interview, which is like a window on the man's soul. 'When I am competing against the watch and against other competitors, the feeling of expectation, of getting it done and doing the best and being the best, gives me a kind of power that, some moments when I am driving, actually detaches me completely from anything else as I am doing it . . . corner after corner, lap after lap. I can give you a true example and I can relate to it,' explained Senna.

'Monte Carlo, 1988, the last qualifying session. I was already on pole and I was going faster and faster. One lap after the other, quicker, and quicker, and quicker. I was at one stage on pole, then by half a second, and then one second . . . and I kept going. Suddenly, I was nearly two seconds faster than anybody else, including my team-mate with the same car. And I suddenly realised that I was no longer driving the car consciously. I was kind of driving it by instinct, only I was in a different dimension. It was like I was in a tunnel, not only the tunnel under the hotel, but the whole circuit for me was a tunnel. I was just going more, going – more, and more, and more, and more.

'I was way over the limit, but still able to find even more. Then, suddenly, something just kicked me. I kind of woke up and I realised that I was in a different atmosphere than you normally are. Immediately my reaction was to back off, slow down. I drove back slowly to the pits and I didn't want to go out any more that day. It frightened me because I realised I was well beyond my conscious understanding. It happens rarely, but I keep these experiences very much alive in me because it is something that is important for self-preservation.'

Senna's account deepened the mystique around him, because he spoke in a language that had not been heard from the lips of a racing driver. Others would have been ridiculed or mocked. But not Senna . . . the intensity of his words matched perfectly the intensity of his driving. Derek Warwick, a man of the people if ever there was one, and intolerant of bullshit, still found himself in sympathy with the essence of what Senna had said. 'I think like all great champions, Senna was able to step up to a level you can only gain with amazing inner confidence,' said Warwick. 'I believe I found that level, but I found it in a car that wasn't as good. I think I found that level like Senna, Prost and Mansell found. It's something you can't explain to Joe Public. Senna spoke about being in the zone. He spoke about that lap in Monaco in a way that he felt detached from what he was doing, because he'd gone outside his own body. So, maybe there is another level of performance I never even saw. I suspect there might be.'

Prost's view at the hour of Senna's wondrous qualifying lap was pragmatic. 'Ayrton's pole time was fantastic,' he admitted that weekend in Monaco. 'But you have to take risks for a lap like that and I am not prepared to do that so much any more.' Had not Lauda reached that same conclusion when a younger man joined him at McLaren, a younger man named Prost? There was one inescapable truth written by Senna over that one lap of the streets of Monaco: he was at his zenith, and he was unafraid to explore the limits of his car or the boundaries of his own brilliance.

Yet we would discover that very same weekend that Senna was still vulnerable to the fallibility of the human condition. As the Brazilian sat on the grid at the start of the Monaco Grand Prix, he must have imagined the race was in his pocket. Prost was far from despondent, though. In the final analysis, Senna's sizzling pole time had only gained him an advantage of seven metres over Prost on the front row. The Frenchman privately backed himself to beat his team-mate in the race to the first corner, Ste Devote. And, whoever had the lead on the climb to Casino Square had control of the race as the streets of Monaco are notoriously hard to overtake on. But Prost's plan to jump Senna backfired from the moment he missed second gear. Senna made a clean getaway and Berger punished Prost's mistake by stealing second place from him into Ste Devote. Senna could not have scripted a better scenario had he penned the plot himself.

By lap five, Berger was invisible in his mirror as Senna opened a lead of 7.5 seconds. Prost could do little about Berger. Senna extended his lead. Still Prost toiled in frustration behind Berger. Senna had propelled himself ahead by forty-nine seconds, when at last Prost mounted an attack that Berger could not repel. Once past the Austrian, from lapping in the low 1 minute 29 seconds high 1 minute 28 seconds, Prost began to bring his times down. The message was relayed to Senna from the McLaren pit wall. The Brazilian responded by lapping faster still; and on lap fifty-nine of the seventy-eight-lap grand prix he set a new lap record, 1 minute 26.321 seconds. 'Once Ayrton knew Prost was in second place, no matter how far behind, he just started going faster,' said Ramirez. When Senna had put fifty-three seconds of daylight between him and Prost, Ramirez recalled how Dennis became alarmed. 'Ron began to panic,' said Ramirez. 'He ordered Senna over the radio, "Slow down, slow down, he cannot catch you."'

Prost was oblivious to the radio traffic between the team and Senna. As Ramirez explained: 'Ron wasn't talking to Prost, he was just left to make his race. You can't say to the guy who is chasing, "Slow down." All you'd get in response would be,

"Fuck you, I'm going for it." But Ayrton wasn't listening to Ron. This is how obsessed he was with beating Prost, the guy who was No. 1.' Senna, briefly, had tried to obey orders by backing off for a handful of laps, but, when he missed a gear at Casino and brushed a barrier, he returned hard on the throttle. Prost's battle plan was uncomplicated – he pursued Senna with every ounce of resilience in his body. 'I was pushing on purpose,' he said. 'Even if you have one chance in a million you try to exploit it.'

On lap sixty-seven, the unthinkable happened. At Portier, the right-hand corner before the entrance to the tunnel, Senna's car slewed across the road and parked nose first into the guardrail separating the cars from the Mediterranean. 'When we saw his car in the barrier, we just couldn't believe it,' said Ramirez. Senna unbuckled his belts and evacuated his car as though on autopilot. He removed his gloves, and looked up the road for Prost to come into sight. He was still looking back as he took off his crash helmet. His face looked drained of blood, he was in shock. Not from the accident, but from the consequences. When Prost duly turned into Portier and took a sideways glance at Senna's carelessly parked car, the Brazilian had been shepherded from the circuit by a group of marshals. As the race continued without him, Senna failed to return to his pit, which was the customary reaction by a driver to an accident. Instead, the Brazilian vanished. 'Ayrton was a guy who didn't tolerate mistakes, and he tolerated his own mistakes even less,' said Ramirez. 'So, he couldn't come back to the pits and face all of us. How could he throw a win away like that? It seemed so stupid – and he was mad at himself.'

Prost motored without incident to the flag to take a victory – a remarkable fourth triumph in four years on these unforgiving streets – that had been destined for Senna. In the McLaren pit there were mixed emotions. The joy for Prost was diluted for the despair a percentage of the team felt for Senna. And where was Senna?

No one had seen him since the cameras had caught him leaving the scene of his accident at around 5.10 p.m., because the Monaco Grand Prix began at the unique hour of 3.30 p.m.; perhaps, it was mischievously speculated, to enable Prince Rainier and his guests to have an unhurried lunch. Ramirez said, 'We didn't know where Ayrton had gone. All I did know was that he would be feeling bad, feeling destroyed . . .' And then Ramirez worked it out. Senna must have returned to his apartment in the Houston Palace, a towering skyscraper which, conveniently, had been but a short walk from where he had crashed his car in such a delicate yet wounding accident.

'He could only be at his home,' said Ramirez. 'I called the number but there was no answer. I called again and again, still no answer.' As Ramirez had eaten with Senna at his apartment just three days earlier, when the Brazilian had not wanted to go out to a restaurant, he knew he had a housekeeper. He just kept on calling . . . someone must answer sooner or later, he reasoned. Eventually, Ramirez heard the engaged tone on the line. 'I thought he might have taken the phone off the hook – but I continued to call every ten to fifteen minutes anyway,' he explained. At last his perseverance was rewarded, when Senna's housekeeper answered the phone. By now, it was around 9 p.m.

'Isabelle, it's Jo,' said Ramirez.

'Señor Ayrton is not here.'

'I know Señor Ayrton is there, he cannot be anywhere else.'

'No, no, he's not here.'

'Please tell him it's Jo. Pass him the phone, he will talk to me. Please.'

At last, Senna came on the line. Ramirez heard him sobbing. Such an elementary blunder in a Formula Ford race would have embarrassed him, but this mistake had been played out in front of a global television audience at the most glamorous motor race in the world. Ramirez knew Senna was utterly distraught. 'Ayrton was crying as he spoke with me,' said Ramirez. 'He said, "Jo, I don't know what happened, but all I can think is I got too close to the apex and the steering wheel got away from my hands with the vibration I received from the kerbing. The next thing I was on the other side of the road in the barrier." I asked Ayrton: "Why didn't you slow down, Prost would never have caught you?" Ayrton was just so emotional. He said he thought he would lose concentration if he had slowed down. "Jo," he said, "I am the biggest idiot in the world."

'Ayrton was blaming himself so much. Much later that night I went to see him at the apartment. He had already tortured himself so much, there was nothing anyone could do or say to make him feel worse.' Later, Prost would reflect: 'Ayrton was really angry when he didn't win this race – but he didn't know against who he was angry. He was always like this. He wanted to have a fight and his biggest motivation was to fight against me and to beat me.' On this occasion, Senna had not been beaten by Prost; he had been beaten by himself. And that was why he had no stomach to face his team, or the outside world.

At the gala dinner after the race, Prost made a short speech when he acknowledged that Senna had the race under control, but that sometimes things happen unexpectedly in motor racing and that he was delighted to have taken victory. According to Prost, Dennis then told the audience, 'Ayrton had been fantastic and there must have been a problem with the car because he couldn't have made a mistake.' Perhaps this was the moment when Prost first detected the momentum within McLaren was swinging towards Senna.

Ramirez, however, thought otherwise. 'The rivalry between Ayrton and Alain was fantastic, but at this point still friendly,' he argued. 'I dismissed the Monaco Grand Prix as one of those things and thought, probably, we are going to have a few more moments like this before the end of the year. But, eventually, we felt we would come up with both championships, the drivers' championship and the constructors. We had an unbelievable car, the best two drivers in the world, the best engine and possibly the best budget and the best organisation. We knew we were almost unbeatable. We just had to get the team running as smoothly as possible and not beat ourselves.'

While Senna's experience had reduced him to tears, he would claim by year end that the incident on the seafront at Monaco had been his spiritual salvation. 'The accident changed me psychologically and mentally,' he said, in an interview republished from the Salvation Army's paper, *War Cry*. 'It was the biggest step in my life, both as a racing driver and as a man. It brought me much closer to God. I have never discussed this before, because it can be dangerous to talk about such things.'

Senna later repeated similar sentiments to Gerald Donaldson. 'I am a religious man,' he said. 'I believe in God, through Jesus. I was brought up that way, was maybe drifting away from it, but suddenly turned the other way. Things that have happened in my racing career contributed a lot to my change of direction. It was a build-up of things that reached a peak and then I had a kind of crisis. Monaco was the peak and made me realise a lot of things. It is something that is difficult to talk about, very touching for me. But it is something unique in life, something that can hold you, can support you, when you are most vulnerable. It has made me a better man. I am a better human being now than I was before this. I am better in everything I am and in everything I do.'

Senna was a Catholic, and a man of devout faith. Yet he rarely attended church. He preferred instead to read and study the Bible in isolation. He read from the scriptures on flights and in hotel rooms. His religious beliefs informed and shaped him as a man and he was comfortable with articulating this in public. He was a man without doubt, firm and insistent that his destiny was at the mercy of God's will. In stark contrast, Prost hardly ever mentioned his own Catholic faith; but he was willing to share with the world that he had received a personal audience with the Pope. They both prayed to the same God only in different voices.

From Monaco the championship crossed the Atlantic for races in Mexico, Canada and the United States. Senna won pole in Mexico, but Prost relegated the Brazilian to second place in the race. A flawless drive from the Frenchman allowed him to open a fifteen-point lead at the summit of the championship. In Montreal, Senna reversed the tables, but not before he had complained to the race organisers. Justifiably, he argued that his advantage at starting from pole position had been compromised by lining up on the right side of the track, which was the 'wrong' side for a circuit with a left-handed corner first. The organisers declared the race began with a right-hand corner – which technically it did, but this was little more than a curve. As Senna feared, Prost pinched the lead at the first real corner. The Frenchman retained first place until, momentarily caught out by a back marker, he granted Senna the opportunity to get ahead. 'Senna's race craft was superb,' said John Hogan. 'He overtook back markers like they weren't there – much better than anybody. Alain was good in traffic, but he just wouldn't run up the inside of somebody and hope that they'd move over. He'd let them have a little sight of the nose of his car. But Senna was extraordinary – for me, Michael Schumacher wasn't in the same league in traffic as Ayrton.'

A week later, the teams had crossed the border into the United States; but the storyline was unchanged. Senna continued to monopolise pole, earning the cherished position for a sixth consecutive time to equal a record held jointly by Stirling Moss and Niki Lauda. With six laps remaining in the first street race since Monaco, Senna led Prost by more than a minute. He had a point to make and he was making it in bold, sweeping brushstrokes. Whereas Prost revels around the harbour front of Monaco, he detests racing on the streets of Detroit. 'I honestly hate the place,' he said. At the chequered flag, Senna's willingness to preserve his brakes and his engine meant that his winning margin over his team-mate had fallen, but it was a still comfortable thirty-eight seconds. It was his third successive win in Motor City, after which he said, 'It was very hard physically and mentally . . . locking wheels into almost every corner, almost hitting other cars. But I'm pretty happy.' He had nudged three points closer to Prost in the championship.

Prost had yet to have any real contentious issues with Senna, but he had detected a mood shift within Honda and, perhaps to a lesser degree, within McLaren, too. 'I had the feeling that I was now seen as the old guy, and Ayrton was the young guy of the future,' he explained. 'I could now see that's how it had been for Niki Lauda when I came into the team. As the young guy you can have the advantage in terms of ambience and support.' John Hogan had observed Senna from close quarters, and he would get a long look at the Brazilian driver over many years. His thoughts? 'You know, it's very difficult to summarise people's characters and you've probably heard someone tell you, so-and-so is shy. And you think, no, he's not; he's a prick. Shy was often a term used about Senna. I don't think he was shy. I think he was emotionally immature throughout his whole career. He was a bit of a spoiled baby at home. His whole *modus operandi* every waking, thinking second was consumed with his desire to win; on and off the track. Anyone who got in his way he wanted to destroy. He just didn't think about anything else. Focus . . . focus . . . focus . . . focus. Just extraordinary.'

Senna was unapologetic about the man he was, or the racing driver he wanted to be. 'The main thing is to be yourself and not allow people to disturb you because they want you to be different,' he insisted. 'Many times you make a mistake due to your own personality, your own character or interference that you get on the way. You learn. You are able to extract more from yourself.' His job was his passion; his passion was his job. Either way he was unlikely to become less intense any time soon. No one calling the shots at McLaren or Honda would have wanted him to be any different.

Senna's domination of qualifying did come to an end, though. At home in France, Prost delivered an inspired lap of his own round Le Castellet to take pole for the first time in two years. An eventful French Grand Prix proved to be just as successful for Prost. Senna took the race lead from Prost after the Frenchman experienced a marginal delay at his pit stop caused by sticking wheels on the left-hand side of his car. Prost refused to be denied, however. On lap sixty-one of the eighty-lap race, he used back markers Alex Caffi and Pierluigi Martini to plot a passage past Senna. Prost had opted to imitate Senna, as broadcaster and journalist Maurice Hamilton described in the grand prix annual *Autocourse*: 'By now the leaders were lapping Nelson Piquet in fifth place, the Lotus driver getting very sideways under braking – right in front of Senna. Piquet, in turn, was about to lap the Dallara of Caffi and Martini's Minardi, but the world champion wisely moved to one side on the back straight as the red and white armada bore down on the Lotus. Going into Signes, Caffi darted out of the Minardi's slipstream and took the inside lane, a move that caused Senna to lift briefly. But there was no problem since Prost had dropped back slightly and would not be a threat. Or so Senna thought.

'As they rushed towards Beausset, Prost saw his chance as Senna remained behind the Minardi. Having taken Signes absolutely flat out, the momentum brought Prost hurtling towards the knot of cars and, seeing the gap down the inside, the Frenchman did not hesitate. In an instant, he was along-side Senna as they hit the brakes, the Brazilian now neatly boxed in behind Martini. It was a glorious move of superb precision, one that would not be thwarted, even as the two McLaren drivers sat it out through the corner. Prost had the line, and the lead.'

Prost too bashful in traffic? Think again. The duel continued for the remainder of the grand prix – and at one stage neither Prost nor Senna responded to radio messages and McLaren team principal Ron Dennis worried on the pit wall that his men could be pushing one another so hard that they might both run out of fuel. But that proved not to be the case and Prost, in triumph, had once again extended his lead to fifteen points. The Frenchman's jubilation at winning at home, at reminding Senna that he was not a pushover, gave Prost a feeling as warm as the summer breeze blowing in from the Mediterranean.

It was a feeling that was soon to be dampened at a sodden Silverstone. On race morning, the heavens opened and never looked likely to close. Senna was third on the grid, Prost fourth, something of a mild shock in itself. The front row had been locked down by the Ferraris of Gerhard Berger and Michele Alboreto in a small triumph at the home grand prix of the all-conquering British team. At the outset of the British Grand Prix Berger led from Senna, who was driving unsighted from the ball of spray created by the Austrian's Ferrari. Prost had made a poor start – and he never recovered. As the rain continued to fall, as pools of water began to collect on the track surface, Prost remembered another day as atrocious as this. He thought of that despicable day at Hockenheim when Didier Pironi never saw his car and sustained such terrible injuries from the ensuing accident that he never drove in Formula One again. So, Prost went backwards down the field, a man unashamedly treating the pools of water lying on the circuit, and the rain blinding him, with the utmost caution.

Martin Brundle was not at Silverstone on this afternoon, having switched to competing in the sportscar world championship, but he had experience of driving a Formula One car in the rain. He described it like this: 'The rear lights on the cars are rubbish in those conditions, there's no point having them. Blind people will tell you that their other senses are developed and I can understand that. Momentarily, your hearing, your peripheral vision is heightened driving in rain; in fact, your whole sense of alertness is heightened. You are mostly listening for the guy in front, listening for him to lift off the throttle.

It's hard. It's worse than driving your road car in thick fog . . . when roundabouts and corners come up and surprise you even if you know the road really intimately. I've known occasions in a racing car when you can't see your own steering wheel, let alone your dashboard; never mind the guy in front. Then you get the weird thing when everyone starts slowing down, because you know roughly where the next corner is. Then the spray reduces . . . and you see there is still 200 metres to the braking point and you all get back on the throttle. That's when you really earn your money.'

At Silverstone on 10 July, Berger and Senna came upon Prost on lap fourteen as they flashed through Abbey Curve. Senna took advantage of Berger's momentary hesitation and zipped down the inside and then narrowly avoided Prost at the next tight left-hander. For a split second, a collision seemed inevitable, but Prost managed to leave Senna just enough room to pass. Senna admitted afterwards, 'Alain and I almost touched. It was a bad moment because the visibility was so bad.' But the Brazilian was both brilliant and fearless in such treacherous conditions, as he had shown in the past and would demonstrate again in the future. He drove with a gossamer touch, an intuition that led him to find the most surface grip and with the ambition to subjugate his rivals.

Senna won on an afternoon when Prost pulled into the pits to retire after twenty-four laps with his car handling badly and his spirit deflated. Prost complained that he had understeer and oversteer in almost every corner as, unbeknown to the McLaren team, he had damaged his car on a kerb at Le Castellet a week earlier. But he also confessed he had been unnerved by the conditions. 'At the end of the day, it's my judgement and my life,' he said. 'If people won't accept that view it's their problem, not mine. I can live with that.'

He elaborated on his reasons for parking. 'When there is a lot of standing water on the track, I don't like it. I have never pretended I do. I can be quick in the rain. But at the start at Silverstone, for example, I was simply swamped in the middle of the field. Okay, it's the same for everybody, but when you are flat out on the straight, you see absolutely nothing at all. Nothing! I'm not worried about driving on a slippery track surface – that is all part of the business we are in. But when you are driving blind, that's not motor racing in my book. My view is that motor racing should be run in the dry. Look at the British Open golf last week. They cancelled the third day because the weather was so bad. And in America, of course, they don't race IndyCars in the rain. Of course, this is purely my personal opinion and I fully understand others may disagree.'

Much of the French media did just that – and poured scorn on Prost's decision to park. More critically, there were those within his own team who questioned Prost's desire, if not his courage. As we drank wine at his hillside villa in Spain, Jo Ramirez admitted that had been the case. 'Alain could drive a good race in the wet, as he did at the next grand prix in Germany when he finished second to Ayrton,' said Ramirez. 'But I think some questions were raised after Silverstone, because if Ayrton was driving all right, there were bound to be questions asked over Alain's reasons for stopping.' Those questions were probably most loudly raised within Honda – where Senna was now regarded with ever-increasing awe. The Brazilian was on a roll: after Silverstone and Germany, he won the next two races in Hungary and Belgium. The manner in which the stakes between Senna and Prost were rising can be gauged from Ramirez, who offered another illuminating insight into their deepening rivalry after the conclusion of the final qualifying session at Spa-Francorchamps for the Belgium Grand Prix. In those times, the drivers changed in the team's truck, not like nowadays at the European grands prix where, in the modern palatial motorhomes, each man has his own dressing room as though on some Hollywood movie set. 'I remember it like yesterday,' said Ramirez. 'I was standing with Alain at one end of the truck looking at the qualifying times each driver had done. Ayrton was at the other end. After qualifying, Ayrton always had to go and sit in the same corner, he needed some minutes on his own and, slowly, he would take off his overalls. Beforehand, he used to get into a kind of trance thinking about what he was going to do. Then, he'd sit in the car in the garage and work through the whole circuit in his mind. After qualifying, he had to come down in his own time.

'Ayrton had taken pole and now Alain was saying to me, "How the fuck . . . where the fuck did he find that time . . . of all places, here. How the hell can he be that quick?" In the corner, Senna heard every word. He looked up and winked at me! Ayrton had a look in his eye that said, "I've done it." Up until then, Prost probably thought he could have managed Senna. But from that moment, he knew it was going to be more and more difficult.'

Spa is a driver's circuit, undulating and fast with corners that demand commitment and bravery over a lap that is 4.3 miles long. Spa is not for the faint-hearted and Prost had won there twice. Again, the Frenchman would have been far from pessimistic at having to start the grand prix from second place on the grid. When Senna created excessive wheelspin on the line, Prost squeezed into the lead at the first corner, La Source, a hairpin. If he could consolidate, get into a rhythm, Prost could yet have the final word at Spa. But less than halfway through the first lap, Senna was alongside, then past Prost at Les Combes. It was a move executed with clinical efficiency and their positions never changed again over the forty-three-lap race. Senna had seventy-five points, while Prost had seventy-two.

'The championship is lost,' said the Frenchman. 'But it is good for the sport that Senna should be champion.' Prost actually offered that opinion, in real time. 'He has driven very well and he deserves it,' he added. 'Also, the pressure is now off both of us so we can concentrate on an even closer working relationship in preparation for next season with our new car and engine.'

Senna was more circumspect. 'It is not over yet as far as I am concerned, and with Alain you can never afford to make a single mistake either in the race or setting up the car. Maybe I am closer to the championship than ever before, but I cannot relax yet.'

Between them, they had won every grand prix and McLaren had private aspirations to deliver a perfect season. However, any hope of them becoming the first invincible team in Formula One history ended when the world championship docked in Italy a fortnight after Senna's last masterclass at Spa. And Ferrari fans will never forget the day a Frenchman called Jean-Louis Schlesser deputised for Williams' Nigel Mansell, recovering from illness. Sometimes, a sporting calamity can be predicted; but at other times, drama arrives completely unannounced as it did on a warm late summer's afternoon at Monza.

Senna had pole once more and he also had Prost for company yet again on the front row. The Brazilian scuttled out in front without any trouble. Prost had a misfiring engine, and that called for some thinking from outside the box. The Frenchman suspected his car would not last the distance, but he still felt that he could manipulate Senna's downfall by taking his influences from Machiavelli, not Nuvolari. Prost increased his turbo boost because he had no need to concern himself with the extra fuel that would cost him. If he could make Senna act in a similar fashion, by encouraging him to run more boost to keep him behind him, maybe the Brazilian might not make the chequered flag either for lack of fuel. Prost's race duly came to an end on lap thirty-four.

By then the Lotus Honda of Satoru Nakajima had also had a misfire, and the Honda engineers at McLaren advised Senna to reduce his speed. His caution brought him back into the clutches of Ferrari partners Berger and Alboreto. All around the circuit, the *tifosi* began to believe a great upset was on the cards. Two laps from the end Senna had just a 4.9 seconds advantage over Berger, with Alboreto a mere 2.2 seconds further adrift. Had Prost's pace in the opening part of the race made Senna now fear for his own fuel consumption after all? Perhaps.

But we will never know as Schlesser unwittingly became a central character in this dramatic plot. Entering the chicane, Schlesser's attempts to get out of the way as he was about to be lapped by Senna for a second time caused him to lose control of his car as he locked his brakes off line on a dusty part of the track. In the confusion, Senna's right rear wheel rode over Schlesser's left front wheel. Senna's car came close to being over-turned, but although he came down on all four wheels he was powerless to prevent himself from spinning out of the race. He was at a standstill facing the wrong way. McLaren's lap of honour around the world had come to an unexpected end . . . and Berger drove the final miles to wild approval from the Italian crowd as the Austrian collected the fourth victory of his career.

★   ★   ★

Senna still led the championship by three points when he arrived in Estoril for the Portuguese Grand Prix. But Prost, despite what he had said at Spa, had clearly not surrendered the championship. During qualifying on Saturday, he engaged in a gripping duel for pole position with Senna. Prost established a benchmark early in the session, but Senna bettered his time not once, but twice. The Frenchman promptly went half a second faster than his rival. Without question, Senna still had time to respond.

Yet Prost changed out of his overalls and returned to the garage in his jeans, a man with no intention of driving his car again that afternoon. Ramirez was startled, as were others in the team. 'Alain, what are you doing?' asked Ramirez, plaintively. 'You still have another set of tyres, there's plenty of time left?' Prost was disinterested. According to Ramirez, this is what he said: 'If Ayrton can make a lap quicker than mine, he deserves the pole. That was my best. I cannot do any better.'

It was a psychological masterstroke from the man they called *Le Professeur*. Ramirez remembered how the sight of Prost drifting around the garage in his civvies had played havoc with Senna's mind. 'The harder Ayrton tried, the slower he seemed to go,' he said. 'The difference between Prost and Senna was this: if you give Prost a car that is one hundred per cent to his liking, there was no guy on this earth who could beat him.' McLaren team policy insisted that their drivers pooled their information on their car's performance, and the settings that they used. By any criteria, Prost excelled in this department. So did Senna replicate Prost's settings?

'Very often,' said Ramirez. 'Prost was much better as a test driver, as an engineer, than Ayrton. Senna used to change so little things on the car, maybe because he was afraid to lose what he had. Alain used to change more, maybe he was more adventurous. Yet Senna would sometimes ask for the smallest of changes. He might, say, take a quarter pound of air from the left front tyre. I'd say, "Ayrton do you really notice that?" He would say, "Yes." But for me, if Prost was brilliant in a car that suited him, Ayrton was the better driver if they both had bad cars. Ayrton could adapt to any car he had.'

This Portuguese Grand Prix would prove to be a chilling prelude for the ugly days to come in the lives of Alain Prost and Ayrton Senna. It was an untidy grand prix, not good for anyone's nerves. The first start had to be aborted when Andrea de Cesaris stalled his Rial as the cars formed on the grid after the formation lap. After a second parade lap, Senna drove off the line more coherently, but Prost harried and hassled him at the first corner without getting past. But behind the McLarens there was pandemonium after Warwick had stalled this time. De Cesaris, Luis Sala and Satoru Nakajima all became victims of the chaos as cars bounced into one another. Instantly, the red flag appeared to stop the race.

Once the wreckage had been removed, the cars formed up once more. Prost again leaned his car towards Senna, on his left on the outside of the track, and they headed into the braking area for the double right-hander almost alongside one another. Senna then swooped to the inside and the Brazilian only avoided Prost because his team-mate plunged on to the brake pedal.

As they the cars swept through the long left-hander at the end of the first lap, Prost had positioned himself to get a tow in the slipstream, from Senna's car. As the two cars passed the pits at approaching 190mph, Prost pulled to his right to overtake. Incredibly, Senna also turned right and ushered Prost towards the pit wall. Only millimetres separated the Frenchman's car from the brickwork and some pit crews had to withdraw their signalling boards as they dived backwards from the track as Prost's car thundered past them. The Frenchman realised he could not brake as his wheels were dovetailed with the wheels of Senna's car. Should they have touched, there would have been a catastrophe. Senna's car could have become airborne with a full fuel tank. Instead, Prost had a split second to react; and he knew he had to meet aggression with aggression to avoid potential disaster. Momentarily, he flicked his steering wheel to the left and back again. This fractional change of direction encouraged Senna to move to his left. Prost then lunged still further to his left to take the line from the Brazilian for the right-hander at the end of the pit straight. The Frenchman made the move stick – and that was the last problem Senna posed for Prost in Portugal. All this happened over the course of a second or two; it just felt like an eternity. Prost was in a dark, unforgiving mood that afternoon after he had secured his fifth win of the season. He felt like a survivor, not a victor. 'If he wants the championship that badly . . . he can have it,' said Prost afterwards. Later, the Frenchman found Senna in the McLaren motorhome. Harsh words were exchanged. Senna argued that Prost had 'squeezed' him at the start of the race – but the Frenchman countered by insisting that the incidents could not withstand comparison. 'What you did was inexcusable,' said Prost.

Ramirez remembers the dialogue was largely one-sided. 'Alain said to Ayrton, "You are crazy! If the championship is so important to you that you are willing to kill or be killed, it's yours. I don't want to be part of it. I enjoy my life and I want to keep on enjoying it." Alain was right – and everyone in Formula One saw that Ayrton was out of order. It would not have bothered him, though. You could say anything to Ayrton, but when he was in the car he wanted to win: at all costs.'

Fundamentally, this was what separated Senna from Prost. In June 2008, Prost replayed this moment in the tranquillity of his home in the 16th *arrondissement*. 'I was really not confident doing this kind of manoeuvre in Portugal,' he said. 'I did not realise how close he could be to pushing me at the pit wall. I thought he would move a little bit . . . but not like this. I was afraid . . . some people were on the pit wall with boards and they had to move. Sometimes, I admit I was frightened by him. He was prepared to do anything, that's for sure.'

Josef Leberer, who maintained his impartiality throughout, even though he was to become such a close friend of Senna, saw the impact this flashpoint had on Prost. 'It scared Alain a little bit, for sure,' said Leberer. 'I think then he realised how much the other guy wanted the championship.' Leberer knew Senna's first priority was to break the will of Prost, his team-mate and immediate rival. 'That's how it always works,' said Leberer. Senna raced to the boundaries of his own creation; and if sometimes that required him to colour his driving with the black arts of his trade he would do that, too. No regrets, no apologies.

Prost kept the championship alive a week later with another victory, this time in Spain. Senna was fourth. His McLaren had used too much fuel – perhaps from attacking too hard earlier – and he had to back off from the throttle to get to the finish. After this race, Senna flew home to Brazil as the drivers and teams had a month at their disposal before the penultimate round of the championship in Japan. In Brazil, Senna gave an interview where he reopened the row that had developed with Prost in Portugal. In a subsequent interview Prost admitted to calling Senna a 'spoiled brat'. The relationship between them was hurtling downhill.

So much so that ahead of the Japanese Grand Prix Honda president Tadashi Kume wrote an open letter to Jean-Marie Balestre, president of the FIA, to reassure him (and the world) that his company would not favour one driver or the other. Balestre, a Frenchman it must be noted, had previously written to Kume in which he declared: 'We should make every effort to ensure that the utmost technical objectivity reigns over these two competitions [the remaining grand prix races in Japan and Australia] and that equipment [car or engine] of equal quality be made available to the two drivers of the MacLaren [sic] Team, for otherwise the image of the World Championship, present and future, would be tarnished. I thank you in advance for helping the FIA to achieve this end of giving the necessary instructions to all the Honda technical executives who may play a part in these forthcoming events.'

For sheer gall, the FIA president was in a class of his own. Kume opted to make his reply public, and his letter was posted on the notice boards in the press room at Suzuka. 'I believe that motor sports should be conducted in the spirit of fair play and safety, in order to obtain the interest and emotional involvement of the spectators and people concerned,' he wrote. 'Honda Motor Co. Ltd sees fairness as the highest requirement of its philosophy for conducting business and sets this quality as an ideology in its corporate dealings.' More lucidly, a spokesman at a Honda press conference stripped bare the message from corporate land. 'We're quite prepared to line up four engines and get the drivers to make their own personal choice, if that's what they would like.'

The championship looked like this: Prost had ninety points and Senna seventy-nine. But, in fact, the bare statistics told a lie as drivers could count only their best eleven results from the sixteen races. The odds hugely favoured Senna. Prost had already finished in twelve rounds; lowest place second. At best, he could leave Suzuka with eighty-one points and, winning the last race in Australia, the highest score he could accumulate was eighty-four. Senna had scored in eleven races, but he could jettison the solitary point he took from Portugal. If he won in Japan, he would have eighty-seven points. And that would make the Brazilian world champion.

Senna was withdrawn, tight and absorbed in his own world. All his life he had waited for this one moment in time: the Japanese Grand Prix on 30 October in Suzuka. He won pole position for the thirteenth time that season and had Prost for company on the front row – again. In Japan, he was revered, a favourite son of Honda if not a publicly favoured one. Prost would dispute that, and he would be vindicated, as we shall learn.

As the clock ticked down towards Senna's date with destiny, it lightly rained fifteen minutes before the start of the grand prix. Prost made a couple of small adjustments to his car to compensate, but the rain stopped and the wet weather tyres were wheeled back into garages. When the light turned to green, Senna was victim to his worst nightmare. He stalled his engine and was passed left and right as he moved at a snail's pace. 'Luckily for Ayrton, the track was downhill and to his great relief the engine started,' said Ramirez. He had paid a heavy price: in a few yards, he had fallen from first to fourteenth. Prost had the lead. Senna began in pursuit like a man possessed. At the end of the first lap, he was eighth. He scythed his way onwards. After four laps, Senna was fourth. On lap ten, he overtook Berger for third place. Ten laps down the road, second-placed Ivan Capelli retired his Judd with engine failure. Senna could now scent his prey: Prost. The Frenchman was powerless to resist, and later discovered he had an ailing clutch. But this was of no consequence or concern to Senna. At the start of the twenty-eighth lap he appeared from the slipstream of Prost and drove beyond the Frenchman into the distance, and into the Formula One record books as a world champion. For the past five laps he had persistently jabbed a finger at the sky each time he passed the start-finish line. Without irony, he was complaining that the light rain was making the track too dangerous. In truth, he just wanted the race to be over and the journey he had charted from a childhood kart in Brazil finally to be completed. Prost was nowhere near being able to catch him. As he navigated the last corner, the one he had envisaged in his dreams a million times, no doubt, he punched a fist out of his cockpit into the air to symbolise his triumph. By the time he crossed the line – thirteen seconds ahead of Prost – both arms were out of the car in triumph. At that moment, Ramirez was on the McLaren team radio. 'Ayrton was screaming, screaming,' said Ramirez. 'I spoke to him in Portuguese. I had to be careful because Ron hated it if we spoke in Portuguese. He would remind me the official language of the team was English. I think I swore in Portuguese anyway – something like fucking brilliant!'

Some time afterwards, photographer Keith Sutton found Senna watching a rerun of the grand prix on a big screen at the end of the pit lane. Senna's friend Reginaldo Leme from TV Globo from Brazil was with him. 'I popped a bit of flash and got some nice pictures of him with the sun breaking through the clouds,' said Sutton. 'All of a sudden, Senna started to cry as he was being interviewed by Reginaldo, who'd been with Ayrton from the early days, as I had. Tears were running down Senna's face. I was shocked, and I wondered what the hell was going on.

What had Reginaldo asked him? After Ayrton had gone, I asked Reginaldo what he had said. Reginaldo told me, "I put it to Ayrton that over the years he had been very ruthless and he pushed a lot of people aside to get where he was. I asked him: Now you have fulfilled your dream will you remember all those people who helped you?" Clearly, Reginaldo had opened some old scars. Ayrton was an emotional man, a deep thinker.' And on the greatest day of his career, and therefore his life, Señor Leme had just invited him to confront some ghosts from his past.

That evening Senna took his McLaren team to a steak restaurant and copious amounts of sake were taken, as well as whisky, which the Brazilian particularly liked. 'Ayrton used to drink and dance, he loved parties,' said Ramirez. Leberer added: 'Oh my God, this was a big party. Fantastic. Normally I have a beer or glass of wine, I am not a guy who gets completely drunk . . . but I think this night was quite nice!' Prost attended, and twenty years later he admitted that he had still harboured a small hope that his relationship with Senna could be spared from a nuclear-scale disintegration. 'Ayrton was so different, so motivated,' he said. 'We had a battle in 1988, it was, let's say, more or less fair even if I knew it was difficult for me. I did finish with more points, but he ended up with one more win and the championship. I was already twice world champion . . . so, I hoped, okay, maybe after this we could continue in a different attitude.' It was to prove a forlorn hope.

Leberer left Japan with Senna. 'I went with him on his plane to Bali as he had invited me with him to Club Med. We played some football, I remember. Ayrton played in goal – that was funny.' Senna managed to slightly sprain his right wrist – but at this point it was little more than an inconvenience.

On the streets of Adelaide, Prost delivered a majestic performance to take victory from pole in the Australian Grand Prix.
Senna's second place meant that McLaren had produced ten
one-two finishes, a remarkable testimony to the magnificence
of their car and Honda's engines. When the engines had died
for a last time, Senna had claimed eight wins, with Prost capturing
seven. The points table looked like this: Senna 94 (90 counting),
Prost 105 (87 counting).

Senna flew to Brazil for a winter's vacation exhausted but
satisfied. 'When you are under a lot of pressure in a championship, or in a particular race, it is the one who can mix when to
be aggressive, and when to be calculating, who will get the result.
To win a championship you need a combination of those
elements.' If his sentiments were not expressed in concise English,
I don't think anything has been lost in translation.

For Prost, the world of Formula One was about to become
even more hostile.

13

BETRAYAL

While Senna headed for the warmth of Brazil, like a migratory bird, Prost had in his diary a succession of testing engagements in southern Europe through the winter months. The turbo era had been interred in Australia, and now McLaren had to get to grips with their latest generation car, the MP4/5, powered by a 3.5-litre Honda V10 engine.

Prost thought the arrangement unfair. 'I had an argument with Ron,' he explained. 'At times in the season, Ayrton had gone home to Brazil while I was testing all the time. Now, he had flown home to Brazil for three months' rest. At this time, we were testing a lot and doing a lot of endurance testing. I was driving, driving, driving and very often I was tired. I'd been in Formula One for almost ten years and I always tested a lot. We had been through such great tension in 1988 . . . and Ayrton was on the beach for months and I was still testing, testing. I was not very happy.'

According to Prost, Senna had been scheduled to appear at least at two tests, yet on each occasion he withdrew. 'Twice that winter,

Ron called me on a Tuesday and said, "Alain, can you help me and come tonight, Ayrton has a problem and cannot come after all." Faithfully, I did. But I found out that Ayrton didn't have a problem at all. I was really upset because I knew Ron would never have accepted this kind of thing with me. I thought Ayrton was going too far.'

By becoming champion Senna had contrived to give himself an edge, with Honda and with McLaren. He cared nothing for offending the sensibilities of Prost. Indeed, it is probable that he relished the Frenchman's frustration and irritability. 'I was tired and very relieved at winning the world championship,' said Senna. 'It was as though I had lifted an enormous weight off my shoulders. It wasn't like night becoming day – but I did need a lot of time to appreciate all the effects that winning the title would have. Everything I have today, everything that I am, as a racing driver, as a man, I owe to my family, to my environment; to the education I was given. I love rejoining my family in Brazil.'

In January 1989, McLaren flew their cars to Rio de Janeiro to test them on the circuit which would host the first grand prix of the new championship in late March. Senna duly arrived at the circuit looking relaxed and reinvigorated by time spent with his family. He told everyone, 'I am prepared for the start of the new season.' This was hard for Prost to stomach. 'It was tough,' he admitted. 'I'd had two weeks holiday and he was doing nothing for three months. I felt we had different jobs.' The test in Rio had been scheduled to last five days, and Senna and Prost had been allotted to share duties. 'Ayrton started the test,' said Prost. 'But after half a day in the car he said to Ron that he didn't want to test any more, because he said that I was so much better than him at setting up the car. Ron came to me and said, "Please can you do the test." I was stupid enough to do the test – but after

I had the car how he wanted Ayrton came back towards the end and said that he wanted to drive again. So he did. That was not correct.'

Prost was feeling slighted on more than one front. His sense that Senna induced greater affection from the personnel within Honda had prompted him to arrange to have dinner that winter with Nobuhiko Kawamoto, president of the company's research and development division; more pertinently, Honda's number one man in Formula One. This rendezvous took place at a golf club, not far from Geneva, where Prost played. Prost recalled: 'Mr Kawamoto said that he wanted to apologise to me. His words were something like this: "We did not do a good job for you. Our engineers were giving more support to Ayrton. They were an after-the-war generation and they liked more the nature of Ayrton because he was like a Samurai." He did not say, in these precise words, but I was seen more as a robot. Mr Kawamoto promised me that the new championship would be completely different.'

When he made that pledge, it has to be assumed that a man as honourable as Mr Kawamoto had not meant it would become worse. But that's precisely what happened.

The Brazilian Grand Prix turned out to be anything other than a benefit for McLaren Honda. Senna had predicted as much when he spoke to a small audience in Rio. To men like Nigel Mansell, the words he offered were more enriching than watching a sunset from Copacabana Beach, more beautiful than the girls who promenade along the shoreline. On the eve of starting the defence of his world title, Senna admitted: 'This weekend, we could be in for some surprises, for some fights with other drivers. Alain Prost and myself lost touch with that situation last year. Perhaps at

Marlboro McLaren we had got into the bad habit of thinking we would always be one or two seconds quicker than the others. Now, we are very similar in performance to the best of the other teams, maybe not even as good as the best just yet.'

Mansell, thirty-five, who was beginning life as a Ferrari driver, embraced those sentiments as a drowning man would cling to a life raft. 'It is of paramount importance to the sport that McLaren do not dominate grand prix racing as they did last year,' he said. 'The sport lost a bit of credibility.' Yet Mansell also saw dark clouds gathering on the horizon for Prost. 'Alain could be disaffected because it is clear that Senna is Honda's No. 1 driver. Senna thinks motor racing morning, noon and night. In him, the Japanese recognise a kindred spirit.' Honda's hierarchy had nothing but praise for Mansell's commitment behind the wheel during their time together at Williams – and they would not have been totally surprised that he should win his first race for Ferrari, even if the Englishman was astonished! In fact, the Brazilian Grand Prix proved to be an unforgettable day for two Englishmen: Mansell and Johnny Herbert. Mansell had been recruited from Williams the previous summer and will pass into history as the last driver to be personally signed by Enzo Ferrari, who died shortly after he had dined with the quintessential Englishman with vowels as flat as his checked cap. Before the grand prix, Mansell's car had failed to run for more than five laps without breaking down. Privately, he had arranged to make a swift departure to the airport for his wife Rosanne and himself as he had little hope of surviving the race distance. Instead, Mansell defied blistered hands, the lurking menace of Prost and the unpredictability of his car's new semi-automatic gearbox to weave his name into Ferrari folklore. In Italy, the church bells rang at Maranello as they always do when Ferrari win a grand prix. And by nightfall Mansell had attained a new name, *Il Leone*, the Lion. His fourteenth grand prix triumph moved him to within two wins of equalling the record of Stirling Moss, who had won more Formula One races than any other British driver. 'It's a great relief and a surprise to win here,' said Mansell. 'Stirling created a great record, but, hopefully, I will be overtake that this season.' In fact, Mansell would need to be patient for another two years before he overtook Moss in the record books; and when he did so he would be driving a Williams Renault, not a Ferrari.

Behind Mansell in Rio, twenty-four-year-old Herbert had an even more courageous story to tell after finishing fourth for Benetton in his maiden Formula One race. Incredibly, Herbert had to be *carried* to the grid, because he was incapable of walking unaided. 'I'd had walking sticks at the test, but a week before the grand prix Flavio Briatore [the team principal] telephoned and told me he didn't want me to use them again,' he explained. 'He didn't think it sent out the right message. So, instead I got carried to the grid. I could move, but I wasn't very attractive.' Herbert had been involved in a horrendous accident in a F3000 race at Brands Hatch eight months earlier. 'It's only when I came round after being operated on that I knew I still had my legs,' he admitted. In the accident, Herbert smashed the heels of both feet; fractured a bone in his right leg, dislocated that ankle and broke other smaller bones in the region. But Benetton team manager Peter Collins had utter faith in Herbert's abilities and persuaded Briatore to gamble on the blond Englishman from Romford, Essex. Somehow, Herbert was granted approval to drive in the Brazilian Grand Prix in spite of still being incapacitated.

'Everyone was shocked that I could finish, never mind score points,' said Herbert, over a glass of wine at the 2008 Monaco Grand Prix on the yacht rented by his friend, affectionately known as Doctor Chocolate. However, Herbert's initial foray into Formula One lasted only another five races before Benetton felt obliged to stand him down. Eventually, Herbert's career would span 161 grands prix races and he would retire with three victories to his name. Everyone in the pit lane liked Johnny; he was the guy with a permanent smile who never took himself or the business too seriously. At least, that was the impression he gave; and it was an image that counted against him when Ron Dennis contemplated putting him in a McLaren in later years. 'Before my accident, I was a little arrogant – partly through shyness – but I came across as perfect for Formula One,' he said. 'I always had the inner belief that I could beat anyone, anywhere, in any conditions. I saw how Ayrton could make driving look, in a sense, like ballet on wheels. He had his car right on the edge, but under control. It was beautiful to watch. I remembered having that same feeling in a racing car, of being on the limit, and knowing that I had everything under control. But after my accident, I never had quite the same feelings again. I don't think it had anything to do with a loss of nerve – the crash wasn't my fault – but all I know is that it was never the same.

'And the only way I knew how to get over my injuries was to joke and laugh about them. Even when I was in pain, I couldn't tell anyone. If I told them, I'd be out of the game. So I put on a mask. People probably looked upon that and frowned and thought to themselves that I was not serious. I think there were elements of that when I went to see Ron at McLaren. The first thing Ron said to me was: "We need to change you." Unfortunately, there was no changing me. That was what I had to do.' Herbert spent his entire career laughing in the face of adversity. Whether it was because Senna recognised in Herbert a particular brand of courage is not clear, but the Brazilian always respected him and always had time for a word or two. 'To me, Ayrton was a nice guy,' said Herbert. 'He had a sense of humour that not everybody saw. Silly things . . . on the way to the drivers' briefing here in 1989 he walked up behind me and pinched my bum. In a drivers' meeting the first thing you'd wait for would be a question from Ayrton. Almost everyone was waiting for it. It wasn't just a random, stupid question. He would almost always give the answer in the way he shaped his question. He was seeing what he would be allowed to do. His English vocabulary was damn good. He'd never hurry when he was questioned, but he always had a cracking answer.'

All pretence that Prost could continue to work with Senna ended at the second race of the 1989 season, in Imola. The San Marino Grand Prix began with Gerhard Berger having to be rescued from his blazing Ferrari and concluded with Prost angrily accusing Senna of breaking a gentleman's agreement. Let us try to place these events in chronological order through, at first, the voice of Prost.

'There is only one version,' he said, during our exhaustive conversation in Paris. 'I would never tell you something wrong. I may not remember a certain moment, or a certain exchange, in which case I will not say anything. But at Imola I remember everything. Ayrton had pole and I was second. But we were not very confident about the start, so we agreed that we would not race one another until after the first corner, Tosa. It was Ayrton's idea. We had this agreement two or three times and it always worked. At the start, Senna got away first and I let him go. Then, Berger had his accident and the race was stopped.' We must press the pause button here, because Berger's accident was monstrous.

At 180mph, his Ferrari went straight on at Tamburello and

thundered into a concrete wall. Berger's car seemingly disintegrated as though detonated by a bomb. Mercifully, aid arrived at whirlwind speed. Within fourteen seconds, marshals were at the scene; within another eleven seconds the fire had been extinguished; and a couple of seconds later Professor Sid Watkins, the chief medical officer, was at work. Watkins later said that the fuel was pumping out of the Ferrari in 'volcanic waves' as he assisted fire marshals in moving Berger to a safer place after he had been extricated from his car. Without fear of being accused of being overly dramatic, Berger had been plucked from an inferno. He was the only one not to appreciate that at that instant. On the ground, out of harm's way, Berger started to struggle so Watkins sat across his chest; and he sustained fuel burns himself as the petrol in the driver's flame proof overalls soaked through his own.

Berger's own recollection, offered in the spring of 2008 at the Spanish Grand Prix in Barcelona, and told in the no-nonsense manner that he brought to the racetrack, is a masterpiece in the art of story telling. 'My day was quite straightforward,' he said. 'I had a proper start, drove three laps and then the car just turned straight into the wall. I tried to steer, but I couldn't. I thought I had a suspension problem in the back, lifting the front of the car. Afterwards, I found out the problem was caused by a front wing failure. Anyway, I had 180 kilos of fuel in the back. I was close to 300kph and the angle that I hit the wall was really shit. I thought to myself, "Well, that's my last moments." For me, it was interesting how the mind switches into slow motion. You say, "Oh, shit, the car doesn't steer." Then you look in the mirror to see if you have had a puncture, or if the suspension has broken. You do all that. You're doing quite a lot of things, it's a capacity of the body to switch into slow motion. But at the same time I thought I was going to die. I still remember the impact; then, for a few moments I was knocked out. Then I remember Sid sitting on my shoulders and trying to put air into my mouth. When I woke up, I thought I was on a beach holiday. It was so funny.'

Berger's accident had been seen by a global television audience of millions – and like those of us in the crowd of more than 150,000 at Imola they feared the Austrian might have become another morbid statistic in motor racing history in front of their eyes. But the strength of Ferrari's carbon-fibre monocoque laminated with a honeycomb layer of Kevlar had saved not only Berger's life, but his career.

Had he thought, as medics attended him, that he was finished? 'Not in the first moments, I was in too much pain,' said Berger. 'My hands, feet and back all hurt. I thought, "I never want to see a shit box like this again." But two hours afterwards I knew I would race again.' After being stabilised at the medical centre at the circuit, Berger was transferred to a hospital in Bologna. From there, he was flown by air ambulance to another hospital in Innsbruck.

Once Berger's blackened, twisted and unrecognisable Ferrari had been removed, and the track swept of debris, the summons was given to the drivers to reassemble their cars on the grid for a restart. Mansell, in particular, had reason to take a deep breath at this prospect. No one within Ferrari could be certain what had caused Berger's car to leave the road, so it required Mansell to demonstrate an unconditional faith in the team's submission that his identical car was safe to race.

On the grid Prost believed his gentleman's agreement with Senna held firm for the second start – he had no reason to suspect otherwise. This is how he recounted what took place once the cars had screamed from the line. 'This time I started better than Ayrton. I looked in my mirrors and saw that it was him closest behind. We were first and second, and I felt there was no risk to have another accident. For me, the race was going to start after the corner. I preferred to take the average best line through this corner, again because there was no need to take a risk, and then, boom, Senna went inside me.'

Senna went through the open door Prost had felt no need to shut, and he soon vanished into the distance. Inside his car, Prost was apoplectic with rage. 'I was furious because of many things,' he said. He thought of how Gilles Villeneuve had telephoned him, day after day, to complain about the betrayal of his team-mate Didier Pironi at this very racetrack. He thought about Villeneuve's anger – and the way it had consumed him until the moment of his death during practice at the next grand prix. And he thought now about Senna's own betrayal of him and he could not concentrate on anything else. 'I think I was much quicker than Senna through this race, but I couldn't drive, not well,' said Prost. 'I spun a few laps from the end in the chicane before the pits. I drove one of my worst races. I was so furious. When I came in second, I saw Senna smiling and all I felt was anger.'

Senna had won by forty seconds, in cruise control, and like the Brazilian, second-placed Prost had also lapped the field. Yet there was no air of celebration around the McLaren motorhome. Prost refused to attend the post-race press conference, and left without a word, which cost him a $5,000 fine. Yet no one in the media centre had a full understanding of what had happened between them; besides, the scale of Berger's accident and his subsequent rescue had already been nominated as the headline story of the day. But behind the scenes, a disgusted and disillusioned Alain Prost had given notice to Dennis that he was of a mind to stop driving.

Jo Ramirez, who tried never to take sides with Senna or Prost, preferring to defrost the atmosphere between them with a joke here, or an aside there, understood the Frenchman's anger. 'Alain said he left because he was so hot with anger that he would have said things that he might later have regretted,' said Ramirez. 'Ayrton was at fault, for sure. But knowing him, I'm sure he would have said the agreement was that neither man would pass the other before the braking area for Tosa. He would say he had not done that. He would argue that he passed Alain after the braking point for Tosa. But Prost said that was clearly not the agreement. He said that the agreement was that they would not pass one another until after Tosa. There was no mention of braking points. There was a big row – had Prost stayed there could have been fists thrown.'

Yet, at this point, Senna was more interested in the health of Berger than the wrath of his team-mate. 'Ayrton was on the phone to me in Innsbruck,' said Berger. 'I said to him, "Ayrton, this corner is shit. If you have a problem there you are dead. We have to do something to move the wall." He said, "Yeah, maybe you are right." When we had the next test at Imola, a couple of weeks after my accident, I took Ayrton and walked to the corner to see how they can move the wall. We looked over the wall and saw the river running behind it. We both realised there is nothing we can do about this wall. And we walked back and we did nothing.' Berger paused, and then reflected in little more than a whisper. 'We stood exactly at the place where he died.'

Two days after the San Marino Grand Prix, Prost and Senna were both required at a private McLaren test at Pembrey, a small race-track near Llanelli, South Wales, with slow speed corners like those on the streets of Monaco, the next race on the calendar. It was not somewhere Ron Dennis would usually appear, but, unsurprisingly, he felt it important to be present. Dennis could see all his plans, all his hard work, under real threat of unravelling at the seams.

Prost recalled the meeting: 'Ayrton and me were always going to Pembrey, but not Ron. The team had a caravan-style motorhome and we went inside, the three of us. Ron started to talk. He said to Ayrton we have to fix the problem we had on Sunday. He asked him, "Is it true you had an agreement?" Ayrton said, "Yes." Ron then said, "Why did you not honour it?" Ayrton said, "It's not me – it's Alain that changed the agreement." This was absolutely unbelievable. Ayrton offered all kinds of excuses. He said the agreement was for the first start, not the second. Ron was not taken in by this.

'Then we had a good twenty minutes, maybe half an hour discussion. I was hardly talking except to say this was not good for the spirit of the team, that the team was starting to break up. Then Ayrton started to cry, started to cry. That is the truth. It is difficult to understand why, again because he is different. He has lied. When he said to me, "You broke the agreement", he was convinced he was right. I said, "Ayrton, you were there." Maybe he cried, because he realised he was wrong and lost his honour.' Was Senna ashamed, do you think? 'It is really possible,' answered Prost.

Dennis fought hard to act as mediator in this escalating row. He had delivered McLaren from the knacker's yard to the summit of Formula One. He had encouraged partners to share his vision, like Marlboro, TAG, Porsche and Honda, and constructed a facility in Woking that was a centre of mechanical and engineering excellence. Boldly, he wanted to have his cars driven by the best drivers: Lauda and Prost; Prost and Rosberg; Prost and Senna. Only this time, he had lost control.

Dennis reached hard to find a diplomatic solution; one that would not insult Senna's acute sense of honour, but one that would appease Prost and prevent him from carrying out his threat to quit. He persuaded Senna – and this was a feat of outstanding diplomacy – to extend an apology to Prost. In hindsight, Senna hated the fact that he had been forced into this action, but he was encouraged to make peace on behalf of the team. In reality, that meant on behalf of Dennis, as 'team' was an abstract concept to a man like Senna.

The Brazilian would later offer a convoluted defence of his action at Imola, which was a piece of opportunism or an act of betrayal, depending in which camp your loyalties rested. 'Last year at Imola he [Prost] had suggested that we should not attack each other on the first bend of a grand prix,' said Senna, who, with rich irony, chose to offer his explanation to the weekly magazine published by France's leading daily sports newspaper, *L'Equipe*. 'It was his idea. I had never found myself in this kind of situation before and I said OK. We respected this agreement for several races. Then, as our relationship deteriorated, we stopped doing so. This year, after the winter break, we were on more friendly terms. Then came Imola. I remembered the agreement of the previous year. And I put the question to myself: what shall we do about the first bend? He replied to me: the same as '88. So that was the situation. On the first start, there was no problem. I was in front. On the second, after Berger's accident, he got off to a better start than me. But I got in his slipstream and accelerated quickly. I was going faster than him. I then started the manoeuvre to overtake him. Not at the first corner, before that. It was when we were braking that we were not to attack each other. We had a momentary confrontation, and then I drove clear. He made a mistake and skidded off the track. He had made a driving mistake, but he was trying to make me take the blame. The original idea was simple: no overtaking as we braked on the first bend. After the race, I had a clear conscience. I didn't think that the whole thing would take on such proportions.'

Perhaps that had something to do with the fact that he had not been in the race when Pironi, blatantly, and inexcusably, betrayed the promise he had shared with Villeneuve. Perhaps that had something to do with the fact that Prost had lived with that haunting memory for seven years and knew that it would never leave him. What was it Prost said? 'Gilles was angry with Pironi and Ferrari, absolutely furious. Later I would fully understand his feelings because I had this with Ayrton. At the next race, Gilles went too far in the car in practice. He killed himself because of that dispute with Didier.' Do you really believe that drivers would enter a pact that involved no overtaking before a braking area rather than a more specific location, such as the first corner? In that little caravan at Pembrey, Dennis did what he could. He brokered an uneasy truce, and he concluded the crisis summit by making Senna and Prost vow that not a word of their meeting be replayed in public.

At this point, Prost accepts that he made a grave error of judgement. Almost immediately, he broke his silence. 'Everyone had heard that we'd had this meeting, and a friend of mine from *L'Equipe* called me afterwards,' said Prost. 'He asked what happened. I said I could not explain everything, but, as I was very close to this writer, I said that I could tell him a few things off the record. I explained to him a few details and then I told him that Ayrton had cried. This was my mistake.'

Prost had been accustomed to giving an 'off the record' briefing to a handful of trusted friends in the media. This had allowed them to report and interpret events from an informed position.

And, it must be said, from Prost's perspective. He was not unique in adopting this position; but nowadays in the modern world, sportsmen and administrators, as well as team owners, have this critical role performed for them by highly paid spin doctors. When Prost arrived in Monaco for the grand prix, Senna refused to acknowledge him. 'I didn't know why,' he explained. 'We just had this strange ambience. Then someone told me that a story about the meeting in Pembrey had been published in *L'Equipe*. I had not seen it myself – and when I did see the story it was really nothing. But I was furious with the writer – and he told me he made a mistake. Ayrton and me had many problems, but I could not expect one of the worst to come in this way.'

Senna had reason to feel aggrieved. *L'Equipe* quoted Prost directly. 'I do not wish to drag McLaren into difficulties caused by the behaviour of Senna,' he was reported as saying. 'McLaren has always been loyal to me. At a level of technical discussion I shall not close the door completely, but for the rest I no longer wish to have any business with him. I appreciate honesty and he is not honest.' Prost did not deny the comments – but insisted they had not been meant for public consumption. It was, he said, an appalling mistake. There was no hope of reconciliation now.

Ramirez understood that. 'Alain always used the press, he had a lot of friends in the press,' he recalled. 'He might say, this is between you and I, and perhaps it was for the first week, but then it would be published. After Imola, the interview in *L'Equipe* was very bad. He called Senna a liar, or words that meant that. It could never be the same between them after Imola. It wasn't easy. It wasn't pleasant. After this, Ayrton never called Prost by his name again. He would refer to Alain only as "him".' Or worse.

★   ★   ★

Damon Hill came late to Formula One, but he was not slow in grasping a fundamental aspect of his trade that went beyond driving a car fast. 'Team owners never get what drivers are about, never get this basic point,' he suggested. 'They think they can provide two cars and pay two drivers to go out there and drive them. Forget it. It's not a team. Every driver has to think of himself. They don't think about being part of the team's history. Forget that, too. You've got to be professional, and do the best you can, but you've got to look out for yourself. It's more like those chess matches at the height of the Cold War when Russia's Boris Spassky played American Bobby Fischer. Before they sat down to play, they argued over everything from the positioning of their chairs, to the placement of the lights. Basically, you've got to get up early if you think you are going to have an edge over any of these guys. That's what it would have been like between Prost and Senna; and Mansell and Piquet. They'd each have been on the phone to their engineers, and their engineer wants their driver to win. It's fascinating – but it can also go wrong. This is where you factor in the Ayrton Senna aspect to all this. I think he took things personally.'

Martin Brundle expressed a similar viewpoint. 'As drivers you're all striving to do the same thing at the same time. I drove when there were quite a few other British drivers in Formula One – Del Boy [Warwick], Nigel, Johnny [Herbert], Mark Blundell and Jonathan Palmer. You're friendly, but you don't go to a lot of trouble to meet. I never got on with Riccardo Patrese or Thierry Boutsen as I never knew them despite racing them for a decade. Then I went to Le Mans and they were my team-mates and we got on like a house on fire. How was it we could have such a good time then, when we could barely talk to one another in F1? I think the answer is pretty clear. Formula One is a super-competitive business and there are so few seats. What are you going to gain from being friends with another racing driver? What's the point? All you can do is give something away. Or find yourself in a difficult position when you want their seat; or when they go after your seat. The first time I met Jonathan Palmer was when I went to punch his lights out because he held me up in Imola. He let [Stefan] Bellof through, but he didn't let me through when I was lapping him. I was incandescent. Now we're really good mates!' And the last time we checked, their teenage sons had been racing against one another.

Sir Frank Williams cast another searching light across this parched landscape of driver cooperation. 'We watched McLaren dominate and decimate,' he said. 'Senna and Prost were like two gladiators fighting it out. Ron allowed them to race as we did with Piquet and Mansell. But we did give our drivers one instruction: "Race as much as you want, but under no circumstances take one another off. You will not be forgiven." Piquet and Mansell got a bit rough a couple of times, but more off the track than on it.

'I couldn't have handled Senna and Prost fighting each other. Piquet and Mansell did not have any feeling for each other except loathing . . . Nigel could be quite physical and he did once attack Ayrton in the Lotus garage and they had to be separated. Between Mansell and Piquet it was tough, aggravating and unpleasant material. Someone like the late Ken Tyrrell would have stood up and intimidated both of them. Probably cowed them a little bit, but I wasn't up to that. You can't really do that when you are in a wheelchair and your voice isn't very strong.'

The atmosphere between Senna and Prost in Monaco had to be measured in minus degrees. Senna refused to acknowledge Prost, never mind speak with him. He felt badly that he had been forced into making an apology to the Frenchman over Imola against his will – and now it was Senna's turn to feel a sense of betrayal after Prost had been quoted in the French media. Senna did not believe, or care, that Prost claimed he had been let down by a newspaperman. He had broken their agreement to keep all that had transpired at Pembrey within the team. Senna dealt with this by shutting Prost out of his mind. He would not even refer to him within McLaren by his name. What had been left of any relationship after the post-Imola post-mortem in Wales had now died. Prost would not lose too much sleep over Senna's obstinacy in recognising him, yet he was a man who disliked conflict and this situation disturbed him for that reason alone. Dennis had no hope of drawing Senna into a second reconciliation with Prost.

On the track, Senna was at his most mercurial. His pole-winning time was 1.6 seconds faster than the previous year. His progress through the habitual traffic on the streets of the Principality was nothing less than majestic, in spite of dealing with gearbox problems. Prost, in contrast, felt his old friend René Arnoux had made his car particularly wide as he baulked the McLaren driver's attempt to lap him; and then Prost came upon Nelson Piquet and Andrea de Cesaris who had accidentally conspired to create a road block at the Loews hairpin. For the first time in a Formula One car, Prost had to select neutral. 'It was laughable,' he said, without a trace of a smile after finishing a distant second to Senna. At the end of another fraught weekend, the Brazilian and the Frenchman were joined in one critical respect: they were locked together at the head of the world championship on eighteen points. But this time battle lines had been drawn without the remotest hope of rapprochement.

14

DRIVEN OUT

Which man would best ride the strengthening wave of bitterness? No prizes for making the assumption that Senna would most easily maintain his intensity. He also continued to plead his innocence. 'I sleep with a clear conscience,' he insisted. His driving never missed a beat, that's for sure.

In Mexico, at the next grand prix, Senna placed himself in the esteemed company of Jim Clark when he won pole position for a record equalling thirty-third time; it was the Brazilian's seventh successive pole, which set a new record. At one point in the race Prost – who opted for the wrong tyre compound – was lapped by Senna, but he was spared the ignominy of ending a lap down when he unlapped himself twelve laps from the flag to finish a distant fifth. Senna jumped out to a seven-point lead in the title race, but the complexion of the championship changed dramatically just one week later, however.

The US Grand Prix had yet another new home – this time in Phoenix, Arizona. The circuit was a concrete jungle, although an array of resort hotels out in the desert, and framed by pink-tinged mountains, offered accommodation of the highest order. On the track, Senna was uncatchable once more in qualifying and the Brazilian removed Clark's name from the records by winning his thirty-fourth pole position. 'I feel rather light-headed with no weight on my shoulders now that I have established this new record,' he said, genuinely overwhelmed to have eclipsed Clark, a man he had never seen race, but one he nevertheless respected by reputation. 'It is a big moment for me.' Just how did Senna repeatedly and decisively annex the prime spot on the grid?

'In qualifying the secret of a quick lap is concentration,' he argued, when we met in Europe a month after his elusive speed had enabled him to create his niche in the history of the sport. 'When I am driving at the absolute limit, I breathe down the straight and hold my breath in the corners. This has nothing to do with anxiety. I hold my breath because it has been proven, medically, that it heightens your powers of concentration. Contrary to what some suggest, I do not take unnecessary risks on a "flying" lap in qualifying or in traffic during a race. Each manoeuvre is calculated, like most things in my life. I weigh up the situation confronting me as quickly as possible, then react. You cannot afford to be hesitant.'

That is not a criticism you will have ever heard levelled at Senna. His race in Phoenix had been ended, in fact, by a misfiring engine. It was the first time in twenty-one races with McLaren Honda that a mechanical problem denied him a finish. Prost took victory – and with it a two-point lead over Senna in the championship. The title race remained unchanged after the following race in Canada as neither Prost nor Senna finished in a grand prix that was staged mostly on a wet track. Senna, who was at last beaten to pole position by Prost in Montreal, had reason to feel most put out. After an eventful race – briefly led by Derek Warwick, at the front of a grand prix for the first time in five years – Senna had charged from sixth into the lead, but to no avail as he stopped his car on lap sixty-seven of the scheduled sixty-nine laps after his McLaren had lost all its oil.

Senna's notoriety had begun to catch the imagination of sportswriters for whom Formula One was a rare destination. In Montreal, Senna came under the forensic examination of Simon Barnes of *The Times*, an award-winning sportswriter with a deep fascination for the cerebral qualities of an athlete. To Barnes, Senna was a gift. 'Sometimes Senna seems not so much driver as driven – driven not by ambition to succeed, but by a purer thing than that: a desire to move into rarified air, to set new limits, to go beyond not only what the rest have achieved, but to go beyond himself as well,' wrote Barnes after interviewing him at the Canadian Grand Prix. 'This makes him a very unusual man, indeed; it is not surprising that people walk a little stiff-legged around him. He is a not a clubbable man. No, Senna is not your everyday megastar. A truly, formidable man.'

And he was the man who provoked Prost into bringing down the curtain on his six-year association with McLaren. After a little more than eighteen months on the same payroll, and driving the same car as Senna, the Frenchman chose Formula One's return to Europe, and more specifically, France, to announce that his plans for 1989 no longer involved being a McLaren driver. Simply, Prost could not reconcile himself with the thought of remaining at a team where his team-mate no longer communicated with him; and one where, to his mind, he was no longer wanted.

Prost's contract with McLaren ran until the end of 1989 and, although Dennis had invited him to negotiate a new deal, his mind was made up. He wanted to leave – an emotionally based decision that any manager would have advised against. But Prost largely managed his own life, and relied on Julian Jakobi only to ensure the fine print of his contracts had been properly written. And Prost had come to his decision: he could not stomach having to work within the same environment as Senna beyond the end of the current season. While Dennis had offered Prost an extension of his contract – and remember these men had built a close and trusting friendship over a period of six years – he had also been responsible, in part, for hastening the Frenchman into making his position known to the team as early as possible. If Prost planned to leave, Dennis wanted maximum notice to recruit a replacement. Sentiment is treated with the disdain for loose change within the paddock.

One man who understood Prost's option to leave was Jo Ramirez, even if he actively attempted to talk Prost into staying. Ramirez recalled how Prost's faith in Senna, McLaren and Honda had dissipated to a point where he thought it counter-productive to stay aboard. Prost had dinner with Ramirez on the night before he called a press conference to make his intentions public. 'Alain told me of his plans to leave and I tried to dissuade him from going through with the decision,' said Ramirez. 'He had already told Ron.

'I said to Alain that by leaving he was admitting defeat. I told him, "You have beaten Ayrton, you can beat him again." Alain's response was that he wanted to carry on winning, but that he also wanted to be happy in his job. He said to me, "I just don't feel happy working with Ayrton. I get on with the team, I enjoy working with everyone; but not Ayrton. It is too much hard work. I know he is going to beat me sometimes, but I know I can win sometimes. I am not escaping because I am not competitive. It's just not pleasant working with him. I don't trust him. He is not a friend. Why should I do it? Life is for real, it is not a rehearsal. You only do it once. I want to be happy, and I've always been happy before."'

Ramirez would have liked to have had the power of argument to deter Prost – but he admitted: 'I didn't have any case to persuade him to stay. I am the same. That's why I stopped – I wasn't happy any more. At the time we didn't know what Prost was going to do next, and that would be another story. But at the French Grand Prix I would say you could see there was an air of satisfaction in Ayrton when he learned Alain was leaving. Senna must have thought: "I've not just beaten him, I've destroyed him. I have pulled Prost out of the team – the team that was Prost's team."'

On 7 July, at Le Castellet, Prost called his media conference after the first qualifying session and announced his departure from McLaren. 'The decision was not an easy one to take,' he said. 'I have had six fantastic years, both from a racing and a human point of view, and I want to leave as friends with a lot of dignity.' Dennis admitted he had applied pressure on Prost to declare his hand. 'We needed a decision early from Alain because we exist as a team to be totally competitive,' he said. 'Other teams were aware that Alain might leave and have been pressing their drivers to sign new contracts in case we approach them. We will announce our choice of replacement sometime in the future.'

In Paris in 2008, Prost relived those moments in his mind and thought he had been placed in an invidious position; a position so uncomfortable that there was no possible escape other than by deploying a parachute. 'I remember I said to Ron even before I made my decision to leave that I would be willing for him to make me the No. 2 driver,' he said. 'I told him you can pay me as No. 2 – but you must tell the people that I am No. 2 and don't tell them that I am No. 1 equal to Ayrton when you don't give me the chance on the track or outside the track.' Dennis wanted no part of such a scenario, of course. Instead, he did try to renegotiate with Prost. 'Ron wanted me to sign a new contract, but after Imola, and then Monaco, I could not,' he explained. 'It was not possible for me to stay any more. I felt the whole degradation of the system. But I must say this was a decision taken with my heart, not my head. McLaren had the best car, the best team, and I was paid very good money. I had no contact with anyone else about where I might go. I was ready to quit for one year.'

In effect, were you driven out of McLaren by Senna? 'Yes, by Senna . . . but also by Honda and by Ron,' answered Prost. 'They all drove me out. I had been very close with Ron – and I think we came back to being close again today – but then Senna meant Honda. And Senna represented the future of the team.' Had Prost really nowhere to go when he made his decision to leave McLaren public? Pino Allievi, a fine, sober journalist, with an enviable contacts book, not least with Ferrari, having represented Italy's leading sports newspaper *La Gazzetta dello Sport* for the past three decades, was convinced some indirect contact with the Scuderia had been made on behalf of the Frenchman. 'I believe there were conversations with the president of Marlboro about Alain at around the time he was leaving McLaren,' said Allievi. 'But a deal was not done, not then.'

Prost's decision to quit McLaren raised pertinent questions. Was he leaving just because he was unhappy? Or was his departure caused through something more fundamental: an admission of defeat at the hands of a faster and more ruthless rival? Gerhard Berger, the man destined to succeed Prost at McLaren, felt the Frenchman had succumbed to the realities of his situation. 'Ayrton always saw the world through his glasses,' said Berger. 'He never had one millimetre of room for anyone else. But, having said this, you look a little closer and you can see that Senna was just the quicker guy. Prost had extreme problems dealing with this, mentally. It was an extremely difficult situation for Alain. Alain is a clever guy, a real champion. He knows that when he was racing with Ayrton here was a guy he cannot beat on the speed side. But his nature and his competitive situation did not allow him to admit to it. I think in the later stage of his career he could see this.'

Berger, who became a close and loyal friend of Senna, had brushed with the Brazilian at the first corner of the first race in Brazil in 1989. 'I was on the inside, Riccardo Patrese was in the middle, and Ayrton pushed in from the outside and everything collapsed. Patrese had gone immediately, I was gone half a lap later as I was missing bits on the car, and Ayrton survived. But I did tell him later he shouldn't try that with me. Never in my life will I back off in that situation. But Ayrton was a real racer, no compromise. I speak not just as his friend, but Ayrton had this South American charm; and when you put that in combination with the brain he had, and with the emotion he had, this is a package that is hard to improve on.'

Damon Hill, who would one day be paired in the same team as Prost, and then Senna, even if his time in the Brazilian's company would be tragically brief, registered the difference in characteristics between the two men in stark terms. 'People want heroes,' said Hill. 'Ayrton fulfilled that role; Alain didn't want to be a hero, he just wanted to do very well. But those who want to look on him as a robot do him a disservice. He was a consummate professional and a risk assessor. That style is not to the liking of everyone, but for some people, like those taking the risks, there is an appreciation of the strength and the sense in that. But a lot of people want to believe in death-defying heroes who are unafraid of anything.'

Was that Senna, when all else was said and done? Certainly, Martin Brundle had watched in fascination as Honda became bewitched by the sorcery of his old rival from F3 days in England. 'You could see Senna galvanise the team,' said Brundle. 'Honda would build Senna an engine for qualifying, with some additional five hundred revs on each of the gear ratios. In the team, they just knew that whatever they did at the factory, Senna could make the most of it. I don't think they felt that about Prost. Senna was quite spiritual, an emotionally powerful man. I think he just drew the team around him with his incredible speed and sixth sense.'

Brundle talked from the experience of being partnered by a man who scaled the ramparts of Formula One in a not dissimilar fashion. Michael Schumacher's charisma had been a force of nature during the season Brundle spent with him at Benetton, as the Englishman acknowledged: 'I don't think someone comes in the factory one morning and says, "Tell you what, guys, don't you think this other geezer is the man." It doesn't happen like that, it is a natural, instinctive change of focus. The problem I had with Schumacher was at the beginning people didn't realise just how bloody good he was. So, while I was small fractions of a second behind him in qualifying in '92, and sometimes ahead of him in races, it was still being reported that the new boy had already got the old boy fixed. Flavio Briatore [team principal] says to me on an annual basis that he was sorry he had binned me at the end of that year because, at the time, he admits he had no idea how good Michael was.

'But I think I know how it must have been for Prost. It's hard. The engineers, the media, the sponsors; everyone gravitates towards one driver. You sit quite a long time in your car in the garage and get to watch how a team operates. You're wearing your helmet and looking out of a letterbox and your senses are quite heightened. You see how people react. David Coulthard was very sensitive to that in his time at McLaren with Mika Hakkinen. You can't help but notice how a group of people are reacting, functioning. If you had two strong drivers trying to pull the team in their respective directions you can imagine it being like a piece of pastry being pulled apart until it breaks. Did Senna break Prost at McLaren? I don't think he broke him, but I think he got the upper hand, didn't he? I don't know if that is effectively the same thing as breaking him – but he won the battle.'

Josef Leberer, who worked in harmony with Senna and Prost, preparing to have them as mentally and physically fit as humanly possible, had acted to retain team spirit as best he could. He admitted this had become increasingly harder after the grand prix at Imola. 'I think I have a good feeling for these things: I know when to say something and when to say nothing,' he said. 'No one wants to hear bullshit. The atmosphere was cooler after Imola. Everyone tries in their own way to gain something. It is part of the game and you get used to this. I tried to bring Ayrton and Alain together a little bit, make a joke, try to balance things up like Jo tried to do as well. But things were not the same any more . . . it was not my business, but I was a little sad. It was an internal matter. I was just there to help in what way I could.

Ron tried to get them together, but to control everything was not so easy at times. Ron had a difficult job.'

Initially, Dennis could not be faulted. In his imitable style, and with his slavish attention to detail, he had deliberately wished to connect with his Japanese partners, Honda. He brought on to the McLaren staff a Japanese-speaking employee and the team's business cards were printed in Japanese as well as English. Dennis explained: 'It seemed arrogant to expect a big company to speak the language of a little racing team.' The Honda Formula One programme had as their public relations officer an Englishman called Eric Silbermann. He spoke several languages, but Japanese was not one of them. 'I worked from Honda's offices in Langley, near Slough, but when I did need to go to McLaren's factory I have to say they did a really good job of bridging the cultural gap,' said Silbermann, a short man with a large personality, who these days is communications director for Toro Rosso. 'Ron is anti-smoking – in spite of all the sponsorship he has had from tobacco companies over the years – but he had a smoking room for meetings that involved Honda staff. I seem to recall little bonsai bushes, too. It was no surprise that the partnership took off the way it did because Ron Dennis invested in doing it right, as he always does.

'As for Senna and Prost, they were a problem every team boss in the pit lane would have wanted to have. But racing drivers are all out to kill one another, metaphorically speaking. I don't think Ron handled the problem particularly well, but at the time he'd probably never experienced anything like it. All drivers are jealous of one another inside the same team; always have been, always will be. But like all people with a commercial interest, Honda wanted the team to be happy-clappy and lovely and, quite patently, it wasn't. But by the time matters blew up, Senna was a god with Honda and as far as they were concerned he could walk on water.

'At the beginning, I got on better with Prost because I'd always speak with him in French. He was always perfectly correct, but he wasn't exactly a laugh a minute; but then nor was Senna. Neither especially liked working with the media, but those were the days when the drivers would wait until the team press officer had buggered off and then go and tell their mates in the press what had really gone on. These were men who had a mind and an opinion of their own. Of course, with the Japanese nothing ever went wrong if you read our press releases of the time. You couldn't have an engine failure. There could be a hole the size of your fist in an engine, but the reason the car had stopped had been caused by an electrical fault. You arrived at this through simple logic. When the piston had gone through the block it had also gone through the wiring, so there you have it: electrical fault. Wonderful . . . !

'Senna was a nice bloke, and I did get to know him. I remember having to meet him at Kidlington Airport, near Oxford, one day and I took my young son with me. I was there because Ayrton was going to drive a Honda road car with a journalist. When the piece came out, the journalist wrote that he had to wait ten minutes while Ayrton spoke with the press officer's son, Jack. Ayrton was good like that – and I always got a Christmas card that was personally signed and specific to me. But he could be a complete prick to work with at times. The classic would be when he would take fifteen minutes to explain to me why he couldn't do a five-minute interview. I'd tell him that in the time he'd been arguing with me, he could have done three interviews and he'd look a bit sheepish. Probably, the main difference between Alain and Ayrton had much to do with their nationalities, one French, one Brazilian, so by definition they were emotionally wired very differently.'

Leberer reinforced that viewpoint. 'Senna was Latin, definitely!' he said. 'Ayrton's heart rate was very high, because he was emotional. His heart rate would be in the range of 170–180; sometimes 190, depending on the characteristics of a race. Alain's rate was lower, in the 150–160 range. Sports scientists like to say that with a heart rate of 180–190 you cannot concentrate. But everyone is different and Ayrton could work at this high level.'

To Prost, there was perhaps some poetic justice that on the weekend he sounded his retreat from McLaren at Le Castellet, he took pole position and then won the French Grand Prix. Senna's car had a differential failure and he never managed to get off the line when the race was started at the second time of asking after an accident. Prost had gained an eleven-point lead. The championship continued to weave across Europe: Prost won in Britain and Senna again retired; Senna won in Germany with Prost second; Senna finished second in Hungary with Prost fourth; and then Senna won in Belgium with Prost second. With five races of the season left, the championship read: Prost sixty-two, Senna fifty-one.

Another twist in the tale occurred as the transporters and motorhomes rolled into Monza. While McLaren had anticipated Prost's announced departure, it is fair to assume they had been caught out by his next move. Just ahead of the Italian Grand Prix, Ferrari informed the world that Prost had signed to drive for them in 1990 as team-mate to Nigel Mansell. There had been those who believed Prost planned a sabbatical – and those almost certainly included Senna. He was reportedly disgruntled by Prost's defection to McLaren's arch rivals. 'Ayrton was mad that Alain was going to Ferrari and taking everything he had learned from McLaren with him,' said Ramirez. 'But Alain was out of contract, he could do what he wanted.'

To Prost and Ferrari the marriage was one made in Formula One heaven; or so it was supposed. 'Ferrari needed a technical guide inside the car,' said Pino Allievi. 'Prost was perfect.' By some accounts, Mansell's bank balance was massaged to accommodate Prost on an equal status. And Mansell, much respected within the Scuderia, is believed at a later date to have taken delivery at a favourable price of a Ferrari F1 car that he had driven to victory; he bargained as hard as he raced, it seems.

To Prost, Ferrari was the one team that he could join after leaving McLaren and feel that he had not downgraded. McLaren had been a *tour de force* in the recent past, winning races and championships, but Ferrari offered Prost prestige and a Formula One heritage without peer. He had definitely made the best of a bad situation − or so it seemed. Predictably, Ferrari's management, with Prost's agreement, chose the weekend of the Italian Grand Prix at Monza in September to announce he had signed to drive for them. This was assured to be great theatre in Italy and beyond.

At the same time, Mansell told British journalists that he was in accord with Prost's arrival at the team. 'Sometimes, you have to make decisions on common sense,' said Mansell. 'I'd done my deal. I was happy with it and I could have been awkward when I heard Alain was coming. I could have blocked it, but there was no point. I had to make some concessions, but I felt it was for the good of the team and I am content.' For how long, though?

Prost's jubilation at the reception he received at Monza soon gave way to anguish and frustration as he realised that the momentum within McLaren and Honda had now swung irrevocably in the direction of Senna. Effectively, he felt the team had deserted him. 'I arrived at Monza and Ayrton had two cars just for him,' said Prost. 'I don't know how many we had in the team, but, let's say, there were almost forty people on one side of the garage with Ayrton, and four or five people with me and my car. Ron hardly talked to me at all.'

In qualifying, Senna was 1.8 seconds faster than Prost: in F1 terms that is like the difference between night and day. 'I always remember this: 1.8 seconds! I always said Ayrton was very difficult to beat in qualifying. He had a way of setting up the car and working with the qualifying tyres that I could not do. But I could not accept I was *that* much slower. It was obvious that I was completely out of the system.'

The Frenchman demanded an explanation from the Honda engineers, as he now felt, as he had suspected for sometime, that he had become disenfranchised. 'They tried to show me on the telemetry that as Ayrton was going quicker than me through the corners that was why he was 12–14kph quicker than me on the straight.' Prost rebuffed the explanation – and he posed an intriguing question of his own: 'In France, Senna never beat me in qualifying, so maybe you have an explanation for that?

'At Monza, after I announced that I would be driving for Ferrari in the future I had no team with me. Ayrton wanted to have everything. He was really unbeatable in this race.' After Senna's qualifying lap silenced the *tifosi*, who at their most vociferous bring echoes of the Coliseum to mind, Dennis said mischievously, 'There was a little satisfaction at seeing the Christian eat the lion for a change.' Overnight, Prost had of course become an honorary Ferrari driver and if Mansell and Gerhard Berger were unable to win, then a victory by the Frenchman driving a McLaren would do just as nicely, thank you. Yet when he took his place on the grid, in fourth place behind Senna, Berger and Mansell, Prost did not have great expectations.

But fate was to play a devilish hand. On lap forty-five of the fifty-three-lap grand prix, and leading by twenty seconds, Senna's race came to an abrupt conclusion as he spun on his own oil when his Honda engine blew up to an extent that even the official press release admitted as much. 'Maybe that's because it had so much power,' said Prost afterwards. 'I am frustrated because I could not catch him. I am not happy with the engine, but what can I do? There are four races remaining and anything can happen with the engines.' On that afternoon, the Frenchman had slowly, but surely, hunted down the Ferraris of Mansell and Berger and, with Senna out, it was ironic that Prost was the man who delivered Honda's fiftieth grand prix win. The drama was not over, however.

On the podium, Prost was greeted with as much enthusiasm as if he had been driving a Ferrari. As thousands cheered him, and screamed his name, Prost responded by tossing the trophy he had just won into the sea of people below. To Dennis, this was nothing less than a treasonable offence. He contracted his drivers to hand over their winning trophies and he was enraged, as Ramirez recalled: 'We were on the podium and all the crowd were chanting, "*Copa, copa*", and they wanted Alain to throw the cup. Honestly, in that moment I think Alain felt kind of obliged to give the cup to his new fans, the *tifosi*. He just dropped it. I saw the cup go in the air and at the same time I saw Ron's face. I thought, "Fucking hell, Alain, what have you done?" Ron really treasures the trophies. They are something tangible that the team has gained and they belong to the team. So Prost was giving away something that was not his. He was showing he does not give a shit about the team. It was just so wrong in Ron's eyes. Ron waited for Alain to come past on the podium. Then he picked up the winning constructor's trophy and threw it at Alain's feet! Fuck, Ron was so mad.'

Ramirez turned to Prost and said solemnly: 'By the look on Ron's face you have upset him very much. I told him to go to the press conference and that, with a bit of luck, by the time you get back to the team Ron will have calmed down.' Ramirez walked with Dennis back to the McLaren motorhome and tried to explain that Prost had meant no offence. 'I said, "Ron you got it wrong, Alain did not mean to upset you." But Ron insisted, "I didn't get it wrong. He threw the cup and the cup belongs to the team." I kept trying to convince him that, not for a second, did it go through Prost's mind that this was McLaren's cup; but Ron was just so mad.'

Prost refuted the notion that he had acted with malice aforethought. 'When I was on the podium I was more a Ferrari driver than a McLaren one, which is understandable,' he said. 'When you have won a race you are not angry. I could hear the crowd chanting, "*Copa, copa, copa*", and it feels like part of my new team. Imagine, I am a Ferrari driver at Monza with all the crowd in front of me. So I threw the cup to them – not on purpose to get at Ron, not because I was angry. I tell you that is not true. I am very much more natural than people think.'

Perhaps, reflected Prost, the angriest man on the podium had been Dennis. 'Ron was disappointed I won the race,' he suggested. 'He wanted Ayrton to win.' Prost had another explanation for his instinctive reaction to the crowd's demand. 'I was never close to the trophies anyway. I gave them away. I have my four cups I received from the FIA for winning the world championship.

I have my four helmets I wore during those championships – that's it.' As journalist and broadcaster Maurice Hamilton wryly observed in his post-race summary, 'It was, you might say, an unnecessary public airing of an increasingly serious dispute over the family silverware.'

The resentment towards Prost had percolated through to the McLaren mechanics, who had been his allies over most of the previous six years. When he returned to the team garage after the press conference, Prost found a Ferrari sticker on his helmet, and a plate of pasta and a bottle of Italian wine in his car. Derick Allsop, a good friend of mine, and travelling companion across the globe, wrote succinctly in the *Daily Mail*: 'Throughout his simmering conflict with partner Ayrton Senna, Prost had remained the popular choice of the mechanics. But now, in that one prank, they had demonstrated their contempt for him. In their eyes, a hero had betrayed them. Prost knew the mechanics' sense of humour had been spiked with bitterness. He was furious. He felt the team and Honda were squarely behind Senna.'

Jo Ramirez cannot explain why Senna had been so much faster than Prost at Monza. 'You know, the arrangement we had was that Honda gave us six engines for the weekend. We used to toss a coin: one weekend the mechanics of Prost would call, the next weekend it was the turn of Senna's mechanic to call. Whoever won would choose engines. But the engines were the same – yet Prost had this thing about them. I don't know why Ayrton was so much quicker at Monza. But Prost – one of the greatest drivers we have ever seen – was never going to be almost two seconds slower than Senna. That weekend was ugly.'

The aftermath poisoned the atmosphere further. Jean-Marie Balestre, unwisely went public in support of Prost in a broadcast on French radio. He said: 'I was furious. Until recent months, we have had a fantastic battle between Prost and Senna. It's clear if Senna's car shows its superiority in the next four grands prix, considerable damage would be done to the value of the world championship.' By now, Honda's patience was exhausted.

Honda informed McLaren that without an apology from Prost they would no longer supply him with an engine. Dennis tried in vain to find Prost – then handed the search over to Ramirez. 'Ron was desperate,' said Ramirez. 'Honda was adamant that unless they had an apology from Prost they would not give him any more engines. I spent all day calling the numbers I had for Alain.' Eventually, Ramirez tracked him down. 'I told him how the situation had become critical,' he remembered. 'You won't be able to drive unless you apologise. Unless you don't want to drive, you must speak with Ron.'

Reluctantly, Prost agreed to fly into Gatwick Airport where he was met by Ramirez driving a company Honda. 'Alain brought his son, Nicolas, with him. As it was a Saturday, there was hardly anyone in the factory. I took Nicolas around and showed him his dad's car. Ron and Alain had a chat. They wrote a letter to Honda together, I believe. I saw them shake hands and then I took Alain and his son back to the airport. He watched me drive and commented, "Oh, you brake with your left foot." I did, but it was an automatic and had only two pedals. Funny I remember he mentioned that. Anyway, I said to him, I guess you are still driving for us! I was glad it was resolved.'

Prost had been backed into a corner, he admitted. 'Honda was furious,' he said. 'I was winning the championship, but it was really a bad moment. To be honest, I didn't openly criticise Honda. I made some comments that Ayrton was much quicker, and that maybe he did not have the same engine. Which I think is true. I did not have too many engine failures, but you can lose your objectivity in this situation. As I have always said, having the same treatment or not – and this was the same situation for Fernando Alonso with Lewis Hamilton at McLaren in 2007 – is not the most important aspect. It's what you feel that is the most important. Because if you do not feel it is the same, you do not drive the same, you do not work the same, you don't fight the same. You can explain to me everything you want, but it's still not the same. You cannot do your own job.'

Yet Prost was still more than a man serving out his time. He was a man in pursuit of the world championship, and that would be motivation enough to continue taking the fight to Senna in the weeks left to him as a McLaren driver.

15

SUZUKA I: ROAD RAGE

Senna arrived in Estoril for the Portuguese Grand Prix in belligerent mood, as to be expected. 'Talk is talk, but what matters are the results and times,' he said in the paddock. 'I have a clear conscience that we are getting equal equipment. What is not true cannot stay alive for long. There are four races left offering thirty-six points and that is enough. We have a big fight in front of us. But with a lot of faith and a clear mind, it can be done. It is only when it is tough that a man's character can be seen in its true light.' Prost, a man in isolation, continued to be circumspect. 'It's difficult when I don't feel comfortable. There is a problem.'

In fact, Prost found an ally in Portugal in the shape of his new team-mate Nigel Mansell. Before business began on the track, the two men shared a round of golf without confiding who had won. They often played a game of golf when time permitted before the serious business of a race weekend got underway. But it was once at the wheel of his Ferrari that

Mansell's aggressive driving had most impact on Prost's weekend. During the grand prix, Mansell, who was leading the race, over- shot his garage when he made a pit stop for fresh tyres. As mechanics rushed to manhandle his car back into position, Mansell panicked and engaged reverse gear, an illegal manoeuvre. The stop lasted twenty seconds and Mansell rejoined in fourth position. But he was soon challenging Senna for second, driving forcefully in his slipstream when the race stewards showed him the black flag to signal his disqualification. As Mansell hounded Senna, the McLaren Honda team watched with mounting anger. Twice more Mansell drove past the black flag, hung out on the start-finish line. At the moment that Dennis was trying to inform Senna by radio that the Ferrari driver posed no threat, as he had been disqualified, Mansell darted to the inside of the Brazilian's McLaren as they approached a right-hand corner. Senna veered to protect his ground and the two cars touched – and the Brazilian's damaged McLaren danced violently out of the race and effectively out of the world championship. Afterwards Senna was dumbstruck as he absorbed the shock of being elim- inated by a man who had no business to be still on the track. 'Why did Nigel stay out after he was disqualified?' he asked, plaintively. Creighton Brown, a McLaren director at the time, said angrily: 'It was appalling and irresponsible behaviour of Mansell to ignore the black flag three times in succession. If it was up to me I'd take his licence away.'

In his defence, Mansell claimed that he had been too involved scrapping with Senna to notice the flag. 'I'm prepared to swear on the Bible that I did not see the black flag,' he said. British driver Jonathan Palmer, who finished sixth in his Tyrrell, offered corroborating evidence. 'I don't blame Nigel at all, it's very hard to see a stationary flag when you are busy in a race,' said Palmer.

Ferrari team manager Cesare Fiorio also absolved Mansell from blame. 'Mansell made only one mistake, to select reverse gear in the pits. We believe him when he says he did not see the flag. We did show him a board telling him to come in, but he could not see it. Nor did he hear us over the intercom.'

None of which appeased the stewards. Mansell was fined $50,000 and banned from the next race, the Spanish Grand Prix, a week later. Dennis said: 'He got what he deserved. If that's the Ferrari management's idea of sportsmanship, they should change the management.' The row dragged on through the media over the ensuing days as Senna accused Mansell of putting his life at risk. 'If there had been a barrier [nearer the track] I could have ended up dead,' argued Senna. 'That is why I say this is serious. Mansell's ban from one race, seen from this point of view, is very far from being the just punishment. In that position he was just not able to take the curve, he was too far in. It's a kind of suicide.' Senna had responded to Mansell's challenge by steering his McLaren across the Ferrari with the inevitable consequence of the cars colliding and spinning off the circuit. Retired world champion James Hunt, working the commentary booth for the BBC, vehemently disputed Senna's version of events. 'The accident was totally Senna's fault. Mansell had won the corner. Nigel has the right to feel aggrieved about being banned. He was right under Senna's wing and driving into the sun. He wouldn't have been able to see the black flag.'

There you have it. Take two drivers, one crash, and collate the evidence to suit your own statement of mitigation and leave it to m'learned friends to make a tidy sum. In this case, there was no time for an appeal by Mansell to be heard so his ban stood. Senna's instant fix was to remedy the ills of Estoril with a win at Jerez in the Spanish Grand Prix, and that is precisely what he did. With Prost third, he had kept the championship alive.

When he arrived at Suzuka in Japan for the penultimate race of that embittered season, Prost told Dennis that he would not, under any circumstances, open the door to Senna if the Brazilian came to overtake him. What was Dennis to do: threaten a reprimand? No, this was merely Prost letting Dennis understand his patience was exhausted. If Dennis wanted to relay that detail to Senna, then fine; if not, at least Prost felt he had gone on the record within the team. In fact, he repeated just that promise to the media corps during the countdown to the race.

As Senna had to win the race to take the championship to the final race in Australia as he was sixteen points adrift of his nemesis, Prost wanted his cards on the table, face up.

He recalled his warning last summer. 'I said to Ron, I said to anybody, there have been times when Ayrton pushed the situation and only my action prevented us from having an accident,' said Prost. 'But I am not in the team for the future and we are fighting for the championship. I have many times before left the door open for Senna, but I will not do that again.' He could not have indicated his position, or his mood, with any greater clarity. Nor could Senna. 'I have nothing to lose,' he said. 'I will drive as fast as I can to win. I like the challenge of racing to win.' Here was a man who held Prost in open contempt – not withstanding the Frenchman's proud record. 'Prost goes only for second places, I race only to win. I have lost my respect for him.'

Senna struck earliest with a qualifying lap, in Honda's heartland, that sent a seismic shock through the pit lane. He covered 5.859 kilometres (3.641 miles) in a time of 1 minute 38.041 seconds.

He had lapped the circuit 1.7 seconds faster than Prost, 2.1 seconds quicker than third-placed Berger and 2.4 seconds faster than Mansell. By seven o'clock on the eve of the race there was a one-kilometre-long queue of people, standing five deep, waiting to get into the track. It was like taking a snapshot from Church Road, London SW18, during the Wimbledon Championships.

An estimated 130,000 flooded the circuit on race day with most of them devoted to Senna. By winning six of the seven rounds of the championship that he had finished during the season, he had outshone Prost. Derek Warwick, the driver with most reason to loathe the Brazilian, other than Prost, portrayed the two faces of Senna when we spoke in the countdown to the race. 'He's probably one of the greatest drivers of all time, but he's also the loneliest man in Formula One,' suggested Warwick. 'I'm still ambitious, but I couldn't bury myself in motor racing the way he has.' Yet the obsession of Senna to win motor races, an obsession that divorces him from the realities of life, is the characteristic that Warwick finds admirable. 'He drives to win and I hope he is champion,' said the Englishman. 'I bear Senna no malice. The reason that he appears to be so unpopular is that he is so dedicated.'

This acrimonious season had been reduced to a duel in Japan over 310.5 kilometres or, if you prefer, 193 miles. Prost revealed ambivalent feelings as the race approached. 'I don't care much about the title because it will always have a bitter taste,' he said. But be under no illusions: this was a man who wanted the title if for no other reason than an appreciation of how much it would hurt Senna to lose it.

Senna began from pole position – but Prost made a lightning

start and took the lead at the first corner. Senna seemed to take an eternity to reach a point where he could place himself as a lurking menace in the mirrors of Prost's McLaren. Once within proximity of his rival, he tracked him at speed to calculate where he might strike. Prost was driving with flawless precision, untroubled by the presence of Senna. The Japanese crowd, and a global TV audience, was being treated to a compelling, epic struggle between two men driving to the edge of human endurance without an ounce of compassion for the welfare of the other. 'I was very fast,' said Prost. 'On purpose, I slowed down at times, then pulled away again. I knew that Senna would never stop fighting, but I felt there was no way he could overtake me in this race without my mistake.'

Where would Senna strike? How would Prost react?

On lap forty-seven, with six laps remaining, we had answers to both questions. With a brash manoeuvre, Senna drove down the inside of Prost at the approach to a viciously tight chicane, entered with a flick of the wheel to the right. The Brazilian had hopelessly misjudged Prost's mood. As he had warned, the Frenchman turned his car to the right in an action known in motor racing as shutting the door. At slow speed, the two McLaren cars interlocked like pieces in a jigsaw. They slid across the entrance of the chicane into the escape road and came to a standstill alongside one another as though in parking bays. Prost flashed a fleeting glance at Senna, then unbuckled his belts and began to climb from his car.

'Ayrton came from very far back, and that meant I did not see him immediately,' recalled Prost. 'At that old chicane, it is almost impossible to overtake in a normal situation. When I saw him I had already started to turn in. I did not move – obviously I did not open the door. Really, almost twenty years later you can say anything you want, but I did not open the door on purpose. I can promise you that. It was not in my interests. I was quick enough to win this race. Easy. In qualifying, Senna had been much quicker, but I had said to my mechanics I wanted to prepare my car for the race. In the warm-up on the morning of the grand prix I was eight-tenths quicker than Senna. I was really, really sure I could win this race. I had no interest to make a crash. I did not want the championship to finish this way. Not at all.'

As Prost made to depart his car, Senna's only movement was to throw his arms in the air to beckon marshals to come to his aid. Four marshals, wearing orange suits and white open-faced helmets, duly obliged. While one waved a flag above his head, the other three pushed Senna's car for as long as it took the Brazilian to catch the engine. At first the McLaren jumped unwillingly, but at the second sign of life Senna had the Honda alive. He drove down the escape road, threw a glance to his right to check the circuit was clear and then rejoined the track. Prost watched this in a state of some confusion. 'I could have stayed in my car, for sure,' he said. 'But I did not understand the situation. I thought my car was damaged – although it turned out it was not. Both our engines were stopped. To be honest, when I saw Senna get going again I thought I did a mistake not to be pushed. But then I thought to myself, "There's no way he can be allowed to keep going because, in the rules, it was forbidden to be pushed."'

Senna had acted by instinct, oblivious of the rule book. His car was still driveable and he had a grand prix to win to remain a contender in the world championship. As he looked to regain racing speed, he sensed his car was mishandling almost certainly because of a damaged front wing and nose. He needed to make a pit stop. As he approached his garage, he waved his right arm in the direction of the problem at the front of his McLaren. His mechanics swiftly replaced the damaged parts and Senna re-entered the race in second place behind Alessandro Nannini. The Brazilian's car was eminently faster than Nannini's Benetton and two laps from the end Senna drove inside the Italian at the precise place where he had come to grief with Prost. Nannini avoided a replica crash by locking his brakes and settling for second place. Senna took the chequered flag with his right fist punching the air as he drove past the McLaren pit crew.

But Senna's elation was short-lived. After a meeting of the stewards he was disqualified for having missed the chicane. On the assumption that he had now become world champion for the third time in five years, Prost went round the McLaren garage and shook hands with every mechanic. The Frenchman said, 'For me, Senna is driving too hard. He is good and he is unbelievably quick. But if you have two drivers like this in Formula One you have an accident every race. The problem with Ayrton is that he cannot accept not to win, cannot accept when someone resists an overtaking manoeuvre. A lot of times I opened the door and if I did not we would have crashed. I said before today's race that would not happen again.'

Season closed.

Not quite. McLaren announced they had lodged an appeal against the result. Senna issued a statement which reflected his determination to be allowed to defend his title in the final race of the year, in Australia in a fortnight's time. 'The results as they stand provisionally do not reflect the truth of the race in either the sporting sense or in the sense of the regulations. I see this result as temporary. It's a pity we had to appeal in abnormal situations like this. It is absurd, but it is the only way when we have a problem like this. We must fight with all our available resources.

Now the matter is out of my hands. What I have done is done and is correct. From now this matter will be in the hands of the lawyers – people who understand the theoretical side. As for the practical side, it was obvious that I won the race on the track – but the taste of victory was taken away. I couldn't go to the podium and celebrate with the crowd – probably my biggest fan club outside of Brazil – or with my mechanics. I would say it is a shame for the sport . . . as to the incident, that was the only place where I could overtake and somebody who should not have been there just closed the door and that was that.'

Note no name just . . . *Somebody.*

Jo Ramirez chastised Prost after the weekend, not for causing the accident but for how he had responded to the crash. 'You can see from the camera Alain turning the wheel before the corner,' he said. 'No one really denies that. But I told Alain that he had made the two biggest mistakes of his career. Firstly, when Ayrton went on the inside you should have left him, not closed the door. He was going so quick there was no way he would have got round the corner. Secondly, once you had crashed you got out of the car. Ayrton had destroyed the nose on his car and he had to come back to the pits. There was nothing wrong with your car. It was perfect. Alain told me he thought he had damaged a front wheel because it was pointed to the right, but once he was out of the car he could see the other one was pointed in the same direction; the direction he had steered.

'I'm sure Prost felt bad about the team's appeal, but the reality was Alain was not in the team for next year. For someone like Ron the past is the past. He never thinks about yesterday, always tomorrow. Is he ruthless? I can tell you he doesn't give a damn about the past and, maybe, this is one of the reasons he has been so successful. When you leave McLaren, with few exceptions, you are in the past, forgotten completely. Ron is a user of people – again perhaps that is why he is successful.'

The appeal was heard in Paris in the week of the Australian Grand Prix – and Senna not only lost but was branded a driver 'who endangers the safety of others'. The sport's FIA appeal court gave him a suspended six-month driving ban and fined him a record $100,000. Prost was world champion – official – but even the Frenchman was astonished at the levy imposed on Senna. 'This penalty is very, very high and may be a problem for all the drivers to discuss,' he said.

I was in Adelaide when Senna reappeared in public for the first time after the court's judgement. 'If I have my licence taken away, probably the values that keep me going will disappear with it and I will not need Formula One any more,' he said. Senna, near to tears, offered this defiant, heartfelt message to those who had placed his head in a hangman's noose: 'I'll drive the way I believe is right.'

'I am supposed to be a lunatic, a dangerous man breaking the rules. But people have the wrong impression. I'll do here exactly the same as I've been doing all my life. Who wouldn't feel threatened? They have tried to intimidate me, to destabilise my mind. When you get in a racing car you have to perform to the limit. Right now, if anything goes wrong I am assumed responsible, the one to blame. Motor racing is dangerous and when I'm risking my life, along with other drivers, is it fair to put such weight on one man? I never caused the accident at Suzuka. It was never my responsibility, but I was blamed for everything that took place there and I was penalised for everything. I was treated like a criminal. Of course, I thought about stopping. I thought about going home to Brazil for good. So many things have gone through my mind. But, as I have said, I am a professional and I have a responsibility to be here. But I am also a human being and the values I have in my life are stronger than many other people's desire to influence those values, to destroy those values.'

In this interview Senna also claimed: 'What we see today is a true manipulation of the world championship.' That accusation would come back to haunt him.

Senna confessed that he had taken excessive risks, but only as part of the contract of his profession. 'I have spent enough time in Formula One to realise you make mistakes, which not only compromise yourself, but sometimes other people,' he said. 'But that's inevitable and you won't find another driver who won't accept that.' But you will find other drivers who accuse Senna of pushing too hard, too often. 'I've always had a team spirit and that means you don't do things with a team-mate that Ayrton's done to me,' said Prost. Mansell, too, was critical. 'Perhaps Senna has it out of perspective. There are twenty-six drivers entitled to pass, but he feels he mustn't be overtaken. Ayrton's got away with so much, it's just come to a head.'

With some inevitability, Senna and Prost featured prominently, for different reasons, in the final action of this embittered season. As the drivers formed up on the grid for the Australian Grand Prix on the streets of Adelaide, the city was being pounded by a rainstorm of biblical proportions. Rivers of water flooded the circuit and an air of unease gripped the city. Nelson Piquet tried to weld the drivers into a protest strike on the grid. Prost's position was entrenched: he objected to racing in such conditions and he declared he would not do so.

'We didn't want to race,' explained Martin Brundle, whose courage behind the wheel of a racing car could never be challenged. Derek Warwick, another persistently brave man, admitted:

'There was no way the race should have gone ahead.' But Warwick felt the decision had to be left in the hands of those paid to steward the sport. Is it too cynical to suggest those are the same people who are answerable to the whim of those with most to lose from lost TV revenues if a grand prix is erased from the schedules? Warwick smiled, 'Well, Bernie Ecclestone always said, "Turn the light green and they'll get in their cars." We all knew the race had to happen.'

Piquet and Gerhard Berger were still lobbying outside their cars when the drivers were given the countdown to begin their parade lap, while Mansell and Thierry Boutsen also made plain their own objections to competing in such atrocious conditions to Roland Bruynseraede and Tim Schenken, joint clerks of the course. Senna remained in his car throughout the submissions being made by other drivers. It was a state of turmoil. It also appeared, from the safe side of the pit wall, utterly insane to contemplate staging a motor race.

Yet the new world champion turned out to be the only man to carry through with a protest. He drove off the line at the start, but never completed a single lap as he peeled away into the pit lane to park. No one at McLaren would dare to question his action. For two hours we watched heavy hearted as the world's best drivers picked their way through a curtain of blinding spray, on a road as treacherous as an ice rink, in pursuit of something more precious than championship points.

We watched them fight for survival.

Mercifully, the carnage was measured in busted cars, not disabled bodies. Only eight drivers completed the race. Senna was not one of them. He had a miraculous escape when his McLaren barrelled into the rear of Brundle's Brabham at 150mph on lap fourteen. 'Senna was driving like a complete idiot, like a demonic man,' argued Brundle. 'Apparently, his team was screaming at him to slow down. On the previous lap, I'd gone down the Brabham Straight and did a triple 360-degree spin. I was only told afterwards it was a triple spin, because I had no idea at the time as there was too much spray around. My Pirelli tyres just got to the point where they couldn't clear the water. I hooked a gear and drove off – then suddenly thought what if I am driving in the wrong direction? All you could see was two perimeter walls . . . It gave me a big scare. I wouldn't think Formula One cars are much good at meeting each other head-on. At last, I saw the braking board for a corner and as the number two hundred was facing me I knew I was going in the right direction. So you can imagine, the next time down the Brabham Straight I was a bit circumspect. I'm in fifth gear, not sixth; I'm on three-quarter throttle, just to see if I can get down the straight this time. Maybe, I should have pulled in. I don't know. The conditions were treacherous, but your mentality is not to pull over until you really have to do so.

'I am thinking this all through, when there is this big thump at the rear of my car and a three-wheeled McLaren goes past me. That's how much faster Senna was driving. He was flat out in top gear. Quite clearly, he didn't see me at all. I don't think he remotely lifted. He just drove straight into the back of me, complete lunacy. What on earth was he doing? If he hadn't hit me, he was going to hit *someone*. Or it might have been me the lap before going the wrong way. Senna was going to hit something before he finished, I can guarantee. I was angry. Where did he come from? But there was no logic to that day at all, though, was there?'

There was not.

But as Brundle flicked through the scrapbook of his memory, he chuckled: 'I can picture Bernie now saying, "Get in your car, the race is starting." You can't just take the high days and the holidays, the sunny days. You have to take the rough with the smooth. And I must say I felt more at risk at Hockenheim on a wet day. That was pretty horrific: trees down the side of long straights. You can't lift for fear of someone hitting you, so you have to go faster.'

Brundle's point is that the show had to go on in Adelaide, for contractual reasons as much as anything else. But it was a frightening spectacle and a question did spring instantly to mind: how in one breath could FISA caution Senna for dangerous driving, then sanction the mayhem that took place on the streets of the capital of South Australia? As Warwick told me afterwards, 'The day is saved because no one is hurt – but that's through luck, nothing else.'

Senna's own account, offered when he returned to the pits, was a reflection of the man. 'We should never have been out there,' he confessed. 'But I am a racing driver and they told us to race.'

Prost had long since dressed and left for the airport, but this championship had been won at a heavy price. '1989 was really a nightmare,' he said. 'I realised in 1989 that Ayrton's motivation was much more than I thought. It was something you could not understand, you could not expect. When you want to be good in life, you need to be challenged. That is a good experience. You can have people challenging you, you can have rivals, but you can't have enemies. I felt from 1989 Ayrton made me an enemy. It was not correct. As I said, I was not prepared to lose my life against another driver.'

But if Prost thought that by leaving McLaren he would escape the attention of Senna, he was very much mistaken.

16

SUZUKA II: REVENGE

Formula One may have gone into winter hibernation, but Senna's name still dominated the headlines. A game of brinkmanship developed between the Brazilian and a Frenchman; not Prost this time, but Jean-Marie Balestre. At the end of the 1989 season, Senna had claimed: 'What we see today is a true manipulation of the championship.' This accusation exploded within the office of Balestre like an incendiary bomb.

In the second week of January – with the first race of the new season just two months away – Balestre made a highly inflammatory statement of his own. He said: 'The World Council will not give a super licence to Ayrton Senna in 1990 unless he makes a public statement taking back the comments which are both false and detrimental to FISA.' With his autocratic style of administration Balestre was outraged that Senna refused to show any contrition – and he was also incensed that the Brazilian had not paid the $100,000 fine imposed on him after he appealed against his disqualification in the Japanese Grand

Prix. This punishment had been deemed excessive in all quarters of the sport, but rather than take Japan in isolation, Balestre had increased the charge sheet against Senna without warning, thereby vindicating the scale of the fine. At the appeal court, McLaren's defence team had been dismayed to be confronted by a whole range of new accusations drawn up by FISA alleging dangerous driving by Senna in previous grands prix in Italy in 1988, and in Brazil, France, Portugal and Spain in 1989; at none of these races had Senna actually been disciplined. This was felt to be unconstitutional by Senna and his team – with perfectly good reason.

Yet Balestre continued to behave as a man who believed he held the moral high ground. Commenting on Senna's appearance in Paris, he said pointedly, 'Senna adopted an arrogant and defiant manner and continually showed gestures of impatience.' When had that constituted a crime, we wondered? Britain's last world champion James Hunt described the developing crisis as a 'witch-hunt'. Hunt, acclaimed for his forthright opinions in his new role as a TV pundit, told me: 'The personal vendetta between Balestre and Senna is their problem. But this is a tragedy for grand prix racing. It seems Balestre is using his personal power to blackmail Senna. I don't see why the motor racing public should suffer. They want to see Senna out there racing. It's a witch-hunt and very bad news.' One Formula One insider suggested dryly, 'This is what you get when one man believes in God and another believes he is God!'

Neither Senna nor Balestre was a man accustomed to conceding ground. The Brazilian had been given until 15 February – the deadline for the issue of a super licence – to apologise. As a precaution, McLaren placed test driver Jonathan Palmer on standby for the season. Who would blink first? Well, Senna's fine was paid at the end of January – by McLaren. One hurdle had been overcome, but there was still one more to clear.

With some inevitability, the game of bluff ended in a fiasco on deadline day. At first, FISA issued a release stating that Senna would not be given a licence as he had refused to retract his opinion that the world championship had been 'manipulated'. Gerhard Berger and Palmer were named as McLaren drivers for the 1990 world championship. Within an hour a message was released on international newswires to disregard this. And a new list was published that included Senna in place of Palmer. A peace formula was reached, it seems, when FISA acknowledged receipt of a letter from Senna, dated 15 February. In his carefully drafted letter Senna wrote: 'During the meeting of the FISA World Council on 7 December 1989 I listened to statements and testimonies from various people and from these statements one must conclude that they provide proof that no pressure group or the President of the FISA influenced the decisions regarding the results of the 1989 FIA Formula One world championship.' Just when that letter arrived in Paris was a jealously guarded secret. In this shuttle diplomacy Balestre also lifted the six-month suspended ban hanging over the Brazilian's head. Honour may have been salvaged all round, but it was an unedifying episode in Formula One history.

At the end of February I flew to Estoril to interview Senna with the first grand prix of the year, in Phoenix, just over the horizon. After his restless winter, he looked at first sight an unchanged man: intense, ruthlessly committed and absorbed in his work testing the latest McLaren. But during our conversation, Senna spoke in a manner we had not heard from him before. 'I am fresh . . . but I am not as keen as I was one year ago,' he said. 'As time goes by things change and you change.

After having one world championship, and having the season I had last year, after so many pole positions, after leading so many races, what else can you aim for? Another three, four or five championships? It doesn't really make sense to my mind. It only makes sense to go as hard as I can while I am driving. I only need Formula One as long as it gives me more pleasure than aggravation.

'My new team-mate agrees that we have to make a special effort to create and maintain a positive environment at McLaren and bring some fun to racing. Otherwise it takes so much out of you that it becomes difficult to justify being a racing driver. At the end of this year my contract expires. I will be totally free, not just contractually, but more importantly morally. As long as I get pleasure this year, for sure I'll be back next year.'

Had Senna's spirit been gale-damaged by the events of the past, stormy year? 'When I am driving the car, no,' he said. 'But when I am not driving . . . maybe a little bit. Only when the season is over will we be able to assess what's happened to me.' Berger brought with him an open mind to McLaren. 'I like Ayrton, the way he is, the way he works,' he explained. 'My good relationship with Nigel Mansell at Ferrari was the same at the end of last year as it was at the beginning and I am proud of that. But I have a rapport with Ayrton that is better than I have ever known and I am telling him things, really deep things, I never told another driver. I have a feeling he is telling me everything, too.'

Senna, of course, did minimal out-of-season testing. He preferred to winter at his Brazilian ranch in Tatui, or his beach home at Angra dos Reis. He liked nothing more than to be with his family: his parents, Milton and Neyde, and his older sister, Viviane, and his younger brother, Leonardo. One day Viviane would devote herself to the Ayrton Senna Foundation which, by the autumn of 2008, had raised an estimated £50 million for impoverished children in Brazil, who had been beneficiaries of substantial private donations from Senna during his lifetime. It is a testament to the man that the Senna Foundation will stand for eternity as a monument to him as much as the records he established or the emotions he stirred.

But this test at Estoril was not as arduous as some. Senna liked to be in Portugal, a country with more than just a language in common with Brazil. He would later buy a villa at Quinta do Lago on the Algarve with its beaches running down to the shore of the Atlantic Ocean and make this his European home instead of Monaco. Senna was never less than compelling company, and he thought hard and long before answering any question. Clearly, the winter had sapped some of his enthusiasm. He agreed this might be the case, but he fully expected to have remedied his mood by the time he reached Phoenix. 'Perhaps I just need to see the green light at the first grand prix . . .' He smiled as he spoke.

Senna saw the green light at the USA Grand Prix and flew to victory. He spoke afterwards about how much that triumph had meant; how he had needed to be seduced again by the thrill of the chase. 'The most important thing I got from that win was motivation,' he explained. 'When I tested the car, at Silverstone and Estoril, it was a matter of instinct to drive it. Only in this race was I able to go, go, go the way I like to drive.' After a winter of polemics, Senna had freed his mind in emphatic style; yet he had not cleared his mind of the antipathy he felt towards Prost. 'I held out my hand,' said the Frenchman. 'But he refused to shake it . . . I won't do it again.'

Prost had spent the winter becoming associated with his new team, with his new car, in a series of test sessions across southern Europe. Uniquely, Ferrari have their own test track close to the team's headquarters and much familiarisation work was done by Prost behind closed doors. He found time for a vacation – but never attracted the French paparazzi.

The next race was of special importance to Senna. The Brazilian Grand Prix had been moved from Rio de Janeiro to São Paulo and Senna had arrived in his home city full of optimism. 'It is my dream to win here,' he said. He captured pole and he was in a commanding lead when he arrived to lap Satoru Nakajima. He misjudged the manoeuvre – and needed to pit for a new nose cone. This was a break from the gods for Prost. He swept ahead and claimed his first, memorable race win for Ferrari. 'Beating Senna in São Paulo made it a fantastic day for Ferrari, but especially for me,' he said. If beating Senna had been pleasurable for Prost, then losing to Prost had been unbearable for Senna. He was a man who hated to lose to anyone – but, as Prost said, 'He just wanted to beat me, nothing else was as important.'

As the season unwound, however, Prost's mood within Ferrari began to change. He grew uneasy with Mansell. The two men who had been friends – perhaps galvanised by a mutual dislike and mistrust of Senna – suddenly found themselves uncomfortable as partners. Matters came to a head for Mansell at the British Grand Prix in midsummer. The Englishman felt Prost was receiving more favourable treatment from the engineers, and getting the pick of cars. 'I had seen for some time now that there was a lot of other business going on between Prost and the management and I didn't have the backing of the team,' claimed Mansell, in his autobiography *The People's Champion*.

After his car betrayed him at Silverstone, an emotional Mansell announced that he would be retiring at the end of the season.

Prost tells a different tale. 'Nigel was difficult,' he insisted. 'He was completely paranoid. He was upset because I was talking Italian. In the team briefing, we spoke English, but with my engineer I preferred to speak Italian as his English was not very good. But Nigel was not working so hard. He was playing golf all the time. Then many times he would come back to the track at night and tell the engineers to put the same set-up on his car that I had put on mine. He was saying I was too political. He was not good within the team. I am not saying it was anything like it was for me with Senna, but we were not as close as we should have been for the team.' Mansell countered: 'Partly through my honesty and partly through naivety, I took him [Prost] at his word and I shouldn't have done. Some of my disappointment was at having been taken in by him.'

Whatever the truth – and a mathematical certainty is that there are always two sides to every story – Prost had positioned himself as the only serious challenger to Senna. At the Portuguese Grand Prix, Prost trailed Senna by a mere six points. Mansell had pole position, though, with Prost alongside him on the front row and the Brazilian immediately behind. At the green light, the Englishman's car came perilously close to putting Prost's car into the pit wall, allowing Senna to snatch the lead. Mansell recovered from his appalling start to win the race, but Prost never did find a way past Senna and had to settle for third. He was incandescent with rage. 'I lost the world championship because of Mansell, because of his attitude at the start when he nearly put me in the wall. At the end of the first lap I was fifth or sixth. It was a race I would have easily won.' Mansell insisted his sideways start was unintentional – and that he still had to negotiate a route past Senna. And that he had.

Pino Allievi from *La Gazzetta dello Sport* had sympathy with both Prost and Mansell, two men he admired for differing reasons. 'Each of them had a mutual respect for each other,' he insisted. 'Mansell knew that Prost was a very strong driver and Prost knew that Mansell was incredibly fast. Mansell was loved inside the team and Prost, at the start, was a little jealous without understanding all the team was with him, too. After a few races, he understood how the technical staff was respecting him. Mansell had a good relationship with Cesare Fiorio [team principal]. Prost had the impression Fiorio didn't like him. These were two men with strong personalities: Fiorio spoke perfect French and Prost spoke perfect Italian. Prost was always a little suspicious. Prost was analytical, very practical about getting results. Mansell was direct. He was loved because of his big heart. In Ferrari, we had a tradition of drivers with big heart and character. Mansell, if you like, was the continuity of people like Clay Regazzoni, Pedro Rodriguez, Jacky Ickx and Gilles Villeneuve. Mansell gave a lot to the people with his courage and heart. Nevertheless, Prost had been faster than Mansell many times. Prost was waiting for Fiorio to decide he was the first driver and that the team would push for him in the championship. But Fiorio never did that. The key man in any struggle was Fiorio. It was up to him to manage the relationship between the drivers, but, unfortunately, the two drivers had to manage the relationship for themselves. That's when it went wrong.

'When Mansell retired at Silverstone nobody trusted him when he said he was leaving. Just for five minutes, perhaps; but then you realised it was bullshit. Mansell was nice because he was changing his mind every minute; it was lovely. I liked him a lot.

I also loved Prost the driver. If the team had been managed Prost would have been world champion – definitely. If Fiorio reflects on his life, he would have to admit if he managed the team in another way, Ferrari would have won the championship.'

Momentarily, on a summer's afternoon in Spain one week later, the world championship seemed unimportant. Ulsterman Martin Donnelly crashed his Lotus so violently after a front suspension failure that he was thrown from his car and left lying in the road like a rag doll.

His team-mate Derek Warwick sprinted to the scene from the paddock at Jerez. 'I ran and ran and was with Martin in about forty-five seconds, a minute at the outside. The Prof [Sid Watkins] got there just after me. Martin had been driving through a flat-out right-hander, probably doing 160–170mph. The front suspension broke, he hit the wall and the car exploded. It sounded like a bomb going off. Martin was lying in the middle of the road, still in his seat. His legs were everywhere, his arms broken. He was dead; I truly believe that. What I remember is that Nelson Piquet – one of the most selfish drivers I have ever known – parked his car in front of Martin to shield him from other drivers to make sure no one ran over him. Ayrton arrived and he pushed a camera crew out of the way. It goes to show there is a lot of good in these people, there really is.

'If you'd had an accident, the Prof used to lay you down, take your helmet off and ask if you were all right. I watched as he ripped Martin's helmet off – and, remember, his body was broken everywhere – and turned him over and beat the shit out of him and brought him back to life. Martin was blue, that's for sure. The only other person I saw like that was Gilles Villeneuve . . . I was first on the scene at his fatal crash. After Martin had been carried back to the medical centre, I went to visit him. I had never seen anyone like that. I was in tears, absolute tears. The hairs on the back of my neck are standing up now when I think I went out and drove the same car. You just don't think about it at the time. But Martin and I drove for a team that was underfunded, and drove cars that kept breaking.'

Only two races earlier, Warwick had survived an enormous shunt at Monza. 'One thing you were aware of in those days was the fact that you were carrying 220 litres of fuel,' he said. 'I always thought to be burned to death would be the most horrific way of dying. Anyway, as I understeered off at the exit of Parabolica – probably because I was too close to Ivan Capelli – I hit a barrier and just knew it was going to be a big one. We were doing 160–170mph and the car power rolled over and skidded along the track on its side. My head was bouncing on the tarmac. I had taken the steering wheel off and turned the engine off. As true as I am sitting here, I thought if I cut the engine there would be no chance of a fire! I was still doing 100mph on my side.

'I thought that before I'd get out I'd wait for the cars that had been behind me to pass. I thought I'd waited thirty seconds – but when I looked at the film afterwards it was more like 1½ seconds! As I got out in the middle of the road, cars passed me left and right. I remember walking back a little dazed, but I was convinced they'd red flag the race and that gave me fifteen minutes to get back to the pits to get the spare out otherwise I'd have to start from the pit lane. It was never a case of thinking, "That's it, my weekend's over." Later I learned that my nieces were screaming at my sister, "Derek, Derek, he's dead."

'Back at the pits, I went into the Arrows garage, not mine, as I was so used to going there after three years in the team. At Lotus, the boys wanted my helmet. I thought they wanted me to stop. But they just wanted to change it for my spare as it was so badly damaged. When I went out in the car again I had a splitting headache. I should never have been allowed to race, but when I drove to my grid position the Italian crowd went absolutely mental. After I'd got on the grid I had to report to the Prof I joined him in the back of the safety car. Bernie Ecclestone was in the front. The Prof said that he had to ask me a few questions. "What's your name?" he asked.

'"Nelson Piquet," I replied. I kept on doing this to all the questions, and Bernie was not amused. He turned round and said, "If you don't answer properly, you're not racing." The Prof asked me where I was and what I was doing. Outside the window, I had a bit of help. There was big sign saying "Monza" and there were a few racing cars around, so I passed Prof's test!'

Was that the most stupid decision of your life? 'Actually, I think what I did at Jerez was more stupid,' said Warwick. 'I knew from Martin's accident that the car was unsafe.' After Donnelly had been taken to hospital in Seville, Warwick returned to his hotel and had some emotional discussions with his dad and his Uncle Stan. 'I didn't think Martin was going to survive,' said Warwick. 'Originally, I told my dad and my Uncle Stan, and a couple of other friends who were with me, that I was not going to drive the following day. But the next morning, my team told me they had been up all night and had put a titanium part to support the bit that broke. They said it couldn't break again, so I agreed to drive. My dad was devastated. But I raced because I thought the team would go bust if I didn't. We were really struggling. On my second lap, the telemetry showed that I had gone through the corner where Martin crashed with my foot flat to the floor. I suppose, that's why we drivers are a special bunch. We have this inner belief – and the ones who don't make it just don't have that faith. How can millions of people understand that when they haven't risked their life, when they haven't found that inner self. I know my gym trainer in Jersey says he has never seen anyone able to go that extra step – even if I am 153 fucking years old.'

Donnelly's life was saved, but his career as a Formula One driver was over. When Senna won his fiftieth pole position in Jerez, on the day after Donnelly's colossal crash, he presented himself at the media conference as an emotionally spent man. 'I seriously thought of not running,' he said. 'I found it hard to cope, to maintain some kind of balance.' This was the first time we had seen in public the sensitive side of Senna's nature; it was not to be the last. The Brazilian's hope of securing victory in the Spanish Grand Prix was dashed by an engine failure – and by winning the race Prost closed the gap in the championship to just nine points.

All eyes turned eastwards towards Japan as, for a second year in succession, Senna and Prost stoked themselves to go head-to-head at Suzuka. Only this time it would become *truly* personal and vindictive. This race remains as notorious today as it was then; as it will do for all eternity.

Trouble brewed from Saturday afternoon. Senna won pole position and he requested that he should start from the left-hand side of the track, the cleaner part of the circuit. His plea was denied, and the cars lined up with Senna on the right of the front row and Prost on the left. Senna was indignant that his plea had been ignored. Prost said, 'Senna wanted to change sides, and because he could not he was blaming me and Balestre. It was always his rules.'

As Senna feared, Prost made a better start on the side of the grid with more traction. With the cars gaining speed in the race to the first right-handed corner, Senna tucked his McLaren under the rear wing of Prost's Ferrari in the centre of the track.

Then he darted to the inside of the Frenchman. When Prost attempted to turn into the first corner, Senna's McLaren collected his Ferrari at around 150mph and the two cars disappeared from the road. Prost's car was on the left without its rear wing, Senna's McLaren was on the right. The two men were only partially visible through clouds of dust as they shuffled away like two gunslingers from a spaghetti Western. Deliberately, they headed in different directions. Prost angry and disbelieving at what Senna had been prepared to risk. Senna avenged – and the new world champion. For a second successive year, they had become embroiled in an accident that had been wholly avoidable and the championship had ended in uproar and controversy.

Allievi was among the first to intercept Senna as he returned to the pit lane. 'Everyone was waiting for Senna at the McLaren pit, but it was the last garage and I went to meet him on his way back,' he explained. 'In perfect Italian, Ayrton said to me, "There are people winning the championship in a chicane, now I won it in a corner." He was very calm, very cold and smiling as he reported to me, "Your Ferrari has crashed!"' Another reporter to get to Senna came from American cable network ESPN. 'Was the accident caused because pole position was on the wrong side of the track and you wanted to change that?' he asked. Unhesitatingly, Senna responded: 'Absolutely! You break your balls to be on the pole and then they put you on the wrong side of the circuit to the benefit of whoever is in second place. I had not such a good start, then we went for the first corner and I went to the inside. He didn't open the door, we touched and we both went off.'

'How do you feel about being the world champion?' asked the TV reporter. The Brazilian shot a big smile straight into the camera. 'It's not a bad feeling at all, is it?'

Jo Ramirez recalled that the first question Senna asked on

reaching the McLaren garage was: 'They aren't going to stop the race, are they?' They were not. But while the race continued almost unnoticed, Prost returned to the paddock to condemn Senna as never before. 'He did it on purpose,' he said. 'He knew he had no chance of winning the race if I got ahead – so he pushed me off. If this is the way the championship is going to be concluded, then the sport is dead. Whatever he may think about me, I can't understand how he is prepared to risk his own safety going into the first corner. I never expected him to do this. I thought he was a member of the human race; that he was hard to race – but always fair. But this? If there is no change in the regulations, if it is not possible to apply sanctions against this sort of driving, then it may not be possible for me to continue in racing. I'm not ready to fight against irresponsible people on the track who are not afraid to die.'

Senna's celebrations were not muted by the controversial conclusion to the championship. 'I don't give a damn what he says,' snorted Senna. 'I can't be responsible for his actions. He moved over on me. As usual, he has his point of view. He has tried to destroy me in the past – but he will not succeed. I have dedicated a lot to winning this championship – and so have my team.'

In France, the television audience included Balestre. The tone of his statement was a mixture of anger and bewilderment. 'It is a scandal that a world championship should be decided on such a collision and I leave everyone to be their own judge of who is to blame,' he said. 'Last year, the race stewards disqualified Senna because he cut short a chicane. This time, they told me on the telephone, that there were no elements to allow Senna's disqualification. In any case, I do think that Senna deserved this world title for his achievements since the beginning of the season. But I regret he did not win it in style.'

At the track, Betise Assumpcao recalled how Senna had remained behind until night fell to make his point known to as wide an audience as possible. Senna had hired Assumpcao to be his personal press officer from the start of the European season that same year. 'Ayrton kept denying the accident was his fault,' she said. 'He was my boss, but I didn't know if he had done it on purpose or not. He denied all blame: in Portuguese, Italian, English. He sat there for hours until dark giving interviews.' At the end of the night, Senna shared drinks with close friends, including Josef Leberer and Karl-Heinz Zimmerman, an Austrian with an impeccable corporate hospitality business within the paddock who these days caters for Ecclestone, VIPS and other Formula One luminaries like Lauda. Zimmerman, a gregarious man, who has a restaurant in the mountains of Austria, remembered mischievously: 'We had some beers and raised our glasses to Ayrton. We used the Austrian word to toast friends: *Prost*!' Zimmerman could be counted in Senna's closest circle of friends. When the Brazilian won a grand prix, Zimmerman fired a salute from a miniature cannon that he transported around the world. 'I think we got on because I was straightforward,' said Zimmerman. Leberer, Berger and Zimmerman formed the Austrian Connection to Senna. 'Everyone thought Ayrton was only focused on his profession – which is true – but he could be a very social guy. He seemed especially to like us mad Austrians!' According to informed sources, Zimmerman kept a list of the good guys and the bad guys in Formula One: Senna was most definitely near the top of the list of good guys and not adverse to taking a schnapps with the Austrian bon viveur.

Senna would later make a public confession about the 1990 Japanese Grand Prix – but we would have to wait a year to hear it.

★　　★　　★

However, when invited to give their verdict on what took place the second time at Suzuka a jury of his peers, interviewed for this book, thought that Senna had behaved injudiciously. 'A lot of people think that was the worst deed ever committed at the wheel of a Formula One car,' argued Martin Brundle. 'He couldn't get the side of the track he wanted – it was an intentional accident.' Derek Warwick said: 'The year before Prost, typically, had chosen a slow corner to have an accident with Senna where he was not going to hurt anybody or anything. But the second crash at Suzuka was an act that could easily have led to death – and should have been immediately stamped on by the FIA. If Andrea de Cesaris had pulled that, he'd have been fucked from here to kingdom come. But Senna could get away with it. It was blatant. It was a 150mph corner and two people could have died there. Not long before, if memory serves me well, a guy had been killed at Suzuka in a F3000 race. But would I have done what Senna did to be world champion? I think I would. Would I have been brave enough? Yes. Would I be proud? No. But for Bernie [Ecclestone] there wasn't a better scenario, was there? He had the greatest driver of all time, this god-like person, as his world champion.'

Gerhard Berger had been forewarned to expect the unexpected. 'In 1989, Prost was not right; he created that accident,' he argued. 'The following year I was with Ayrton, preparing ourselves in the area where we changed our clothes, when he told me: "I am going to have a good show in the first corner." I was in the first row for this show, right behind them. I didn't know what was going to happen. But Ayrton was right: the show was good! Of course, he was to blame for the accident. But, like I said, he was not a guy for compromise.'

Damon Hill had been at Le Mans for a F3000 race that weekend.

'I remember turning on the television in my hotel at around 3 a.m. – and I was racing later that day,' he said. 'But I wanted to see this great race, or that's what I'd hope it would be. Instead, crash, bang, wallop and that was it. I felt really angry. I'd got up in the middle of the night and been denied any kind of race. I was staggered there was no action taken against Ayrton. Some people actually went, "Nice one, you got him back." Senna had no regard for the other twenty-four guys behind on full fuel tanks. It was a completely selfish, irresponsible act. Sorry, but that is a fact.'

Murray Walker said solemnly, 'I think Senna initiated a lot of the ruthless moves you have seen in Formula One. He was a much revered, idolised world champion and drivers that came after him thought, if he can act like that, why couldn't they? But the reason I don't respect him totally was because he was prepared to put his own life, and the lives of others, at risk. The potential consequences of what happened at Japan in 1990 were quite terrifying. He could have taken the whole lot with him – it was a miracle he didn't. When people say it was *quid pro quo*, that Prost did that to him in 1989, my answer is that the circumstances were entirely different. Prost had been aggravated by Senna the whole bloody season in '89 and he'd reached a point where he said, "To hell with you, mate, you're not coming through this time." And he did it at a 40mph corner. Senna had this incredible gift – but he believed he was right whatever he did. He had created this image with the other drivers that if they saw his yellow helmet coming they got out of the way, because if they did not, they knew there was a fair chance he'd drive through them or over them; or do whatever it took.'

And what of Prost? 'I almost stopped and retired the same day,' he admitted last summer. 'Senna's engineer from Honda did resign the same day. Ayrton did not think about other people – he just thought about me. He was prepared to be in a crash and maybe kill himself, or hurt himself. He did not think about this: he was not afraid to kill himself. I think that year we should have been world champions with Ferrari and that would have changed a lot of things.' Senna ensured that we would never know if Prost's intuition had been correct.

After the events that day in Suzuka, Senna wore the crown of Fangio, Clark, Stewart and Lauda. It should have been an aching fit. Senna had told us that he was a champion with values; from that moment we could never confuse them with instincts of sportsmanship and principle established by men like Fangio, Clark, Stewart and Lauda. In a split second, he revealed himself to the world as a man whose obsession with winning, and crucially his obsession with defeating Prost, knew no recognisable boundary.

It was a point that Jackie Stewart, in part, raised with Senna a fortnight later during an interview with him for an American broadcasting company at the final race of the season in Australia. Senna barely retained his renowned composure. Stewart said: 'If I was to count back to all the great champions, and this is the 500th grand prix, the number of times they made contact with other drivers is less than you have done in the last thirty-six months. Why?'

Senna responded curtly, 'I find it amazing for you to make such a question, Stewart. You know a lot about racing, so you should know that by being a racing driver you are under risk all the time. By being a racing driver, it means you are racing with other people. If you no longer go for a gap that exists, you are no longer a racing driver because we are competing to win. And the main motivation for all of us to compete is for a victory. I race to win. Sometimes, you get it wrong for sure; it's impossible to get it right all of the time. Some take risks, some don't. In the end I am the one who is driving. I can only do what speaks from my mind.'

Off camera, Stewart was heard to remark later: 'Kid, you need to grow up.'

As usual Senna headed down to Brazil at the end of the season, a drained but contented man. He enjoyed a long break. 'Winning is done thousands of kilometres away from the racetrack,' as he once put it. The winter was designed to rest his mind and train his body. 'I run always in the middle of the day when the sun is at its hottest,' explained Senna. 'That best approaches the circumstances during a race. It's sticky. It's muggy. It is so tight and sultry in the car and you have to be focused one hundred per cent. Concentration – that's what it's about. Mentally, you have to be very strong. That means you have to be in good physical shape.' Often he ran twelve miles at a stretch.

At the start of the 1991 season, Senna won the first four races in succession, at the time a record. At last, he had his prized victory in the Brazilian Grand Prix in São Paulo. His partnership with Gerhard Berger, in its second season, had moved from strength to strength. 'Gerhard was good for Ayrton,' said Leberer. 'I must say Gerhard was working very hard with the engineers, and stayed longer and longer at the track. Gerhard accepted it was no sense to start a fight with Ayrton. Anyway, he had decided Ayrton wasn't an asshole, he saw that he was someone with real character and Ayrton was good to him.' Jo Ramirez watched the partnership blossom as well. 'We were under no illusions that Berger could take Prost's place,' he said. 'The team had lost one of the two best racing drivers in the world. We were just hoping to have a good relationship between Ayrton and Gerhard, which we did. Gerhard was quick, good and honest and a lovely guy to work with; a friend, then and now. At the end of 1990, Ayrton said to us don't call me until the new car is ready. Gerhard said that he would do all the tests. He worked really hard all winter. Senna came to Silverstone for one test and went to the first race at Phoenix; and Senna was a second quicker and took the pole. Berger was so depressed, I can't tell you. We told him that he was racing the best, and that he would not beat him; but if he was close to him that would be good enough for the team. Berger said that in their time together Senna taught him how to improve as a Formula One driver while he taught him how to have fun.'

One area where Berger held all the aces – at least to begin with – was as a practical joker. 'One time Gerhard called Ron's pilot and told him that Ron didn't need the plane that night,' recalled Leberer. 'Ron turned up at the airport, not knowing about the call, and found it in darkness. Ron got his own back, of course.' The most famous prank of all involved a helicopter and Senna's briefcase. 'Some stories take on a life – and so many people tell this story now as if they were there,' smiled Leberer. 'But the only ones in the helicopter, flying from the team's hotel beside Lake Como to Monza, were Ayrton, Gerhard, Ron and me. Ayrton was the co-pilot and had put his briefcase in the back. Gerhard was trying to open it over Lake Como, because he wanted to throw out the contents. This guy *would* have done it, but he couldn't open it in time. When we came into the circuit over the Royal Park at Monza, there were thousands of people around. As we came in to land, Gerhard threw the briefcase out. Ayrton knew nothing as he was at the controls. After we landed, Ayrton reached for his briefcase and, of course, it was not there. Gerhard said nothing. Suddenly, out of the trees a guy from security is running towards us with the briefcase. As he came closer, Senna recognised it. Can you imagine how he looked? Fuck, I was crying!

It was totally destroyed. Ayrton looked at me, then Gerhard. He was not very happy. Gerhard was saying, "No, no, it wasn't me." Everything was destroyed. He was not very happy at all.'

Berger laughed at the memory. 'It is my favourite joke,' he said. 'But I must say it took Ayrton a while to laugh about it; but he did, eventually.' Frogs, snakes and Super Glue all featured in a stream of preposterous practical jokes that went round like a revolving door. Leberer said Senna ultimately called a halt. 'Ayrton said that we had to stop as Gerhard has no borders,' said Leberer. And Berger? 'The only guy I was afraid about joking around was Keke Rosberg, who was competing on the same level as me,' he said. 'Even I thought twice about doing anything with him.'

As Senna made his immaculate start to the 1991 season, Prost was growing impatient with the performance at Ferrari. He voiced his disappointment in public, and continued to do so. The two men clashed again at the German Grand Prix – with Prost again accusing Senna of underhand behaviour at high speed. 'Next time I'll try to take him on the inside and I'll run him off, that's for sure,' Prost told French journal *La Cinq*. Prost received a suspended one-race ban for his outburst, while Senna was given an official warning for his driving.

By this time, Prost and Mansell tolerated one another, but they no longer played golf. Rather than retire, Mansell had left Ferrari to rejoin Williams Renault for this season and, with a sterling second half of the season, the Englishman became the most serious threat to Senna in the championship. At the Spanish Grand Prix at Barcelona, Mansell and Senna drove down the pit straight wheel-to-wheel at almost 200mph before the Brazilian finally conceded the corner with little to spare. After Mansell won the race, he said with a huge grin: 'Ayrton said I am blip-blip crazy! I laughed. It may have taken this long, but now he thinks *I'm* crazy I am going to be okay!'

With two races left, Senna, who in the autumn had signed to remain with McLaren for 1992 on an estimated £10 million contract, led the championship by sixteen points from Mansell. Prost was in the doldrums, and his future at Ferrari was the subject of much speculation. For the first time since his debut season in 1980, he failed to win a race. His new team-mate, compatriot Jean Alesi, a wonderfully flamboyant driver bulging with charisma, fared even more grimly as Prost at least salvaged three second places from the season.

Once again the championship was on the line at Suzuka; only the protagonists this time were Senna and Mansell. Ramirez recounted the critical elements of the Japanese Grand Prix: 'We produced a fantastic team effort. We came up with an extended nose, which gave the car better balance. Honda came up with more horsepower and Shell came up with "rocket" fuel. We ran this package at Silverstone and were 1.5 seconds faster than we had been before. On the day, we had to beat Mansell. Berger had pole, with Senna second and Mansell third. The plan was for Berger to lead the race from Senna. The idea was just to control Mansell, who had to win the race to stay in the championship. Berger was a second a lap faster than Senna. Mansell was desperate. He went left . . . he went to the right. Senna was driving on his mirrors. Berger was building a lead. In the end, Mansell tried to overtake on the outside of the first corner. Senna left him a little room – and knew that Mansell would have to go off. As soon as Senna saw the big cloud of dust in his mirrors, he must have had a smile inside his helmet. Then Senna went quicker and quicker, and he got past Berger. We planned it all like that – but Berger was to win the race. Not just to thank him for what he did in this race, but to thank him for what he had done all year. Ron was on the radio to Senna: 'Remember, Gerhard is going to win the race.'

Senna: 'What? What? I can't hear you.'

Ron: 'Slow down, Gerhard is going to win.'

Senna: 'I can't hear you!' But he knew exactly what was going to happen, he was just teasing. On the last lap, in front of everyone, he let Gerhard past. Gerhard wasn't happy with the way it was done. That was Ayrton – you couldn't change him.' For a third time in four years, Senna had become world champion. But Mansell, Williams and Renault had shown McLaren that they had galvanised themselves into a force to be feared in the future.

At the press conference at Suzuka Senna rewound the calendar one year, then two. He had a platform and he had much to say; so much. 'Before you ask me . . . 1989 was a disgraceful year here,' said Senna. 'I still today struggle to cope with that when I think about it. You all know what took place: I won the race, and I was robbed of it. And that was not justice. What took place over that winter was really shit.

'Then, 1990 was . . . to prove a point, to show everyone that what you do here, you pay. When we came to Suzuka I was in the lead of the championship. Before practice, myself and Gerhard went to the officials, to change pole position, because it was in the wrong place. They said, "Yes, no problem." I got pole – and then what happened? Balestre gave an order and the officials said, "Oh, no, no, we don't change the pole position." And we said, "But we agreed before that it should be on the left." It was an order from Balestre and I know that from inside the system.

'I said to myself, "OK, you try to work clean, to do your job properly, and you get screwed by stupid people. If at the start, because I am in the wrong place, Prost beats me off the line, at the first corner I am going for it – and he'd better not turn in ahead of me, because he's not going to make it. And it just happened like this."'

There was more, as Senna gathered steam. 'He [Prost] took a chance – and it didn't work, because I went for it. I didn't care if we crashed. I went for it, and we crashed. That was a result of what happened in 1989. It was unavoidable. Why did I cause the accident? Because . . . if you get fucked by the system every single time you try to do your job cleanly and properly, what should you do? It was a result of a bad decision, influenced by Balestre. It was not my responsibility – I contributed to it, yes, but it was not my responsibility.'

It was, however, Senna's revenge.

Prost's season was doomed to end with the ignominy of the sack. His crime? He publicly declared his Ferrari uncompetitive. Towards the end of the year in which he accumulated thirty-four points, while Senna filed ninety-six points as he won his third title, Prost likened his Ferrari to 'a truck'. He was not the first racing driver to so comprehensively abuse his car with such a withering condemnation. It was only a figure of speech – but this was the moment the Ferrari management had been waiting for to hang him out to dry. How dare anyone be so irreverent about a *Ferrari*? It was much easier for the management to blame the team's slump on Prost's performance. But had Prost really become such a bad driver over the course of a season? And what of Alesi, whom everyone within the paddock acknowledged was fast, fearless and a driver of immense potential. Alesi won twenty-one points in 1991.

But Ferrari is unlike any other racing team. It is an inviolable institution within Italy, just as the Vatican is.

Prost would be made to pay for his perceived insolence. Before the final race of the season in Australia, the three-times world champion was informed that his contract had been terminated with immediate effect. He was to be replaced at the Australian Grand Prix by Gianni Morbidelli. Who? Actually, he was Ferrari's test driver who revered Prost.

Pino Allievi instinctively felt that Prost had been treated unfairly and unreasonably. 'Prost probably arrived in the wrong moment for Ferrari,' he said. 'There was a lot of change inside the team, a lot of people without experience and a lot of people who spoke too much without knowing anything about Formula One. They came only with a big ego and arrogance; but without experience. First, the car was not competitive. Second all these people who had arrived started to say Prost was not good, instead of saying we had done a shitty car. No one wanted to take responsibility. They took the excuse to fire Prost because he said his car was like "driving a truck". It's normal for a driver to speak these things without offence. I remember Regazzoni said it a thousand times; Lauda said it. They took this excuse to end a story that was already ended months before.'

To shame Prost? 'It was disgusting, a bad moment for Ferrari,' said Allievi. 'Prost had been hurt by this situation. Morbidelli was put in the car and he was the biggest fan of Prost. It was surreal. It was a big, big story in Italy because Prost was one of the most respected men of the sport; and Ferrari was Ferrari.'

Alain Prost would play no part in the 1992 world championship – a man fired and with no natural home to take his talents at such short notice. Sometimes, even the great men of history are dumped on their backside for no conceivably good reason.

17

HOW SENNA MOCKED PROST
WITH ROAD KILL

As a signal of his intentions, Mansell had established a base in Florida on the Gulf of Mexico. He wanted a warmer climate to train for the 1992 season, a season he believed would be a watershed in his life. He bought a colonial-style property in Clearwater, and moved his family with him from the Isle of Man to escape the British winter. He also vowed to lose weight by altering his diet and training harder than ever. He declined to have surgery on a damaged foot as a two-month rehabilitation timetable would have interfered with his fitness programme. Mansell opted to live with the pain.

He had sensed that he had a car to win the championship – at last. His faith was not misplaced in the Williams car designed by technical director Patrick Head with an aerodynamic package perfected by Adrian Newey, a boffin who would later command driver-size salaries at McLaren, and Red Bull where he is currently employed. The '92 Williams FW14 had 'active' suspension and electronic wizardry that allowed drivers to change settings from inside the cockpit to suit conditions on the track.

Mansell won the first race of the year in South Africa, and he stood proudly to attention on the podium as they played the British national anthem. It was to become the soundtrack for the season. 'Plan one was to lose weight and arrive here fit,' said Mansell. 'Plan two was to come out of the box and win here. I think everyone knows plan three.' Senna had been disappointed – but not critical – that McLaren had not delivered a new car for the new season in South Africa. 'Sometimes, it is better to have a result like this,' he said, speaking solemnly after his third-place finish. 'Hopefully, it will push people, get them motivated. Perhaps, later in the season, we can fight Williams again. But, for now, we have no chance.'

While Prost had his nose pressed against the paddock window, assessing his future options as he attended grand prix races for French television station TF1, Senna soon found himself with a new protagonist: a young German called Michael Schumacher. At the third round of the championship in Brazil, Schumacher ran in close proximity with Senna before the world champion retired after eighteen laps. Afterwards Schumacher publicly accused Senna of playing 'dangerous games'. Senna had left the track before the twenty-three-year-old German, driving in only his ninth grand prix, spoke to the media, but he later heard what had been said. Senna dismissed him as 'just a stupid boy'.

The tables had been turned on Senna, no question. Just as the Brazilian had targeted Prost, Schumacher had clearly chosen to make himself a nuisance in the presence of Senna. The atmosphere between the two men, the great champion and the young pretender, became increasingly tense as the summer unfolded. On the first lap at the French Grand Prix at Magny Cours,

Schumacher and Senna collided after the German made a failed and uncompromising overtaking manoeuvre at the Adelaide hairpin. The race was stopped, but Senna's car was damaged beyond repair. By the time the debris had been cleared to facilitate a restart, Senna had changed out of his flame-proof overalls into a pair of jeans. He approached Schumacher on the grid, telling Jo Ramirez as he left the McLaren garage: 'Watch this.' Ramirez dutifully did as he was requested. 'As Michael was pulling on his helmet, Senna was pointing at him,' he said. 'I was too far away to hear what he was saying, but Schumacher was very attentive. I could tell that Schumacher was for Senna what Senna had been for Prost. Ayrton came back past me with a big smile, and said, "You watch!" After the race began for a second time he [Schumacher] crashed his Benetton Ford into Stefano Modena's Jordan. Ayrton had completely destabilised Schumacher – but he knew it was temporary because he could see Schumacher was the up and coming star.'

Even then, two years before he won the first of his seven world titles, Schumacher was a man without fear of picking a quarrel. 'If someone is making a mistake in my eyes I have to tell it the way I see it,' he said, untroubled by how Senna would react to such blatant provocation. 'They all know what I think of them. They cannot just do what they want with me.' Two weeks after the contretemps in France, Senna took exception to Schumacher's driving during a test session at Hockenheim, in Germany. The two of them took it in turns to spoil each other's testing programme by playing cat-and-mouse on the throttle and brakes.

Senna's patience snapped. He walked down the pit lane to confront Schumacher, as Mansell had once done to him. According to whom you believe, the Brazilian threw a punch at Schumacher or else grabbed him by the neck of his overalls and gave him a hard shove. Whatever actually took place, Senna's displeasure had been expressed face-to-face with Schumacher. Several mechanics intervened to prevent an escalation of the trouble. Senna was heard to yell, 'You show some respect.'

Schumacher's later controversial and ruthless collisions with Damon Hill in 1994, when he won the world championship, then with Jacques Villeneuve in 1997, when he failed to win the title, can be traced perhaps to those exchanges with Senna. James Allen, who commentated for ITV in succession to Murray Walker, has written two books on Schumacher. 'Senna's gift as a racing driver was sublime, but his self belief was the thing which made him the driver he was,' said Allen. 'The same was true of Schumacher, even though he had done comparatively little at that point he knew he belonged in the highest echelons of the sport.'

As Senna dealt with a fresh rival and Mansell ran away with the world championship, Prost had not been idle. He had known from the previous year that Williams and Renault had created an impressive and ultra-competitive car. His currency may have been devalued by Ferrari's insensitivities to what he believed was constructive criticism, but within Renault and Elf, a French oil company also in partnership with Williams, Prost was still a driver of immense worth. Frank Williams had long admired Prost's talent. 'An understated and quiet man,' said Williams. In April 1992, Prost signed a two-year contract to drive for Williams Renault from the following season. And it seemed, in the bargain, Prost had outwitted Senna. The Frenchman's negotiations included one specific clause to be written into his contract – the right to veto Senna from joining the team. 'After the bad situation with Ayrton, I asked Frank and the Renault people that I cannot accept to be in a team with him again,' said Prost. 'I did not care about being No. 1 and I was okay with being with Nigel again. It was written in my contract that Senna would not be able to drive with me. I remember the French press was against me again after this. I tried to explain that I can work to be world champion against Senna as a rival, but not as a team-mate. I cannot accept this any more.'

Whether Senna knew of the deal or not, he courted Williams that year as Mansell, and his team-mate Riccardo Patrese, obliterated the opposition in a simply magnificent car. The Brazilian was shameless. On the very day that Mansell clinched the world title in Hungary – five races from the end of the championship – he made an open plea to be given a seat for 1993. Williams has a vivid memory of how Senna approached him. 'It was Nigel's big day, the team's big day,' he said. 'We arrived at the little heliport by the medical centre at the track to get a quick ride out – I think I was with Patrick – when, fuck me, in front of everybody, Ayrton is running after me shouting, "I want to talk to you, stop, stop, STOP." I was astonished by his behaviour; I was affronted, but it was ballsy. He pursued Patrick and me telling us he wanted to drive my car. I mean, take it easy; it was Nigel's big day, but that was Ayrton, wasn't it?'

Reportedly, Senna made a later attempt to get himself into the Williams team by offering to drive for nothing. It has to be admitted, this did sound a little unlikely; but what was not in dispute was that he was now actively thinking of leaving McLaren and he had his eye firmly set on getting a Williams contract. 'It is no secret that I have been trying very hard to get some deal with Williams,' admitted Senna. 'If I cannot get a competitive car I would rather take a year off.' Betise Assumpcao recalled,

'Ayrton was pissed off that Prost had beaten him to the Williams drive.'

Ironically, Mansell's own future with Williams suddenly became the issue of the hour. His negotiations with the team for a new improved contract, as world champion, faltered on Williams' unwillingness to meet his demands. Mansell's position had been weakened by Prost's recruitment – but he stubbornly persisted in demanding what he thought was a fair deal. Williams told me how talks with Mansell finally broke down. 'The team was well funded, but we spent everything we got on the drivers and the team won championships,' he said. 'That was great – but we felt a need to be a bit more profitable. Does that sound bollocks? We had to save for a rainy day and keep developing the car as there was a lot of technology around in those days. We were just cautious with our money – and Nigel was outrageous in his demands for 1993. At the end of the day, Nigel came down a bit, we went up a bit and Renault also came up with some money. But we had already signed Prost and that made retaining Nigel less than a priority. Nigel chose not to accept the terms offered.'

Mansell was bitterly disappointed. In his hour of triumph, at the end of the season of his dreams, at the culmination of a life-time's blood, sweat and tears, he knew he had effectively signed his resignation papers from Formula One when he declined Williams' final offer. As events transpired, Mansell decamped to the United States on a permanent basis and won the IndyCar championship to create motor racing history by winning major titles on both sides of the Atlantic in successive years. It was his due reward for his fortitude, as well as his undeniable courage and speed.

Senna's own contractual negotiations had fared little better. He won three races in 1992 as Mansell triumphed nine times and came second on three other occasions in the sixteen-race championship. At the end of the season, McLaren lost their Honda engines as the Japanese company withdrew from the sport due to recessionary pressures at home – does that sound familiar? Senna was so emotionally distraught when he heard the news of Honda's withdrawal that he actually had to halt an interview with a television station while he wiped tears from his eyes. Honda had been behind the Brazilian's rise and rise to the pinnacle of the sport and there was no knight in shining armour to ride in to replace them. McLaren had to revert to Ford Cosworth power for 1993. For Honda's British PR man Eric Silbermann the company's retreat from Formula One had a more profound effect. 'I was out of work,' he said. 'I had to get a train home from Langley because I had to leave my office car behind!' At this time, Senna was generally unimpressed with the whole scenario of Formula One. He was disillusioned by a generation of cars governed by technological aids. The Brazilian, now thirty-two, had not reached an agreement with Ron Dennis on a new contract and that winter he returned to Brazil with much on his mind. At his office at São Paulo, on the top floor of a tower block where he was able to land the helicopter that he personally flew, Senna told *The Times* Chief Sports Correspondent David Miller in February 1993, 'I want to be challenged by my own limits together with someone else's limits, by someone who is made of the same skin and bone, where the difference is between brain and experience and adaptation to the course; not challenged by someone else's computer. I don't want a car from Ron Dennis to let me win, but a car to let me compete.'

In essence, Williams had a jump on the opposition and Senna found it hard to stomach that he would not be able to persistently challenge their dominance: or be able to inflict further pain on Prost. But Williams had problems of their own to overcome after missing the deadline to enter the championship. Benetton Ford were one of two teams who opposed their re-admission, as team principal Flavio Briatore tried to use the moment to leverage cost-cutting proposals like banning the use of a spare car and a reduction in testing. Again, is this a familiar sounding story from the times we live in? While Prost waited to be granted a super licence for his return, as Williams battled to overcome the political shenanigans, McLaren took the precaution of naming three drivers for the '93 championship: Michael Andretti, Mika Hakkinen and Senna.

The Brazilian's contract negotiations had also reached an impasse. Senna and Dennis no longer enjoyed the same relationship that had prevailed in earlier years. Contractual negotiations had become protracted and increasingly unpleasant. Senna had long since shredded the idea of a standard team-driver contract. The more he won, the more privileges he demanded. Dennis countered by being just as finicky over each clause. I am reliably informed that at this stage Senna's contract ran to over 140 pages – each one sent backwards and forwards from Woking to São Paulo for forensic examination. Bernie Ecclestone identified another stumbling block. 'Ron normally finds a way to upset his drivers,' said Ecclestone. 'Ask Niki Lauda; ask Prost. In the end, I think that's what happened. Ayrton wasn't very happy at all. I saw the relationship between Ron and Senna deteriorate, it was obvious to everybody. Exactly the same happened between Ron and Fernando Alonso in 2007.'

Ron Dennis is a man of towering achievements. 'I came from

a humble background,' he said, speaking at the McLaren Technology Centre in the aftermath of the celebration surrounding Lewis Hamilton's coronation in November 2008 as the youngest world champion in Formula One history. 'But my parents fed me, clothed me and put a roof over my head until I was twenty-two, or twenty-three years old and that left me without a worry. That was a struggle for them – but that was my break in life.' Immaculately preserved cars driven by Lauda, Prost, Senna and Hakkinen, all world champions, are on display in the entrance boulevard of the McLaren HQ to symbolise the team's enduring success under Dennis. Trophy cabinets are bursting with silverware. (The team's collection was restored to full complement at Christmas 1995 when Prost presented Dennis with a newly made replica of the 1989 Monza trophy that he had thrown into the crowd to the great pain of his boss.)

Dennis is a racing man through and through. Yet he is also a complex man. He is demanding of himself, and all those around him. He also likes total control at all times. Over the past twenty-eight years I have watched Dennis build a motor racing team of enviable strength, and a company of burgeoning horizons. If that has offended some rivals, he is unapologetic. 'Most people like a winner, but they don't like consistent winners,' said Dennis, in an interview with Gerald Donaldson at a time when Senna and Prost reigned at McLaren. 'If I walk around with a grin on my face I am smug. If I walk around with a scowl people say I'm miserable. It is so disheartening to try so hard to do a job well, then achieve success and feel it should logically attract recognition of a job well done, then not get that recognition. When people perceive you as an underdog, they are very supportive. Then when you're on top they turn you from a David into a Goliath and immediately try to tear you down.'

His basic philosophy is the same today, as it was then. 'The secret is attention to detail,' he told Donaldson. 'Everything is important. You have to start with really fundamental basics. When someone walks into a room I notice straightaway such details as fingernails, whether they are cleaned and manicured; how the person is dressed, whether they're scruffy, or neat and tidy. If you don't have any respect for your own body, then I think you tend to have a lack of personal discipline.' In another passage from the same interview Dennis revealed: 'The only way I measure my performance is by my own values. It's very similar to the methods Ayrton Senna uses to get his performance. Ayrton is tremendously demanding, both of himself and his team. You really have to keep your mind focused and watch that everything functions in an optimum way. It's damn hard, and very wearing, and very fatiguing, and not made any easier when it's criticised.'

Over the winter of 1993, the fight Dennis had on his hands was from within; and from his star asset, Ayrton Senna, who refused to sign a new deal. John Hogan, from paymasters Marlboro, reacted to the crisis by hosting a meeting for Dennis and Senna in Lausanne in January. 'To cut a long story short, we wheeled and dealed all day,' said Hogan. Was Senna really going to walk away, you ask. 'Would you have taken the chance?' replied Hogan. 'Would you have taken a chance knowing this emotionally crippled, focused, demonic, best driver in the world? I wasn't. It might have been one of the greatest bluffs of all time, who knows.' Finally, with Senna's manager Julian Jakobi in attendance as well, a compromise was brokered. Hogan explained: 'We assumed if we all worked together we could persuade other sponsors to up the ante, including Shell as well as ourselves.' Senna would race through 1993 on a race-by-race – for the princely sum of one million dollars a race.

Hakkinen was stood down to the role of test driver at McLaren – but his day would come. The Williams team was duly re-admitted to the championship and Prost received his super licence. Normal service could resume. And it did: Prost won on his Williams debut and Senna came second at the South African Grand Prix. Yet from this point, the Brazilian majestically took command of the championship. Senna won at home in Brazil in a race that was staged in worsening rain. Prost spun out. The result could not have been better choreographed in a city that needs little excuse to start a carnival. Adriane Galisteu was one of the promotion girls working for Shell at the race and Senna met her for a second time at the post-race party. 'I think Ayrton picked out one or two other Shell girls before he met Adriane!' smiled Assumpcao. Senna had a discreet, if not obvious, charm around women, and he dated Australia's supermodel Elle McPherson as well as a succession of strikingly beautiful girls from Brazil. There had been perhaps two who stayed with him for longer than most. After his divorce, his first serious girlfriend was Marjorie Andrade, a brunette, who was seen with Senna in the period he drove for Lotus. But the woman who had been closest to Senna – before Adriane Galisteu – was Brazilian TV presenter Xuxa Meneghel. She rarely travelled to races with Senna as her commitments with TV Globo prevented her from doing so, but Xuxa was closely associated with him between 1988 and 1992. Meneghel, according to writer Tom Rubython, who is the author of a comprehensive biography of Senna, was 'adored by the da Silva family'.

No one had taken a permanent place in his life, however. 'I think Adriane turned up at a time in Ayrton's life when he was receptive to the possibility of a relationship,' explained Assumpcao. 'Before that, he would not commit himself. He wasn't like David

Beckham, always seen at the "in" parties. He wasn't that chatty or spontaneous – but Adriane was. As the months passed, he agreed to picture shoots with Adriane that he had never entertained before. One set of pictures included Ayrton hugging Adriane from behind while she was wearing a bikini. The family wanted to veto those pictures from being published – but Ayrton insisted that they should be used. Through that year, Ayrton started to change.' His trainer – and much more besides – Josef Leberer said, knowingly: 'Ayrton cast a spell on women, it's that simple.'

But one aspect of Senna's persona remained consistent: he still wanted to be the architect of Prost's downfall, even if he felt he was at a disadvantage in a McLaren that was inferior to the Frenchman's Williams. One of Williams' major sponsors that year was computer games company Sega, whose character Sonic the Hedgehog was a motif on the cars of Prost and his team-mate, Damon Hill. Mischievously, Senna's car at the next race, the European Grand Prix at Donington, was adorned with a flattened hedgehog embossed on the side of his McLaren's nose. The message was unequivocal: Senna had crushed Prost beneath the wheels of his still raging ambition and the cartoon road kill was his way of mocking his nemesis one more time.

At Donington, Senna's drive in the wet passed instantly into the folklore of Formula One's colourful history. 'If I take one lap to my grave, it's going to be the first lap at Donington in 1993,' said Murray Walker. Senna had been fourth on the grid, and dropped back a place after the start. It mattered little to the Brazilian. The track was treacherous from rainfall, showers peppered the circuit, and he was about to illustrate the beguiling range of his brilliance. First, the Brazilian appeared through a cloud of spray to pass Schumacher. Next to be overtaken was Karl

Wendlinger, devoured at breakneck speed. Then Hill was caught and passed. 'I remember the spray when Senna went past,' smiled Hill. 'When everyone else was being cautious, he was off... gone. Brilliant – but he knew he could do that.' With almost indecent haste Senna closed down Prost, whose lead of the grand prix lasted only as far as the hairpin on the first lap. Senna slid through on the inside – and was never troubled again. Prost, in contrast, searched continuously to find the correct tyres for the conditions. Astonishingly, he made seven pit stops, yet Prost still finished third with Hill second, both of them obliterated by the brilliance of the Brazilian's driving. 'In the press conference, Ayrton took the piss out of Alain,' said Hill. 'He gloated and it was slightly unattractive. Poor old Alain, his uncertainty that afternoon certainly got the better of him.'

Afterwards Senna acknowledged that, even by his standards of excellence, he had driven an exceptional race. 'I don't remember a grand prix won in such a style,' he said. 'You think you have a limit, as soon as you touch that limit something happens and suddenly you go a little bit further with your mind power, your determination, and your instinct. You can fly very high.' That day Senna soared across the heavens – and he had another flattened hedgehog attached to his car. Berger, re-signed by Ferrari from McLaren at the end of 1992 and placed on an exorbitant contract, laughed knowingly at what his friend had done. 'Ayrton was pissed off having a Ford engine,' he said. 'He had to wait for special circumstances to compete – and he made everyone look stupid!'

Hill, who had been promoted from test driver to take the second Williams seat after Mansell had departed, had found Prost to be an easy, undemonstrative man to learn from. Later, he would also have brief exposure to being inside the same team as Senna. His observations are educational: 'Alain was the professor, an alchemist trying to concoct something in his car,' said Hill. 'He never said too much. My vague recollection with Alain was that if Ayrton's name came up, he'd give a knowing smile. I don't think Alain was malicious – he might be quite a good operator, let's say. I don't think he liked the animosity; I don't think he understood it. You can only put it down to the fact that Ayrton knew he was a threat, and so Alain became his target. I remember being at a karting event for Formula One drivers at Bercy, in Paris, and Ayrton was all the time watching Alain. He couldn't take his eyes off him. Alain's style was sublime in an F1 car, that's the only way I can put it. You just didn't see him do anything. He hardly used a kerb, he didn't put it in the dirt.' Hill deliberately affected a mock-French accent to accentuate his point. 'Alain was just a leetle beet of zis, a leetle bit of zat,' he smiled. 'You watched him and his hands aren't moving.

'Nigel Mansell was dramatic, a passionate man, who swung one way then the other. Ayrton, however, created an impression that if you were around him something really important for the world was taking place. This was not just confined to racing. In England, we have this self-effacing trait. We don't like self-importance, aggrandisement if you like. But if you are carrying the hopes of a vast nation, like Brazil, which is what Ayrton was doing, he was not just a racing driver, not just any old sportsman. From his perspective, he had a big responsibility. He was very intense. He wanted to know the message that he was conveying had got across. It was that passion, that concern for what he was doing that struck you. He treated himself seriously; he wanted almost to coach his engineers to engage them to get to the same level of intensity.

'Prost was cordial, very polite. He was very sweet, not slow to give you recognition. It's not easy to go up to someone and say, "Hey, well done for beating me." There is never any let up in Formula One. Even if you are a three-times world champion, like Alain, there is always some little bastard trying to bite your ankles. I can imagine what it was like for him with Ayrton in the same team. Ayrton did create the idea that he had a God-given right to dominate the sport. I took issue with that side of his thinking. It's a sport; you try to be in front, but no one has a right to be in front.'

Hill later sampled an embittered rivalry of a kind with Schumacher. 'I did get involved, I suppose, in a similar rivalry as Prost and Senna,' he said. 'I did my best against a guy who had no idea how good he was going to be. At times, I was beating myself up. I'd liken it to boxing; it always comes down to a showdown. Was I taken off by Schumacher in Australia for the world championship in 1994? I think there is a pattern to Michael's career that supports that theory is all I'd say. In motor racing things happen. I think it was Michael's loss that he wouldn't allow a competitive team-mate to be hired alongside him. If he had wanted to show he was better than anyone else he would have benefited from having an Alain Prost to his Ayrton Senna in his own team. But he didn't and that was when the sport lost a lot of its appeal because Michael had a whole team to himself. He was like the lone champion – and that deprived a lot of us of an important ingredient in Formula One.'

Senna's race-by-race agenda was not without its drama, as Jo Ramirez recalled. 'Ron had to rob banks between races to get Ayrton's money!' said Ramirez, dryly. 'Ayrton wouldn't leave Brazil until his money had been deposited. I remember how he almost missed the San Marino Grand Prix at Imola. Ayrton arrived from São Paulo in Rome on the morning of the first session of the weekend. I went in the company plane to collect him and Ron said, "You better have him here by the start of practice or you've lost your job." We couldn't land at Fiumicino Airport, in Rome, as they didn't allow private planes. So we landed elsewhere and I asked the pilot to keep the engines running while I took a taxi to meet Ayrton at Fiumicino. At the airport, I asked the taxi driver to wait. I trusted him and left my briefcase with him. When I came out of the terminal with Ayrton there was no sign of my taxi driver. Senna had arrived first class by Varig [Brazil's national airline at the time] and the driver hadn't been allowed to stop where I had got out; this was normal, but I wasn't thinking. I assumed that he was probably doing a lap of the airport and on his way back, but Ayrton didn't want to wait. He wanted to take another taxi. I told him I couldn't leave without my briefcase. "Fuck your briefcase," said Senna. I told him it held company tickets, money and important documents. My life is in that briefcase, I told him.

'In that case, Senna wanted to know, why I had left it with the taxi driver? He was really twitchy, and complained that we were going to be late. I lost my head then. "Fuck it, it's your fault," I said, loudly. "Everyone has to run around like chickens without a head because of *you*. If you'd got in the night before like a normal driver this wouldn't happen. Now you ask me to lose my briefcase because of you."'

In the event, Ramirez weakened, as most people did in the presence of Senna's authority. 'We took another taxi and carried on arguing,' he recalled. 'At the other airport, the plane was geared up to leave as soon as we had arrived. But as we taxied out to take off I looked out of the window and saw my original taxi driver running towards us with my briefcase. In this moment, my belief in human nature was completely restored. I stepped from the plane, took the case and gave the driver some lire. When I came back inside the plane, even Ayrton was smiling. He didn't quite say sorry, but his smile said it for him. Once we had landed at Bologna, a helicopter was waiting. At the circuit, we had to land in the football stadium next door. We had a little scooter waiting for Ayrton. When he reached the paddock, he didn't have the chance even for a coffee. He had time only to get to the motorhome and change into his overalls for the first practice. Senna went out in his car – and promptly crashed! He was just overtired. He didn't score a point that weekend. But Ron couldn't do anything about it – he just had to find the money.'

Hogan watched this debacle, when Senna unusually spun three times during two days of practice, and took counsel from James Hunt. 'James was a great reader of an athlete,' said Hogan. 'He was a great tennis player and knew all these guys and how they worked. I said to James, "He's asleep, he's knackered." James disagreed. He argued that blokes who are as fit as Senna don't get knackered. James explained that Senna hadn't been focused, but he assured me that Senna would pull it all together. I trusted his judgement. Actually, James and Ayrton got quite friendly. I remember a funny story. James had an Austin A35 van by then as his main mode of transport. One night he went out to dinner with Ayrton and Julian Jakobi. He parked the van in Cadogan Square, or one of those posh squares in the West End. After dinner they walked back to their respective cars and Ayrton took one look at James's van and said, "*What's that?*" Well, the night ended with the two of them doing laps around the square in the van, tyres screeching and belching smoke! They became big mates and when, sadly, James died, Ayrton said to me, "The bloke was an absolute lunatic, but what a great guy.'"

Senna's third win of the season came at Monaco, where he won for a sixth time to establish a new record. And this was accomplished after a heavy 160mph accident on the first day of practice. 'Ayrton hit his thumb hard on the steering wheel,' said Leberer. 'I treated him, of course, but it was still difficult especially at a track like Monaco with all the bumps and gear changes. But for the race I fixed the taping on his hand so that he could change gear. I was doing no more than my job, which was why I was there.' Prost, on pole, had been penalised for jumping the start. Once again, Senna had revelled in the embarrassment of his nemesis. He wore a wide smile when he was accompanied to the black tie gala dinner that night by Adriane, the woman who was broadening his perspective on life.

As that summer unfolded, there was an unseen amount of business taking place. Senna was in deep discussions with Williams, even as Prost had constructed a commanding lead over the Brazilian in the championship by winning in Canada, France, Britain – his fiftieth grand prix victory – and Germany; which turned out to be his last. Leberer was privy to some of the calls that Senna received. 'Ayrton trusted me one hundred per cent, and in the evening he took telephone calls in my company sometimes,' he said. 'Once Ayrton called me from his home in Brazil – it was 2 a.m. in Europe. He talked to me about what could happen if he changed the colour of his team. Then he realised I had been sleeping – but it was on his mind and he needed to speak. He wanted me to know that it was clear that I would come with him wherever he went.'

For Prost the call that would change the direction of his life came from Frank Williams in July. 'It was during the summer break in the season and I was in the South of France,' said Prost, as we lunched at his apartment in the 16th *arrondissement* in the summer of 2008. 'He asked to see me – but I explained that I was on holiday and needed the break. But Frank said that he *needed* to see me the next day and would come by plane to meet me in Biarritz. I realised it must be important – yet at the same time I was under contract to Williams for 1994 so what could be that important? When Frank arrived, he told me that he was under increasing pressure from Renault to have Senna in his team for 1994.'

Prost requested time to clear his mind. He held a contract that specifically prevented Senna from driving a Williams while he was in the team. But, then, as history has shown, what real value does a Formula One contract have when the bargaining becomes hard ball? Prost said, 'I wanted to see for myself what Renault wanted to do. I know they wanted to win the championship with me, but they also wanted to show that they can win a championship with Nigel, with me, and then in the future with Ayrton and probably Michael. The driver was not so important for them. In the end, I said, "Okay, let me have three weeks, then I will decide if I accept Ayrton or not." I had plenty of power. If they hired Ayrton without my permission, they would be in breach of contract.'

The Frenchman thought through his options in the weeks he asked to deliberate. Then he placed a call. 'In August, I told them, "Okay, you want Ayrton, and he wants to drive for nothing, he drives for nothing! Then you pay me my contract for 1994. That is the only deal – you pay me and I go away." I'd had enough of all their stories, of all the politics. I think this was a deal driven more by Renault than Williams. You know, the funny thing is I talked about this with Patrick Head from Williams at Monaco this year, fifteen years later. Patrick is a racing man and I am a racing man and we had a good relationship, but he explained to me he was not really aware of all the politics. There were a lot of things he did not know.'

Williams met Senna in his hotel room during the Hungarian Grand Prix in mid-August, when the two men came to a verbal agreement. Negotiations were completed with Jakobi some time not long afterwards. However, the actual news was not made public until the Portuguese Grand Prix in late September. Prost announced his retirement – only to be upstaged when Senna declared that he would leave McLaren at the end of the season after six seasons with the team. Prost said in Estoril, 'It is a difficult decision, but it has been growing all year. I made it about a month ago, I wanted to make it after winning the championship, but the way circumstances have developed, it is better for me and the team to do it now and concentrate on the title. There is no one reason. I think it's enough. After thirteen years, I will finish driving. There will not be another comeback.'

Senna's own disenchantment with Dennis had reached a nadir a week earlier when an 'off the record' briefing had appeared in a Brazilian publication. The tenor of the message was that Dennis felt Senna's demands had made him 'unemployable'. The Brazilian's press conference shone a light on his feelings. 'I wish Ron was beside me now, because there were some negative comments from him,' said Senna. 'It's very sad and I feel sorry. We have worked together for six years and won three championships. You need respect and it has not always been there. I did as much for the team as they did for me and for him to say those things is very unfortunate and I think he will regret that.'

Frank Williams had his man – at last. And in the summer of

2008, against the weight of history and the passing of time, Williams thought wistfully of some of those who have driven for him with panache. 'Alan Jones [1980 champion] was a man's man with an Australian swagger, just getting on with it with an Australian attitude in the car,' said Williams. 'Keke Rosberg was flamboyant, always on the power, always hanging his car out. Nigel had sheer physical and mental strength, and more than enough skill. Alain was the daintiest driver we ever had. He drove as slowly as he could get away with and Damon, at times, pressed him hard. But when Alain was really pushed, he was a pleasure to watch. Ayrton . . . well, he was just a world-class event. I can't say that I'd waited ten years, since that early test he had in our car at Donington, but Williams was an inevitable destination for Ayrton, wasn't it?'

On an open telephone line from Brazil in mid-October Senna's own enthusiasm for his new challenge was perceptible. 'This is a great dream come true for me,' he said. 'Since that first test at Donington, we have talked and we have negotiated over the years and now finally we have come together. But winning the championship will be tough. It is so long since my last one, I have almost forgotten what it feels like.'

Senna won his last two races for McLaren at the end of the 1993 season, in Japan and Australia. After the race in Suzuka, Senna took exception to the driving of debutant Eddie Irvine from Ulster. The Brazilian burst into the Jordan team room at the track – and threw a left hook at Irvine. 'Ayrton whacked him in the face,' said Betise Assumpcao, who had run after Senna, who reacted furiously after he had been told that Irvine had been disrespectful towards him in an interview broadcast on television. When Senna had lapped Irvine, the Ulsterman barged back past again. 'Irvine was a shit – I'd have hit him,' said Assumpcao. 'Ayrton was furious – I realised this was not the right time to tell him he'd done the wrong thing.' Senna had to be pulled away by his engineer, Georgio Ascanelli. Irvine was unrepentant. 'Senna can't talk,' he said. 'I remember the stories about him at the start of his career.' Senna eventually escaped with a two-race suspended sentence for his misdemeanour.

Having finished second, Prost was in company with Senna before the podium presentation and press conference. 'It was quite a long time since we had spoken and I suggested to Ayrton that we might show the people that our relationship was getting better,' said Prost. On the podium, Senna flatly ignored the privately made request. 'In the press conference he was just aggressive,' said Prost. 'Only when we were in Australia did I understand why.'

Before his final grand prix for McLaren, I interviewed Dennis at his office at Woking. 'Ayrton detracted from one of the team's best grand prix wins,' he admitted. Yet Dennis, with no brief for further loyalty, arranged an array of mitigating circumstances in a case for Senna's defence. 'There were a whole range of circumstances that led to Senna's behaviour – incompetent flag marshals, stewards who failed to give Irvine a stop-go penalty for holding up the race leader in contravention of two articles of the Sporting Code, and Irvine's continuing arrogance after the race,' he argued.

Dennis then talked of the man he had known and worked with for the past six years. It was an illuminating experience. 'All athletes, especially those who are the best in the world, normally carry with them character traits which are difficult to handle and accommodate. That especially applies to those in team sports. The successful ones, those driven by an intense desire to succeed at all costs, occasionally make mistakes which they subsequently regret. That observation can be applied to the greatest sportsmen who have ever existed. It's a legacy of the beast. And, as a company who exist to win, we reluctantly have to accept that is occasionally the case.

'Overall, I feel his desire to win every grand prix sometimes detracts from his greatness. But the overwhelming memory will be of good times shared, be it sometimes expensive! We both feel it is better for us to have a spell not working together. We are so hard on each other. But I don't consider next weekend the end. Just an interlude.'

In Adelaide, Senna fittingly won pole position for his last drive with McLaren. 'Just before the race, Ayrton called me to him from the cockpit of his car,' said Jo Ramirez. 'Normally, he did his seat belts himself, but I thought maybe he wanted some help. But it turned out he wanted to speak with me – in private that couldn't be heard over the team radio. Ayrton grabbed my arm very hard and said to me, "I feel strange to do this with you for the last time." I told him: "If you feel strange imagine how we all feel about you going. We don't want you to go, but you are the one going because we didn't send you."'

Senna's mission was to deliver McLaren's 104th grand prix win – a milestone to take them beyond Ferrari into the record books as the most successful team in Formula One history. 'I said to Ayrton, "If you win this for us I'll love you forever!" Then I looked in his eyes and I saw the emotion of the man. I am glad Ron didn't see what I had done. Ayrton looked at me, and said, "I will do my best."'

Senna won the race – the forty-first and final grand prix win of his life. Prost had taken second place in his last-ever grand prix and he would leave Formula One as world champion for a fourth time. 'Ron came to me on the podium and said, "Nice work!",' recalled Prost. 'Then I saw Ayrton. I did not want to say anything because of what had happened two weeks before in Japan. But this time Ayrton had been the one to decide what to do on the podium. He asked me to come up on the top step with him – it was his decision, you see, not mine. This is how he thinks. After this podium, there was a very strange press conference. He told me that I'd become fat, bored. All kind of nice, fun things to say. He was completely different. Before we went to give interviews to television stations, we talked in private. Suddenly, from the end of the race something changed in his attitude completely. It was really, really something. Slowly, I understood more and more the way he is thinking. Only when we were in Australia did I understand why.'

Suddenly, Senna appreciated Prost had been removed from the picture. Forever. That night the McLaren team partied at an Italian restaurant in Adelaide. 'A couple of years before we had a big party in Portugal when Ayrton realised he wasn't going to get the Williams drive, and that Prost had got it,' explained Ramirez. 'Ayrton's world was closed and he got pissed at that team dinner. This time I delegated one of our girls, Katie, to keep Ayrton supplied with Haigh Whisky, his favourite. I had a little speech for him. "If you can better this with another team, you are welcome to try!"' Karl-Heinz Zimmerman that night fired a one-gun salute in honour of Senna from his miniature cannon.

Senna would later give Ramirez his overalls, gloves and racing boots from that last race with McLaren. He has them at his home in Spain.

* * *

Alain Prost flew from Australia to an uncertain future. He had won the world championship by winning seven races and claiming pole position thirteen times during the season in a fabulous racing car. Yet, somehow, Prost felt hollow; even in triumph he had somehow been beaten by Senna. 'I did not want to stop,' admitted Prost in the summer of 2008, in contradiction to his statement made in Estoril. But he could not handle living within the same team as Senna again – so he banked the money from the outstanding year of his Williams contract and walked reluctantly into the sunset after driving in 199 grands prix.

18

MAY DAY

To Senna, Prost may have gone, but he was clearly not forgotten. Over the winter months, Senna did something he had never done previously: he dialled a number belonging to the Frenchman. 'He had asked for my number from Julian Jakobi, and Ayrton was calling me from Brazil many times,' said Prost. 'He was pleading with me to drive again. I was laughing, and told him, "You are really unbelievable!"'

Prost cannot begin to psychoanalyse what drove Senna to telephone him. All he can confirm is that the Brazilian relentlessly asked him to come out of retirement. Imagine the confusion in Prost's mind. On the phone, almost begging him to drive again, was the same man who had spent years of his life doing his damnedest to destroy Prost as a racing driver; and as a man. Clearly, he had not thought for a moment what might happen to the Frenchman that afternoon in 1990 when he drove his car into him at Suzuka. Clearly, he did not care for him when, with a calculating mind and a cold heart, he negotiated his way into the Williams Renault team for 1994 knowing that Prost would feel duty bound to quit rather than share a team with him again. Clearly, Senna had undergone an incredible change of heart. He wanted Prost back to give meaning to his own life and career.

The truth is that Prost did seriously consider making a comeback – with McLaren. In mid-February, I was reporting for the *Mail on Sunday* from the Winter Olympics in Lillehammer, Norway, when I was invited to meet Prost at the old home of the French Grand Prix, at Le Castellet in the South of France. Ostensibly, the invitation had been extended to promote the 230mph McLaren F1, the fastest, most technologically advanced road car in the world; and, at £540,000, undoubtedly the most expensive. As Prost was going to be at the wheel, and as there was growing speculation that he was mulling over a return to Formula One, it seemed eminently sensible to take a three-day sojourn from the bitter cold of Lillehammer. McLaren had entered into an alliance with French car manufacturers Peugeot to provide them with engines for the 1994 world championship – and Prost seemed to be the perfect man to succeed Senna. You lose Prost because Senna becomes all-empowered; then you lose Senna as he is disillusioned; so, if you are Ron Dennis, you compensate by trying to entice Prost out of retirement. No one ever accused Formula One of being a rational business.

At Le Castellet, Prost told me: 'I still love Formula One, I still have the passion, but that alone is not enough. I need to feel something different. In a way, yes, I have to fall in love again.' Prost had spent the winter skiing, surfing and motorcycling and had not actively searched for gainful employment. 'It's very important to me that, if I return to Formula One, it will be in a different ambience,' he argued. 'And, if I win a race, it is not just because of my car, like everyone was saying last year. I still cannot bring myself to talk publicly about how I feel inside about this championship.' Prost, just days from his thirty-ninth birthday, added, 'I am not trying to play political games. I have had two other opportunities to return to Formula One, but only the McLaren Peugeot team could perhaps put me in a position I might enjoy.'

Prost duly tested the McLaren Peugeot at Estoril. 'Ron had asked me for two reasons,' he said. 'He wanted me to drive again for the team and he wanted me to evaluate the car. It also allowed me to clear my mind – as I told you I did not want to stop.' Senna had heard of this test on the grapevine and that was when he intensified his plea to Prost to return. Senna's calls to Prost were always about Formula One, but he was cordial if a little dispirited. 'I asked Ron for a bit of time to think, and Ayrton knew that. Ayrton told me in one of his calls that he was not motivated to race against the other drivers. As I say, I laughed with him about how unbelievable he was to be making this suggestion. But I also told him that I was not going to be a punch bag for him. I knew that there was no way I could compete against Ayrton with that car, or, especially, that engine. It would need a lot of time to develop the car and the engine and I was not ready to do that again.' Prost informed Dennis that he would not be coming back to the team.

Two weeks after I had met Prost, I returned to Le Castellet to interview Ayrton Senna and Damon Hill during a Williams test to smooth out the wrinkles from the team's latest generation car now stripped of electronic driver aids under the new regulations. 'Senna is a man totally absorbed,' said Hill. 'You get the feeling his work input will have a motivating effect on everyone in the team. It's like putting in new batteries.' But Hill was not deluded about what he faced. 'It's a funny business, Formula

One,' he said. 'It's like putting Chris Eubank and Nigel Benn in the same team, asking them to work together . . . and then setting them loose to punch one another's lights out. You are asking the almost impossible.' But Hill did not anticipate slugging it out, toe-to-toe, with Senna as Prost had done during their tension-filled couple of years together at McLaren. 'I'd be a fool to go head-to-head with Ayrton in a team environment,' he insisted. 'I've got so much more to gain by cooperating and exchanging information and I am thinking long term as I want to be driving in F1 in the year 2000 and beyond.'

The two men had barely got beyond the point of strangers shaking hands at a cocktail party. These were men born just six months apart chasing a common dream from separate worlds. Senna had arrived by private jet with Josef Leberer to tend to him and with his own private publicist, Betise Assumpcao to relay to the Brazilian media his thoughts on a daily basis; Hill was alone. On the night I spent at Bandol, Senna arrived back at the hotel at 10.45 p.m. after a day spent driving and debriefing with engineers. Leberer had prepared his dinner at the circuit. As he collected his key from the reception desk, he was given an armful of faxes relating to his business interests. He still had to accommodate a massage from Leberer. The next morning Senna confessed: 'I am stimulated by a new team and a new car. But I am tired, too, because there are many things to consider, to feel, to judge.' The first grand prix of the year, in Brazil, was just over three weeks away.

Prost continued to hear from Senna through this period. 'Ayrton told me that he had many problems with the Williams,' said the Frenchman. 'He was complaining about his position in the car, he just did not feel good with it. He did not like how the steering wheel was positioned – something I had complained about the year before. The car had been really done for Nigel and I never felt quite comfortable in it. Ayrton was also a little disappointed with the car in general terms.'

In Brazil, Senna, for all his misgivings claimed pole position. Alongside him on the front row was Michael Schumacher's Benetton Ford. Already there were suspicions within the pit lane that Schumacher's team had found a way round the new regulations, which had banned among other aids launch control, a system which allowed a driver to start without needing to pay heed to wheelspin or gear changes. Senna actually led the race, but Schumacher emerged from an identically timed pit stop in front of the Brazilian. Then Senna spun out of the grand prix later in proceedings in an attempt to get after the German, who drove unhindered to the chequered flag.

If that was not a bad enough start to Senna's career with Williams, worse followed at the second race, the Pacific Grand Prix at Aida in Japan. Once again he was on pole, but this time Senna's Williams caught too much wheelspin and Schumacher drove past him into a clear road. As Senna negotiated the first corner, his car was touched in the rear by Mika Hakkinen's McLaren and this pushed his Williams sideways, placing the Brazilian in the path of Nicola Larini's Ferrari. Senna and Larini ended in a heap in the gravel. Schumacher's victory meant that after just two races he had a twenty-point lead in the championship to take with him to the next round, at Imola in Italy.

And still Prost took calls from Senna. 'Each time Ayrton's mood was going down, about the car, about the performance,' said Prost. 'He was also convinced that the Benetton car was outside the regulations. He had a problem with the safety of the sport, too. The week before Imola he asked me if I wanted to be president of the drivers' association, but I didn't want to do this job again. But it's important to know, Ayrton was a completely different man and a completely different driver. He was not happy for sure. He was alone, and telling me he was not motivated to fight against Michael and the other drivers. It was a combination of many things and I had a lot of sympathy for him because he was feeling so bad. Obviously, I had some very tough moments with him, but I felt it was good to have these discussions and this was also part of our history. We talked two days before he was to be in Imola. I never heard Ayrton telling me about his concerns for safety like this in my entire career. He was concerned when we had Martin Donnelly's crash at Jerez, but after that he didn't talk any more about this. On the telephone, he said, "Let's meet." I should have arrived in Imola on Friday, but, in fact, I did not arrive until Saturday.'

That was the day Roland Ratzenberger was killed during qualifying, a tragedy that had such a profound impact on Senna, as we have seen. He went to bed that night with a troubled mind having earned the right to start from pole position for the sixty-fifth – and last – occasion in his career.

1 May 1994: Senna was aroused from sleep by a familiar voice on the telephone in his room at Castel San Pietro. 'Baggage service,' said Owen O'Mahony, his pilot, who acted as Senna's wake up call when he rang wanting to know what time to collect his bags. Senna gathered his belongings together – he travelled light whenever he could but always with his Bible – and flew by helicopter to the circuit at Imola that hosted the San Marino Grand Prix.

Senna had already departed when Josef Leberer checked out and went to the hotel's car park. When he switched on the ignition of his VW Golf with 400,000 kilometres on the clock, the oil light glowed red. Leberer looked anxiously at the instrument panel, then selected gear and drove off in defiance of the oil warning light. 'I never missed a race,' said Leberer. 'It was unthinkable for me not to be there; anyway, Ayrton needed his breakfast.' Leberer nursed his ageing car over the ten kilometres he had to drive to the circuit, and admitted he felt a relieved man when he arrived. 'I was expecting every minute that the car was going to blow up,' he recalled.

At the track, Frank Williams understood that Senna had been brooding hard over the first two races of the year even before Ratzenberger's fatal accident caused him to grieve in front of the world on the previous afternoon. Ratzenberger's death during qualifying at Imola had awoken emotions in Senna that he did not recognise. He found it hard to deal with the loss of the life of a man who had been doing, for all intents and purposes, the same job as him in the same place at the same time. He had been required for the first time to examine his own mortality. It was not something he had enjoyed or wanted to experience. In addition, he harboured dark thoughts about the technical hardware under the skin of Schumacher's Benetton at a time when all electronic aids had been outlawed by regulation. 'We were up against an unusually competitive Benetton,' said Williams, selecting his words carefully in 2008. 'Ayrton being perceptive, experienced and shrewd knew that he was not racing on an equal footing. He believed that to be the case, I know.' Benetton, however, maintained their car conformed to the rules. No one ever proved otherwise.

There was another complicated strand in his life: his family continued to challenge him over his relationship with his Brazilian girlfriend, Adriane Galisteu. They felt she was unsuitable for him, a girl deemed to be from the wrong side of the city, a girl who had been looking for her Henry Higgins and found him at a Formula One party in São Paulo where she had been booked as a model promoting the Shell Oil company. That weekend his brother Leonardo had travelled to Imola to tell him that they had evidence of her unsuitability that he needed to hear, at least those were stories that ran in Brazil. What was indisputable was that Senna had been an emotional wreck when he spoke with Galisteu, after she had arrived at his home on the Algarve to await his return after the San Marino Grand Prix. 'Ayrton telephoned me on Saturday and he was shaken,' she said. 'Crying, really crying . . . he told me Roland Ratzenberger had just been killed and that he did not want to race. He had never spoken like that and I didn't know how to react.'

But after a quiet, sombre dinner with Josef Leberer and a few close friends, Senna had returned to his hotel at Castel San Pietro, where he had stayed in the same room for many years for the duration of the San Marino Grand Prix. At the hotel, Senna visited Williams in his room to try to clear his mind. Williams thought he had been successful, because on Sunday morning Senna had pitched up at the team's motorhome in purposeful mood. 'Ayrton was determined to beat Schumacher at Imola, absolutely determined,' said Williams. 'He was in unstoppable mood.'

Williams' No. 2 driver Damon Hill had not been blind to Senna's discomfort even before Ratzenberger lost his life. 'There was a whole number of factors at play,' said Hill. 'Ayrton hadn't settled into the Williams team yet – and Schumacher was a dimension in all this, too. Ayrton was concerned about the legality of the Benetton. He didn't say anything specific to me, but we were all thinking: *How did they do that?* At Aida, after he had been taken out, Ayrton stood on the track and watched Schumacher for a long time. On the way back from Japan, there was some muttering going on about the Benetton. Ayrton's response was to fight people who were not "correct". That was a word he used a lot – actually so did Alain.'

Yet in the warm-up on Sunday morning, a thirty-minute session when drivers searched for an optimum set-up to race their cars in the actual grand prix that began at 2 p.m., Senna had been electrifyingly fast. It was an illustration – another one – of the Brazilian writing an unchained melody at the wheel whenever challenged, mentally or physically. He had been disturbed by the mournful events of the previous afternoon, but within his race car he was cocooned from the reality of what had taken place. Senna was just different, as Prost has maintained. Had he not once defended his right to behave belligerently in a racing car, while being intolerant of others doing the same, by declaring, 'But I am Senna'?

Richard Williams, the chief sportswriter of the *Guardian*, and an astute and extremely knowledgeable man on Formula One down the decades, wrote in an outstanding book, *The Death of Ayrton Senna*, 'That remark sounded preposterous, until you thought about it. He was indeed Senna, and the cultivation of humility in his working life would not have taken him to the places he found. And for all the occasionally dubious nature of his intimidatory manoeuvres, it also has to be said that on many occasions his sheer brilliance deformed the behaviour of his competitors, which could hardly have been held to his account.'

And on that spring morning in Imola, with so much heaviness in the air, Senna put down a marker. 'Ayrton was clearly out to stamp his authority, and was about a second a lap faster than me in the warm-up,' said Hill.

An hour or so later, Berger joined Senna and they walked together to the drivers' briefing at a room in the inner sanctum of the control tower. Senna asked his friend to bring up a point about the safety car, new to Formula One; he did not want to be the one to mention it as he appeared to be in frequent conflict with the authorities. A safety car had been introduced into Formula One at the start of the season and was to be used during a race if an accident, or an incident, endangered the lives of the drivers. Its function was to slowly lead the cars around the circuit in single file until the danger had passed as a preferred means to stopping the race altogether. Hill explained: 'It wasn't called a pace car, because pace cars are what they have in America, so it was called a safety car, but its purpose was the same.'

Senna had disliked the fact that the safety car had been used to lead the cars around the circuit on the formation lap as he feared the drivers would be unable to warm their tyres sufficiently and could also risk losing tyre pressure as the car could not maintain a fast enough pace. 'This is an example of how Ayrton pushed for things all the time,' said Hill. 'He was quite a challenge for the authorities. He didn't raise it at the briefing, though. He didn't want to make himself the target. That's why he had arranged for Gerhard to mention it, and then we all piped up.' In the briefing, the drivers had observed a minute's sombre silence in a private tribute to Ratzenberger.

Afterwards, Jo Ramirez from McLaren saw Senna and reassured him that the helicopter the Brazilian had asked for had been booked to allow him to make a swift getaway after the race. 'I wished Ayrton a good race, as always,' said Ramirez. 'Ayrton spent quite a long time walking with Michael Schumacher after they left the briefing.' They were putting in place plans for all the drivers to attend a meeting to discuss safety issues at the next race in Monaco, when it was expected that the safety car would disappear from the formation lap. Niki Lauda had also been invited to offer his contribution to the debate on the drivers' behalf.

On this morning, Prost had arrived at the circuit with a twin role to perform. He was there to act as an ambassador for Renault, who had a substantial guest list for this first race of the year in Europe. He was also there to broadcast for TF1. Prost stopped by the Williams motorhome, which was on the neighbouring site to the Renault one, to have a word with his old bosses and friends, Frank Williams and Patrick Head. Senna was with them. 'I smiled and said, hello,' said Prost. 'You know, when I had come to the track the guys at TF1 had shown me a film that Ayrton had been recording for Elf [Williams' French fuel partner]. He was supposed to drive round and say things about the track through a microphone in his helmet. But Ayrton began by saying, "I would like to say welcome to my old friend, Alain Prost. Tell him we miss him very much." It was a nice moment.'

Prost did not overstay his welcome. He could tell Senna, Williams and Head had much to discuss and he left to keep a rendezvous for lunch with some of Renault's guests. He had the last table under the awning of a tightly packed dining area that had been created in the lee of Renault's motorhome. In the midst of the meal, Prost suddenly became aware of excited chatter around him. 'I saw Ayrton leave the Williams motorhome, but instead of going to the garage he came through the crowd of Renault guests having lunch to come to where I was sitting with around ten other people,' explained Prost. 'A driver doesn't usually do that so close to the start of a race – especially not Ayrton. But he wanted to talk with me. It was very abnormal. He talked a little about the car, a little about safety again. Everyone was looking and listening to what he was saying. It was a shock for the guests to see Senna and myself. It was an unbelievable moment – you can talk about this, but it is hard to describe. I was astonished. He left to go to the garage – and I said that I would see him in five minutes.'

'I did not finish my lunch. When I went into the garage he was completely alone. He was doing some stretches. We spoke a little more about the same things, but I did not want to disturb him. He wanted me to stay, though. He was talking again about Michael and Benetton. He asked me what *I* was doing. The words were not very important; he just wanted to share time with me.'

Senna may have been blindingly fast during the warm-up, but Prost had detected that his old rival was in some part unrecognisable. Usually, Senna had no time for meaningless small talk before a grand prix. Usually, he walked through the paddock from his motorhome to his car in such a state of heightened awareness that they say he could have passed his mother and not known she was there. But on this morning Prost had seen another side of Senna, one he did not know. 'I had never seen him like this, not in the same mood ready to fight as usual,' said the Frenchman.

Prost felt a little uncomfortable on his behalf. He would not have wanted some old ex-driver to be hanging around him when he had other more important matters to think about. So, Prost shook hands with Senna, wished him good luck and walked out of the Williams garage. He did not know it then – but he had also walked out of his life. So much had been said, and so much had been left unsaid between them. This was not supposed to be how they parted . . .

When Senna climbed into his car he had with him a small Austrian flag. He may have been in an unfamiliar mood to those who knew him best, but Senna still believed that he was about to win the San Marino Grand Prix. And that was when he would fly the Austrian flag from his car in tribute to the memory of Roland Ratzenberger. Why? 'Because I am Senna', as he might have said.

After bringing his car round to its place at the front of the grid, Senna continued to behave strangely. He removed his crash helmet – something he rarely did. As always, Leberer was with him until the one-minute board was held at the front of the grid in a silent order for everyone to depart in preparation for the cars to be released on their formation lap. Before this, Bernie Ecclestone's wife, Slavica, went over to see Senna and knelt down to speak with him as he sat in his car. 'She was to be the last woman that kissed him,' said Ecclestone.

Leberer observed, 'Normally, Ayrton never took off his helmet, but he did that day. He looked very serious. You could almost hear him thinking as he sat in the car. But then they announced Gerhard Berger's name to the crowd and they all cheered loudly. This was the only time he smiled this day, the only thing that took him out of his mind. He was laughing; it was lovely to see.'

Did you always have the same exchange before the start of a race? 'No, just eye contact,' replied Leberer. 'No words were necessary.' Were you ever afraid that Senna would never come back? 'No . . .'

Berger can still remember being on the grid that afternoon, at a circuit that might easily have claimed his life five years earlier when his Ferrari hit the wall at Tamburello and exploded. 'As a Ferrari driver in Imola you have a lot of fans!' he said. 'They were chanting my name and Josef came over to me and said Ayrton was laughing about this. This is the last picture I have of Ayrton in my mind . . . it is a nice one.' They had perpetrated dozens of practical jokes on one another, they had raced and lived as rivals and friends, and they had expectations of growing old together. It was supposed to be just another grand prix.

As the clock edged towards 2 p.m., the cars filed from the grid on their formation lap behind Senna's Williams. He was on racing driver autopilot when he stopped his car in the zone reserved for the man on pole. What was it he had said, two races down and with no points in the championship? 'The season starts here.'

His mind had been stripped clean as always – and when the lights turned green Senna had the lead of the San Marino Grand Prix from Schumacher in close attendance. But behind them chaos reigned. J.J. Lehto, who had arrived at Imola in the company of Ratzenberger, had stalled his Benetton on the line and his car was struck by Pedro Lamy driving a Lotus. A wheel from Lamy's car whizzed into the crowd and injured nine people while debris flew across the circuit. Instantly, the safety car was ordered on to the circuit and Senna fell in behind it with the other drivers obediently holding station in his wake.

'There was lots of tension, real tension,' said Hill. 'With those cars, when the tyre pressure went down the ride height went down. It was a tough car to drive. Refuelling had been introduced for that year. If I am correct, Ayrton was on a one-stop strategy and Schumacher was on a two-stop. Ayrton was faster than Michael on a heavier fuel load, which shows you how hard he was pushing. Ayrton was determined to stay ahead, but he didn't need to do so, but he didn't know that. As it was, Ayrton's car was heavy and much more difficult to control in high-speed corners.'

For five laps, the Brazilian stalked the safety car before it slipped off the track. In the medical car, parked at the corner near the entrance of the pits, Professor Sid Watkins watched his friend Senna apply full, screaming power as he passed. When they came round the next time, on lap seven, Watkins disliked what he saw as Senna wrestled to keep his Williams under control. 'I thought, "Fuck, Ayrton's going to have a big accident."'

Behind Senna, Schumacher and Hill pounded after him along the pit straight and out of view of Watkins. At exactly 2.17 p.m.,

Senna's car entered the left-handed Tamburello at 190mph, but instead of sweeping through the corner his Williams careered right across the track. Somehow, in the fractions of seconds at his command, the thirty-four-year-old Brazilian, the fastest, most obsessed and most committed racing driver the world had known, scrubbed as much speed from his car as was humanly possible. Inside the car, he could only pray to his God.

Yet he was still travelling at 130mph when his Williams violently struck the concrete wall set back from the track and sheltering the river that Senna and Berger had discovered on their reconnaissance visit to Tamburello a couple of weeks after the Austrian's crash at this same corner. On impact, Senna's car ricocheted and the right front wheel shot skywards, higher and higher into the air, but to the naked eye it looked a much kinder contact than when Berger's Ferrari exploded.

As Hill passed Senna's car behind Schumacher, he caught sight of the wreckage and thought to himself, 'Bloody hell, not again. That's three races he's been off, it's not going well for Ayrton . . .' Betise Assumpcao grabbed her handbag, without waiting to see the end of the accident, and readied herself to absorb the details for a press release on the Brazilian's third successive failure. 'Fuck, Ayrton's going to be in such a bad mood,' she thought. In the BBC commentary box Murray Walker had not been overly alarmed by the pictures that he was viewing. 'My immediate reaction was, "Wow, that's a big one." But in no sense did I think it was a fatal accident. I had seen Michele Alboreto go off at Tamburello in seemingly terminal circumstances and get away with it. I'd seen Gerhard Berger go off there and sit unconscious in a car on fire; I thought the bloke was being done to a crisp before my eyes. In between Alboreto and Berger I'd seen Nelson Piquet go off at Tamburello at great velocity and only hurt his foot. All had gone off in identical circumstances to Senna and got away with it . . .' In the TF1 commentary booth, Prost looked at his monitor and froze. 'In this case, you don't know what to say,' he admitted. 'It was a tough moment, you see it is a serious accident, but you never know.' In the calm of his high-ceilinged dining room in central Paris, he still found words difficult to find, difficult to describe properly how he had reacted. 'You have no judgement, you are not in a rational situation,' he explained. His voice was soft, softer even than usual. 'We had one man dead the day before. When you comment, you remember what happened in the day, what happened in the days before, what had been happening in the months earlier. You think about all these different things. You are confused. Ayrton was losing some motivation, and he had some personal problems. Life had been not only racing now . . .'

He looked anguished as he remembered those images from Imola, when a perimeter wall was turned into a tombstone and he had a microphone pressed to his lips. While his broadcast was being heard across France, commentators from Brazil were informing the country to be prepared to be plunged into national mourning; and without knowing, Prost and Hill, Berger and Derek Warwick would soon be aboard flights to São Paulo to be pall bearers at a State Funeral.

But in the confusion, and as Professor Sid Watkins and a team of local medics hurried to the accident scene, television cameras looked for life on that spring weekend from hell at the San Marino Grand Prix. And Ayrton Senna's head could be seen to move, briefly.

But then he was still, so shockingly still.

EPILOGUE

Thirty-eight minutes after Ayrton Senna's Williams cannoned into the wall at Tamburello the San Marino Grand Prix was restarted. No one had declared Senna dead – so the show went on as usual.

Just beforehand, Williams' public relations officer Ann Bradshaw, a woman of vast experience in motor racing, approached Damon Hill on the grid. He asked for a bulletin on Senna and remembered that she replied: 'He's not good.'

Medical chief Professor Sid Watkins had feared from the extent of Senna's head injuries, caused on impact, that he could not survive. Yet a helicopter was called to the crash scene anyway to transport the Brazilian to the Maggiore Hospital in Bologna and the gravity of his injury was kept quiet from all but a few. Confusion reigned in the paddock – but the drivers were informed that the race would be resumed and dutifully complied. Watkins stayed at the track to fulfil his obligations with a heavy heart.

Prost looked on the scene from a commentary booth. 'You don't know what to say,' he admitted that afternoon in Paris when we had pieced together and rearranged the jigsaw of his life when it interlocked with that of Senna. 'There were rumours that Ayrton was dead. There were rumours that he had only broken a shoulder. You have no judgement any more.'

On the track, Hill had to put his faith in his team when he took his place on the grid in an identical car to the one Senna had crashed, because no one at that moment could be certain as to the cause of the accident. 'We were using power steering at the time and, as a precaution, the team asked me to turn mine off,' recalled Hill. 'That was responsible – but it was chaotic and my engineer John Russell spoke with me to give me what assurances he could. It sounds absurd – almost immature – but there was a sense to our response that simply said, "We're going to fight on." Sometimes, life is horrible; but you can't sit down and give up. You've got a job to do. I didn't feel it was the right thing to withdraw. I'd made a commitment; I'd signed the contract and I took the money. But I admit through the whole race I was wondering what had happened to Ayrton's car. I was absolutely fucked at the end.' Murray Walker later suggested: 'Damon was a very brave man getting back into the Williams car.'

Michael Schumacher duly won the race, but the world was paying no attention to the outcome of a grand prix. Gerhard Berger had already left the circuit, his Ferrari having developed a mysterious fault, to get to the bedside of his friend in Bologna. He found Senna on a life-support machine. 'When I saw him, Ayrton's heart was still beating,' said Berger. 'But he was not alive, though.'

At 6.40 p.m., the world was officially informed that Ayrton

Senna had died. In Brazil, President Itamar Franco announced three days of national mourning.

At Imola, Prost had collected his belongings and been driven the short journey to Forlì Airport, where he had a seat on a chartered flight to Paris. Senna's own plane had been waiting for him at the same airport. He was together with the president of Renault when news reached him that Senna had been declared dead. 'The president started to write a tribute with a press officer,' said Prost. 'I was in shock, real shock.' On the plane home to Paris, the other passengers consumed the in-flight meal with wine, but Prost felt nauseous to the pit of his stomach. 'Everyone else was eating and drinking and laughing,' he said. 'I could not eat – I could not talk.'

The next day Prost was harangued against his better judgement into appearing in a television programme that was broadcast by TF1. 'It was a serious analysis and inquest into Ayrton's crash and I didn't want to do it at all,' said Prost. 'But I had the president of TF1 and Renault pushing me to appear. In my opinion, it wasn't nice at all.'

Twenty-four hours later, Prost was still in a quandary as to whether or not he should fly to São Paulo to attend the State Funeral that had been planned in Senna's honour for Thursday. On advice from influential French entrepreneur Jean-Luc Lagardère, who had a Brazilian wife, Prost gained the necessary self-confidence to book a flight to São Paulo. 'I always had good relations with the Brazilian people,' said Prost. 'But I just wanted to hear from Jean-Luc and his wife that I would not cause offence by my presence. He called me back to say that it was clear that I must go.'

For Josef Leberer, Senna's final flight was one of great poignancy. He had flown from Salzburg to Paris to connect with a Varig flight RG723 to São Paulo. 'I sat next to Ayrton's coffin in business class,' he explained. He had for company Betise Assumpcao and Galvao Bueno from TV Globo. 'Otherwise, the business class cabin was empty,' said Leberer. 'This was not easy, and it was the longest flight of my life. But it was also a time for me to face the reality of the situation and to make peace with everything.' The 30-kilometre route into the city from the airport was a sea of people wanting to pay their respects to a national hero now carried in a coffin draped in a Brazilian green and yellow flag on a fire engine. Police motorcycle outriders provided an escort.

In São Paulo, Prost was among the pall-bearers. 'I had a fantastic reception from the family, from the people,' said Prost. 'They were happy for me to be there. It meant a lot to me.' Along with the Brazilian nation, and the world of motorsport, Prost shed tears during the emotional service in commemoration of the extraordinary life of Ayrton Senna, a man who lived and died for his passion to drive racing cars as fast as humanly feasible.

At Imola, the bells chimed in sympathy. And the local authorities began what was to become a long drawn out and fruitless investigation to apportion blame for his death on three principal members of the Williams team: Frank Williams, Patrick Head and Adrian Newey. Eventually, all three were exonerated of any culpability. Meanwhile, the FIA, the governing body for motorsport, accelerated and improved a campaign to increase the safety of Formula One cars and the tracks on which they raced. Tamburello corner had become a chicane by the time Formula One returned.

All manner of theories speculating on the cause of Senna's death have been aired over the years, but none are worthy of divesting with any integrity by repeating them. Hill is comfortable that Senna died in an accident – and not through any sinister circumstances. 'I am completely satisfied in my mind that I know what happened,' he said, over coffee at a pavement café in Godalming, Surrey, fourteen years after his team-mate had been killed. 'All the hysterical press reporting about what happened was created because, in a lot of people's minds, they could not accept Ayrton Senna was fallible. I'm saying that if racing meant taking risks he would do that. That is what he had consistently done throughout his career. If the car was very difficult to drive, and very difficult to keep ahead of Michael Schumacher because it was on low tyre pressures, cold tyres and higher fuel, he would have done that. And that's what he did.

'People do not understand the forces involved in cornering in a Formula One car. They relate it to driving on the road – get that out of your head. You are being slung around and you are under 4G going around Tamburello. If that car starts to wobble, it's going to get out of your hands very quickly. Ayrton was taking a tight line on that corner. You can see quite clearly from the onboard camera on Schumacher's car that Senna's car bottoms out. When it does, it slides; then rises up, which means it settles on the nose. Then his car settles down again – and he hit another bump. This time, it's a bigger one. From his onboard camera, you can see him putting left lock on, and he literally gets a monster slide on that corner and the car pointed towards the wall. He got on the brakes, but by that time he was on the grass. That was it. There was so much pressure on Ayrton that weekend – he was not going to come second to Schumacher.

'The death of Roland Ratzenberger had heightened his passion to be Ayrton Senna – and to win. That's coming right back to the beginning of his career; it was how he approached his sport. And his life. He was a deeply, deeply compassionate person.

He had a vision, an understanding of life which was way more mature than most of us. It was his mission not to give into any form of fallibility.'

To Alain Prost, the funeral in São Paulo had been like dropping a veil over a part of his own life. 'I would say that was the end of the story for me, as well as for Ayrton,' said Prost. Together, they had hardly been out of the headlines. The numbers alone are impressive: Prost claimed four world titles, fifty-one wins, and took pole position thirty-three times from 199 grand prix races compared with Senna's three championships, forty-one victories and sixty-five starts from pole position from 161 races.

'Life is very difficult,' said Prost. 'Ayrton had everything: money, success. But you can lose everything in a moment – in an accident or with an illness like my brother Daniel. We must never forget life is short.'

Too short in the case of Ayrton Senna. But in company with Alain Prost, his legend will never die.

ACKNOWLEDGEMENTS

I am hugely indebted to Alain Prost for opening his home and his memories to me to bestow upon this narrative a contemporary review of his extraordinary rivalry with Ayrton Senna. He was a generous host – as well as a formidable champion.

It was my good fortune to have reported on Formula One from Rio de Janeiro to Adelaide, from South Africa to Monaco in the years when Prost and Ayrton Senna enriched motor racing with their talent and the strength of their personalities. I had the privilege of interviewing them independently as well as being in attendance when the stories they manufactured, at the wheel, or in the paddock, became headline material around the world.

I am grateful as well to those from within the Formula One fraternity, who willingly gave of their time and recollections of the period to assist my quest to recreate this story from the embers of history. In no particular order, my thanks to Bernie Ecclestone, Sir Frank Williams, Professor Sid Watkins, Gerhard Berger, Damon Hill, Martin Brundle, Derek Warwick, Nigel

Mansell, Jo Ramirez, Josef Leberer, John Hogan, Betise Assumpcao, Tony Jardine, Murray Walker, Johnny Herbert, Eric Silbermann, Karl-Heinz Zimmerman, Andrew Longmore and James Allen.

I am also thankful for the friendship, the knowledge and the companionship at the bar from fellow members of the travelling press caravan: Nigel Roebuck, Maurice Hamilton, Alan Henry, Gerhard Kuntschik, Gerald Donaldson, Christopher Hilton, Richard Williams, Simon Barnes, Derick Allsop, Ollie Holt, Tim Collings, David Tremayne, Ray Matts, Stan Piecha, Bob McKenzie, Kevin Eason and Byron Young; and to those who have joined more recently, Jon McEvoy, Ian Gordon, Ed Gorman and Kevin Garside.

I must thank my agent Jonathan Harris for his enduring belief and Tim Andrews, the commissioning editor at Century, for his continual support, enthusiasm and encouragement. Malcolm Vallerius, sports editor of the *Mail on Sunday*, warrants my gratitude for allowing me to pursue this project beyond the scope of my day job. I have to give special thanks to Cara Sloman from the *Mail on Sunday* for her editorial support.

Finally, but by no means least, I must extend my thanks to my wife Rachel and our daughters, Sian and Megan, now women of the world, for pretending for the most part that I am easy to live with.

BIBLIOGRAPHY

Autocourse, 1998/9, Hazleton Publishing, 1989.

Jacques Deschenaux, *Grand Prix Guide*, 2007 edition, 2008.

FIA Formula One Championship Yearbook, Virgin Books, 1987.

Alan Henry, *McLaren Formula 1 Racing Team*, Haynes, 1999.

Christopher Hilton, *Ayrton Senna: As Time Goes By*, Haynes, 1999.

— *Ayrton Senna: The Hard Edge of Genius*, Patrick Stephens, 1990.

— *Ayrton Senna: His Full Car Racing Record*, Patrick Stephens Limited, 1995.

— *Alain Prost*, Corgi, 1992.

Nigel Mansell, *My Autobiography: The People's Champion*, Ted Smart, 1996.

Alain Prost, *Life in the Fast Lane*, Stanley Paul, 1989.

Sid Watkins, *Life at the Limit*, Macmillan, 1996.

Richard Williams, *The Death of Ayrton Senna*, Bloomsbury, 1999.

DRIVING RECORDS OF ALAIN PROST AND AYRTON SENNA

Key to Races:

ARG – Argentina

BRE – Brazil

EUR – Europe

RSM – San Marino

ESP – Spain

MON – Monaco

CAN – Canada

FRA – France

GB – Great Britain

GER – Germany

HON – Hungary

BEL – Belgium

ITA – Italy

POR – Portugal

JAP – Japan

AUS – Australia

MEX – Mexico

USAE – United States East

USAW – United States West

SA – South Africa

HOL – Holland

VEG – Las Vegas

SUI – Switzerland

PAC – Pacific

Ayrton SENNA DA SILVA (BRE)

Born 21.3.1960
Died on 1.5.1994 (GP San Marino, Imola)

Grands Prix contested: 161

1984	Toleman Hart Turbo:	BRA – SA – BEL – FRA – MON – CAN – USAE – DAL – GB – GER – AUT – HOL – EUR – POR
1985	Lotus Renault Turbo:	BRE – POR – RSM – MON – CAN– USAE – FRA – GB – GER – AUT – HOL – ITA – BEL – EUR – SA – AUS
1986	Lotus Renault Turbo:	BRE – ESP – RSM – MON – BEL – CAN – USAE – FRA – GB – GER – HON – AUT – ITA – POR – MEX – AUS
1987	Lotus Honda Turbo:	BRE – RSM – BEL – MON – USAE – FRA – GB – GER – HON – AUT – ITA – POR – ESP – MEX – JAP – AUS
1988	McLaren Honda Turbo:	BRE – RSM – MON – MEX – CAN – USAE – FRA – GB – GER – HON – BEL – ITA – POR – ESP – JAP – AUS
1989	McLaren Honda:	BRE – RSM – MON – MEX – USA – CAN – FRA – GB – GER – HON – BEL – ITA – POR – ESP – JAP – AUS
1990	McLaren Honda:	USA – BRE – RSM – MON – CAN – MEX – FRA – GB – GER – HON – BEL – ITA – POR – ESP – JAP – AUS
1991	McLaren Honda:	USA – BRE – RSM – MON – CAN – MEX – FRA – GB – GER – HON – BEL – ITA – POR – ESP – JAP – AUS
1992	McLaren Honda:	SA – MEX – BRE – ESP – RSM – MON – CAN – FRA – GB – GER – HON – BEL – ITA – POR – JAP – AUS
1993	McLaren Ford:	SA – BRE – EUR – RSM – ESP – MON – CAN – FRA – GB – GER – HON – BEL – ITA – POR – JAP – AUS
1994	Williams Renault:	BRE – PAC – RSM

Pole position: 65x
1985: POR – RSM – MON – USAE – ITA – EUR – AUS
1986: BRE – ESP – RSM – USAE – FRA – HON – POR – MEX
1987: RSM
1988: BRE – RSM – MON – MEX – CAN – USAE – GER – HON – BEL – ITA – ESP – JAP – AUS
1989: BRE – RSM – MON – MEX – USA – GB – GER – BEL – ITA – POR – ESP – JAP – AUS

1990: BRE – RSM – MON – CAN – GER – BEL – ITA – ESP – JAP – AUS
1991: USA – BRE – RSM – MON – HON – BEL – ITA – AUS
1992: CAN
1993: AUS
1994: BRE – PAC – RSM

Front line: 87x
1985: POR – RSM – MON – CAN – USAE – FRA – ITA – BEL – EUR – AUS
1986: BRE – ESP – RSM – CAN – USAE – FRA – HON – POR – MEX
1987: RSM – MON – USAE – GER
1988: BRE – RSM – MON – MEX – CAN – USAE – FRA – GER – HON – BEL – ITA – POR – ESP – JAP – AUS
1989: BRE – RSM – MON – MEX – USA – CAN – FRA – GB – GER – HON – BEL – ITA – POR – ESP – JAP – AUS
1990: BRE – RSM – MON – CAN – GB – GER – BEL – ITA – ESP – JAP – AUS
1991: USA – BRE – RSM – MON – GB – GER – HON – BEL – ITA – JAP – AUS
1992: SA – CAN – BEL – ITA – AUS
1993: SA – JAP – AUS
1994: BRE – PAC – RSM

1st: 41x
1985: POR – BEL
1986: ESP – USAE
1987: MON – USAE
1988: RSM – CAN – USAE – GB – GER – HON – BEL – JAP
1989: RSM – MON – MEX – GER – BEL – ESP
1990: USA – MON – CAN – GER – BEL – ITA
1991: USA – BRE – RSM – MON – HON – BEL – AUS
1992: MON – HON – ITA
1993: BRE – EUR – MON – JAP – AUS

2nd: 23x
1984: MON
1985: AUT – EUR
1986: BRE – BEL – GER – HON
1987: RSM – HON – ITA – JAP
1988: MEX – FRA – AUS
1989: HON
1990: HON – POR
1991: ITA – POR – JAP
1992: GER
1993: SA – ESP

3rd: 16x
1984: GB – POR
1985: HOL – ITA
1986: MON – MEX
1987: GB – GER
1990: BRE – FRA – GB
1991: MEX – FRA
1992: SA – RSM – POR

4th: 7x

1986:	POR
1987:	FRA
1988:	ESP
1991:	GB
1993:	FRA – GER – BEL

5th: 6x

1986:	CAN
1987:	AUT – ESP
1991:	ESP
1992:	BEL
1993:	GB

6th: 3x

| 1984: | SA – BEL |
| 1988: | POR |

Fastest Lap: 19x

1984:	MON
1985:	POR – CAN – USAE
1987:	MON – USAE – ITA
1988:	MON – CAN – JAP
1989:	USA – GER – ESP
1990:	MON – ITA
1991:	ITA – JAP
1992:	POR
1993:	EUR

Not qualified: 1x

| 1984: | RSM |

Accidents/Left track: 24

1984:	USAE – DAL – GER – EUR
1985:	USAE – FRA
1986:	FRA
1987:	BEL
1988:	MON – ITA
1989:	GB – POR – JAP – AUS
1990:	RSM – JAP – AUS
1992:	ESP – FRA – AUS
1993:	ITA
1994:	BRE – PAC – RSM

Laps in the lead: 2982

Miles in the lead: 8510 *miles*

Classifications and Drivers' World Championship points:

1984:	*9th* – 13 pts		1989:	*2nd* – 60 pts
1985:	*4th* – 38 pts		1990:	*1st* – 78 pts
1986:	*4th* – 55 pts		1991:	*1st* – 96 pts
1987:	*3rd* – 57 pts		1992:	*4th* – 50 pts
1988:	*1st* – 90 (94) pts		1993:	*2nd* – 73 pts

Alain PROST (FRA)

Born 24.2.1955

Grands Prix contested: 199

1980	McLaren Ford:	ARG – BRE – BEL – MON – FRA – GB – GER – AUT – HOL – ITA – CAN
1981	Renault Turbo:	USAW – BRE – ARG – RSM – BEL – MON – ESP – FRA – GB – GER – AUT – HOL – ITA – CAN – VEG
1982	Renault Turbo:	SA – BRE – USAW – RSM – BEL – MON – USAE – CAN – HOL – GB – FRA – GER – AUT – SUI – ITA – VEG
1983	Renault Turbo:	BRE – USAW – FRA – RSM – MON – BEL – USAE – CAN – GB – GER – AUT – HOL – ITA – EUR – SA
1984	McLaren TAG Turbo:	BRE – SA – BEL – RSM – FRA – MON – CAN – USAE – DAL – GB – GER – AUT – HOL – ITA – EUR – POR
1985	McLaren TAG Turbo:	BRE – POR – RSM – MON – CAN – USAE – FRA – GB – GER – AUT – HOL – ITA – BEL – EUR – SA – AUS
1986	McLaren TAG Turbo:	BRE – ESP – RSM – MON – BEL – CAN – USAE – FRA – GB – GER – HON – AUT – ITA – POR – MEX – AUS
1987	McLaren TAG Turbo:	BRE – RSM – BEL – MON – USAE – FRA – GB – GER – HON – AUT – ITA – POR – ESP – MEX – JAP – AUS
1988	McLaren Honda Turbo:	BRE – RSM – MON – MEX – CAN – USAE – FRA – GB – GER – HON – BEL – ITA – POR – ESP – JAP – AUS
1989	McLaren Honda:	BRE – RSM – MON – MEX – USA – CAN – FRA – GB – GER – HON – BEL – ITA – POR – ESP – JAP – AUS
1990	Ferrari:	USA – BRE – RSM – MON – CAN – MEX – FRA – GB – GER – HON – BEL – ITA – POR – ESP – JAP – AUS
1991	Ferrari:	USA – BRE – MON – CAN – MEX – FRA – GB – GER – HON – BEL – ITA – POR – ESP – JAP
1993	Williams Renault:	SA – BRE – EUR – RSM – ESP – MON – CAN – FRA – GB – GER – HON – BEL – ITA – POR – JAP – AUS

Pole position: 33x
1981: GER – HOL
1982: BRE – BEL – USAE – SUI – VEG
1983: FRA – MON – BEL
1984: MON – GER – HOL
1985: AUT – BEL
1986: MON
1988: FRA – POR
1989: CAN – FRA
1993: SA – BRE – EUR – RSM – ESP – MON – CAN – GB – GER –
HON – BEL – ITA – JAP

Front line: 86x
1981: ARG – GB – GER – AUT – HOL
1982: BRE – RSM – BEL – USAE – HOL – FRA – GER – SUI – VEG
1983: BRE – FRA – MON – BEL – CAN
1984: RSM – MON – CAN – USAE – GB – GER – AUT – HOL – ITA
– EUR – POR
1985: POR – AUT – BEL
1986: MON – GER – ITA
1987: FRA – JAP – AUS
1988: RSM – MON – MEX – CAN – FRA – GER – BEL – ITA –
POR – ESP – JAP – AUS
1989: RSM – MON – MEX – USA – CAN – FRA – GB – GER –
BEL – JAP – AUS
1990: MON – ITA – POR – ESP – JAP
1991: USA – FRA – BEL
1993: SA – BRE – EUR – RSM – ESP – MON – CAN – FRA – GB –
GER – HON – BEL – ITA – POR – JAP – AUS

1st: 51x
1981: FRA – HOL – ITA
1982: SA – BRE
1983: FRA – BEL – GB – AUT
1984: BRE – RSM – MON – GER – HOL – EUR – POR
1985: BRE – MON – GB – AUT – ITA
1986: RSM – MON – AUT – AUS
1987: BRE – BEL – POR
1988: BRE – MON – MEX – FRA – POR – ESP – AUS
1989: USA – FRA – GB – ITA
1990: BRE – MEX – FRA – GB – ESP
1993: SA – RSM – ESP – CAN – FRA – GB – GER

2nd: 35x
1981:   GER – VEG
1982:   FRA – SUI
1983:   RSM – EUR
1984:   SA
1985:   GER – HOL
1986:   CAN – FRA – POR – MEX
1987:   ESP
1988:   RSM – CAN – USAE – GER – HON – BEL – JAP
1989:   BRE – RSM – MON – GER – BEL – POR
1990:   BEL – ITA
1991:   USA – FRA – ESP
1993:   POR – JAP – AUS

3rd: 20x
1981:   ARG
1983:   MON
1984:   CAN
1985:   CAN – FRA – BEL – SA
1986:   ESP – USAE – GB
1987:   USAE – FRA – HON
1989:   ESP
1990:   POR – AUS
1991:   GB – ITA
1993:   EUR – BEL

4th: 10x
1982:   VEG
1983:   GER
1984:   USAE
1985:   EUR
1989:   HON
1990:   RSM – GER
1991:   BRE – JAP
1993:   MON

5th: 5x
1980:   BRE
1983:   CAN
1989:   MEX
1990:   CAN
1991:   MON

6th: 7x
1980:   ARG – GB – HOL
1982:   GB
1986:   BEL – GER
1987:   AUT

Fastest lap: 41x
1981:   FRA
1982:   SA – BRE – USAE – SUI
1983:   FRA – GB – AUT
1984:   BRE – FRA – GER
1985:   BRE – GB – AUT – HOL – BEL
1986:   MON – BEL
1987:   BEL – JAP
1988:   RSM – MEX – USAE – FRA – HON – ESP – AUS
1989:   RSM – MON – BEL – ITA – JAP
1990:   MEX – BEL
1991:   MON
1993:   SA – RSM – MON – HON – BEL – JAP

Accidents/Left track: 20
1980:   MON – CAN
1981:   USAW – BRE – ESP – CAN
1982:   USAW – BEL – MON
1983:   HOL
1984:   DAL – AUT
1985:   POR – USAE
1986:   HON
1987:   MEX – AUS
1989:   JAP
1990:   JAP
1993:   BRE

Laps in the lead: 2712

Miles in the lead: 7841 miles

Classifications and Drivers' World Championship points:
1980:   *15th* – 5 pts
1981:   *5th* – 43 pts
1982:   *4th* – 34 pts
1983:   *2nd* – 57 pts
1984:   *2nd* – 71½ pts
1985:   *1st* – 73 (76) pts
1986:   *1st* – 72 (74) pts
1987:   *4th* – 46 pts
1988:   *2nd* – 87 (105) pts
1989:   *1st* – 76 (81) pts
1990:   *2nd* – 71 (73) pts
1991:   *5th* – 34 pts
1992:   did not compete
1993:   *1st* – 99 pts

INDEX

Pembrey, meeting at, 260-3, 264,
267
Penske team, 52
Peterson, Ronnie, 48
Peugeot, 11, 12, 352, 353
Philip Morris organisation, 41,
59, 127, 132
Phoenix, Grand Prix races at
1989, 268-9
1990, 305
1991, 320
Piccinini, Marco, 134
Piquet, Nelson
1980 season, 57
1981 season, 67-8, 70, 72
1982 season, 77, 81, 83, 84, 90
1983 season, 117, 123, 124,
125, 127, 129, 130-1
comments on Mansell, 140-1
contract with Williams, 140-1
1984 season, 152, 153
1986 season, 176, 177, 179,
180, 181, 184, 185
1987 season, 194, 195, 200,
201, 209, 211-12
signs contract with Lotus, 202
visits McLaren headquarters for
discussions, 203-4
Prost favours Senna over, 5
insults Mansell and his wife,
221
1988 season, 221-2, 234
1989 season, 267, 297, 298
and Donnelly's accident, 309
brief references, 27, 165, 188,
265, 266, 365-6
Pirelli tyres, 147, 299
Pironi, Didier, 7, 8, 30, 46, 78, 79,
80, 84, 85, 86-7, 88, 90, 94-5,
96-8, 122, 148, 235, 259, 263
Platini, Michel, 13
Playboy, 221

Pook, Chris, 65-6
Pool, 99
Porsche, 126-7, 131, 135, 144,
145, 261
Portier corner, Monaco, 227
Portuguese Grand Prix
1984, 152-3
1985, 161, 162-3
1986, 179-80
1987, 209-11, 212, 216
1988, 6, 241, 242-4
1989, 287-9, 302
1990, 307-8
1993, 345
Price, David, 105
Procar series, 44, 73
Project Four, 44, 54, 57-8, 59
Prost, Alain
early career, 45
test drive with McLaren, 45,
46
signs contract with McLaren,
46
Jardine's recollections of, 47-8
1980 season, 49-51, 53-4, 55-6,
57, 58
approached by Renault, 55, 56
leaves McLaren and signs for
Renault, 58-9
1981 season, 60, 64-5, 66, 67-
8, 70-1
1982 season, 75, 77, 80, 81, 83,
85-6, 90-3, 94-6, 97, 101
driving style, 76-7, 95-6, 122,
174-5, 346
friendship with Villeneuve and
Pironi, 84-5
comments on Villeneuve's
anger with Pironi, 87-8
and death of Villeneuve, 88
and Pironi's accident, 94-6
and Pironi's death, 98